Living and Dying with Dignity

*A Daughter's Journey
Through Long-Term Care*

Part of death means reflecting back on a life well lived.
Here are my parents in their 1945 wedding photo.
(Andrew Skilling)

Living
and
Dying
with
Dignity

*A Daughter's Journey
Through Long-Term Care*

Jennifer A. Jilks

GENERAL STORE PUBLISHING HOUSE
499 O'Brien Road, Box 415
Renfrew, Ontario, Canada K7V 4A6
Telephone (613) 432-7691 or 1-800-465-6072
www.gsph.com

ISBN 978-1-897508-11-4

Copyright © Jennifer Jilks, 2008

Design and layout: Magdalene Carson / New Leaf Publication Design
Printed by Custom Printers of Renfrew Ltd., Renfrew, Ontario
Printed and bound in Canada

Library and Archives Canada Cataloguing in Publication

Jilks, Jennifer A., 1956-
        Living and dying with dignity : a daughter's journey through
long-term care / Jennifer A. Jilks.
ISBN 978-1-897508-11-4
        1. Jilks, Jennifer A., 1956-. 2. Aging parents--Care--Canada. 3. Older
people--Long-term care--Canada. 4. Parents--Death. 5. Adult children of
aging parents--Family relationships--Canada. 6. Caregivers--Canada--
Biography. I. Title.
R726.8.J54 2008   649.8084'60971   C2008-904979-9

I dedicate this book to my parents.
The salt of the earth, they gave of themselves through
their personal and professional activities throughout their lives.
They provided strong role models to which I aspire daily.

Disclaimer

Other than those of immediate family members, I have withheld last names in order to protect the privacy of those intrinsic to my story. In many cases, I have made up first names to further protect the privacy of health care workers. With 640 LTC homes in Ontario, 533 of them for profit, I have deliberately been vague about what occurred, but this is not a unique story.

Contents

Acknowledgements

Much appreciation must be expressed to my brother, Robin, AKA "Rich Uncle Robbie"! His role as caregiver was immense and profound. His strong presence and unconditional emotional support helped me through a very tough time. His financial support in publishing this book commends him as my silent partner!

It is with great joy that I am blessed with the infinite love and support of my three adult children, Terrence, Jesse, and Caitlin, and her husband, Jean–Luc. I have learned much from them and have been blessed with their incredible support. My mother gave me both roots and wings; I hope I have provided these for you.

To my husband, Brian, without whom little of this could have been possible, I express my deepest love and inexpressible thanks. You have been, and continue to be, my rock and my pillow. My father, I know, is eternally grateful for your tender loving care.

I would like to thank my friends and acquaintances; you have provided much-needed encouragement. I felt reassured that I had a story to tell.

Laura Anderson provided me with a reader's report that helped me focus the book's lessons and its tone. My editor, Jane Karchmar, brought clarity, precision, and accuracy to the language and the content.

We owe much to my parents' friends and neighbours in Muskoka. Some of Dad's neighbours in the Manor and LTC were incredibly supportive; Dolly and Michelle were extraordinary in patiently tolerating much noise and the biopsychosocial impact of Dad's dementia. As well, there were many health care professionals who helped my family, and to them I owe a debt of thanks.

Many researchers encouraged me and provided much-needed copies of research papers that added to the body of knowledge I could make accessible to my readers. Many family members will benefit from their work. I hope, too, that those readers who work in health care might have a better understanding of what their exemplary work means to residents and family members. Many of you have a great gift and a calling.

Thanks, all of you.

Jennifer Jilks, October 6, 2008

We were healed of a suffering only by expressing it to the full.

—Marcel Proust, Novelist (1871–1922)

There was in every true woman's heart a spark of heavenly fire, which lies dormant in the broad daylight of prosperity; but which kindles up, and beams and blazes in the dark hour of adversity.

—Washington Irving (1783–1859) American Writer

Introduction

It is possible to live and die with dignity, but it isn't always certain. My mother denied to all that she was either ill or in pain. She died at home. My father raged angrily against his brain tumour.

I chose to document this story of caring for my ailing parents, as I could find little in the literature to help me on my journey. To keep ourselves organized, and to keep track of my parents' appointments, our trips to Toronto, their cancer treatments, and their prognoses, we wrote every appointment on our calendar. Eventually, I created a journal.

Journalling is a highly recommended means by which a writer can come to terms with the events of her life. An autobiography is an excellent way to capture a life well lived.[1] Some new studies have reported the benefits of writing a memoir to come to terms with your own story. There is healing power in such a process.

Dr. Gary Reker's (2002) work on spirituality and his autobiography, as well as the work done by Pennebaker (2004), convince me that the writing process is a healing one. In *Writing to Heal*, Pennebaker cites research that demonstrates reduced visits to medical professionals for those who disclose their emotional trauma and try to make sense of it. Writing about one's emotions is associated with general enhancement of immune function and reduced physiological indicators of stress. His research finds that one's mood and behaviours change after writing, and that expressive writing can help those dealing with stressed interpersonal relationships. His work gives the reader many ideas about basic writing technique, constructing and editing your story, changing perspective, and experimenting with context. Certainly, when teaching writing to my intermediate students, we found much healing in working through the writing process in fiction, both poetry and prose. Natalie Goldberg's *Writing Down the Bones* gives terrific strategies for opening up your mind and helping the words flow off the pen.

I was inspired to write this memoir in order to share my stories with others. These are lessons that I wanted to share. While my parents were fighting for their lives and trying to deal with the vagaries of

---

1   See **www.jilks.com/articles/AutobiographyTherapy.htm**.

age, I looked for human and physical resources through the Internet, sought out various counsellors, and contacted the Canadian Cancer Society. I scoured bookstores and found few resources. This book outlines the human and physical resources, the personnel, and the publications I found during my journey; and the frustrations of the bureaucratic process of dealing with health care professionals, long-term care facilities, and even extended family members.

These difficulties were compounded by my own diagnosis of clinical depression. I found during my research that as a woman going through menopause, with symptoms of stress, I was at great risk for depression. I am now receiving hormone therapy, after a saliva test showed that my estrogen levels were low and that my progesterone was minimal. This imbalance, due to surgical menopause in 1995, resulted in menopausal symptoms that included depression.

I worked hard to advocate for my parents, while working full time and caring for my adult children. After facing depression, a year on antidepressants and a focus on healthy eating and daily exercise have me feeling better. Depression is a difficult disorder, as it is unspoken, unnamed, and often undiagnosed. Many things can trigger it, including adolescence, hormonal changes, moving through life passages, a new job, or perceived job stress. I went into a mild depression and sought counselling after my divorce; having been in a marriage of sixteen years, it was a shock. I used the Employee Assistance Program to find someone to talk to about the issues I had been facing. The research says that depression can return with new stressors, such as work pressures, perimenopause, worrying over young or adult children, ailing parents, or bereavement. I have done extensive research on it to understand it better. It was quite a learning experience.

I had a fairly normal family life. Adopted as an infant into a loving working-class family, I had the usual teenage angst. A large amount of my leisure time was spent singing in choirs, attending church, and participating in a close, extended family network with cousins galore. I was always a good student and had no trouble in school. My parents really wanted me to get a good education. They encouraged me to go to university. I pursued a degree in Early Education from Ryerson, married in second year, and graduated pregnant. I earned my B.Ed., and then an M.Ed. Reading, writing, and research have taken up a better part of my life. I have always liked to ask questions.

Here we are: a loving, '60s family at Robin's first birthday. He was adopted at two weeks of age. I was adopted when I was six months old in 1957.

My younger brother, Robin, was adopted when he was two weeks old. Robin now lives in British Columbia. He works in Northern Ontario as a miner for two weeks at a time, spending the alternate two weeks on Vancouver Island where he lives with his son. Robin is a big man. Not tall, but a sturdy man of Scots descent. His dark, curly hair usually needs a trim. He is a "go to it" type of person. He works hard as a miner. We never talked much, not until our parents' ill health, but we love one another.

I was very proud of my mother. She was a very strong and determined woman. Her father died when she was fifteen years old and she dropped out of school to work and supplement the family income. Old photos reveal a beautiful young woman, especially the old, old black and white photos dating from 1940—obviously taken when she and Dad were courting. She worked and played hard all of her life. At the age of fifty, she learned to use a computer in her office. For twenty-seven years she managed a Rotary Club of 500 members with aplomb and panache. She was one of my best friends, despite living in separate cities. She listened to me and gave me unconditional support. We spoke every few days.

I did not talk to Dad very much. In his later years, he couldn't hear me on the phone. A strong, silent type, with many tools and a well-appointed workbench, he always had a project on the go and seemed to be able to fix anything. He loved his plants, his goldfish pond, his pets, and his lovely waterfront home. In my youth, he and Mom attended every track and field meet, every concert, and every other important event in my life. I always felt loved unconditionally and totally supported all my life. My parents were always there for me. I suffered little, other than having a huge lack of self-confidence.

We were a busy family that lived in the bustling inner city. I grew up taking the subway everywhere. Summers were spent in marvellous Muskoka. I adored the lake, the water, and the wind. We built a cottage, which still stands nestled in the trees by the lake. Dad loved his cottage. In the summer he would leave early on a Monday morning to nip into the busy city, and we would meet him at the highway when he returned on Friday nights for the weekend. In 1991, Mom finally retired after Dad had lost a series of jobs in the construction bust of the eighties. They were both sixty-six years old.

Part 1

My Parents' Final Years

2002: The Ravages of Old Age

The ravages of age were familiar to me. My elderly aunts and uncles had passed on. Listening to my parents describe aches and pains in their seventies, I had myself realized aches and pains of middle age in my forties. Getting up in the morning could be slower than before. Mom and Dad had fought arthritis, cholesterol, and weight issues since their fifties and were pretty careful with their health. They would work long hours at events in town supporting the volunteer network. They slowed down in their sixties and I began to monitor them more and more during this time. There were clues that their visits to the pharmacist were becoming more serious by the sheer volume of medications they were on. Mom had lactose intolerance and debilitating colitis: a stress-induced diarrhea. She was an extreme worrier, and it resulted in her having to wear adult diapers when driving a long way or going to church or choir practice. The smallest stress would send her off to the toilet. Dad was taking eight pills a day, a polypharmacy situation that put him at great risk.

Mentally I had already looked ahead to the last chapter in my parents' lives after my first husband's mother developed lung cancer. She was a heavy smoker, so it was not a surprise. I read all I could at that time and began to understand the philosophy of Elizabeth Kübler–Ross's five stages of grief: denial, anger, bargaining, depression, and acceptance. I had developed such strong bonds with my mother, I knew we could honour the past while accepting the present. I could foresee that time coming, as my parents began recognizing and showing signs of the aging process. Slowly they began giving up the physical activities they could no longer manage: mowing the lawn, shovelling snow, raking snow off of the roof, stacking the cords of wood they needed for their wood stove, and so on. They began to hire people for those purposes.

Dad found caring for his precious garden much more difficult
in his seventies. His knees were ravaged by arthritis,
he was in pain, and needed much more sleep.

I, too, was beginning to prepare for the last chapter in my life. I had always been an active member in my teachers' federation,[2] serving as executive member, secretary, treasurer, and branch president. I enjoyed trying to give something back to my profession. I took student teachers under my wing and mentored them while contributing articles to educational publications and planned and presented workshops on curricula, special education, and technology. Finally, I joined a professional organization (Ontario Association for Supervision in Curriculum—OASCD) and began doing work with this provincial group to help plan workshops and organize conferences. It was exciting work, planning, preparing, and facilitating the professional development opportunities so crucial in the field. I took the principals' course in order to find new challenges beyond the classroom. It was rewarding work and gave me great joy.

---

2   The federation became a union in 1997.

I had been divorced for ten years. This kind of time commitment gave me a purpose, especially as my children found their own friends and their own interests. I was content to carry on with my personal and professional goals. One December, I met a special man. The week we met, we were scheduled to visit Mom in Muskoka. She told me to bring this dear man. Imagine driving five hours in a car with three teenagers. He is not a tall man, and I am not a tall woman. My children are fairly tall, and when we would stop on the way for a bite to eat, we looked like a peculiar family. But the visit was a success. After a busy spring and summer, we became engaged.

Brian, my second husband, is a delightful man. He was in the middle of a successful business career, with much responsibility related to the transportation industry. He has an open heart, a genuinely honest disposition, and is loved by almost all. I adored seeing him take off for work in his business suits. He looked like the businessman he was at the time. His generosity extends from the financial gifts he made to my struggling children while in university, to the generosity of spirit that moves him to do Meals on Wheels in his retirement in this community. My mother always called him "a pet"!

Mom put off her surgery until after our wedding in 2002. (Terry Hrynyk)

Mom's first surgery — September 23, 2002

A month after our lakeside marriage ceremony in 2002, my mother phoned to let me know that she'd had her surgery and that it had gone very well. "What surgery?" I asked. She had had a hard lump excised. It was more uncomfortable and irritating than painful, she told me. It was difficult for her to describe where it was, since she really did not know the terminology, but she could feel it somewhere between her vaginal opening and her anus. The surgery went well and they thought they had gotten most of the lump, which was to be tested for cancer. She explained that she had not wanted to have it dealt with until after the joyous ceremony. She had told my groom about the problem, swearing him to secrecy. He did not say a word. This was the beginning of their relationship, which remained a special one. It was the first of their wonderful secrets and a bond that held them fast.

At this point I wish I had seen Mom's secrecy as a foreshadowing of things to come. She did not want me to ask her questions. She was resolute in appearing in charge, in control, and able to handle the entire medical requirements that a cancer diagnosis entails. It did not frighten me at the time. I had a strong faith that all would unfold as it should. I trusted, then, that this was a mere blip in the landscape. The media reports were full of stories of lumpectomies and successful treatments. Much of the literature explains the progressive treatment of cancer and how many cancer patients respond to treatment. I read autobiographies of people like Dr. Marla Shapiro, Wendy Mesley, and other famous folks who wrote of their success in conquering cancer. These women could direct their care, did the research, and generally put a positive spin on the whole affair. My mother had little information and clearly did not understand all that was told to her; nor did she know much about the process. There is little in the literature that talks about dying from cancer.

The biopsy on Mom's lump, which took a week to process, told her doctors that she had "leukoplatia on the vulva" — or so she told me. (The vulva is the skin surrounding the vaginal opening.) Mom told me that this was a cancerous lump. She knew little more than this and I went to the Internet to find some information. There was nothing much available on this topic. It was only years later that I figured out she had *leukoplakia*, a cancerous legion that usually forms in the mouth, can be associated with HIV, but also forms on external female genitalia. I had more questions than Mom wanted answered at the time. She was adamant about doing this alone, unlike my husband's mother, who accepted his help and interventions with health care professionals. After consultation with her original surgeon, Mom was sent for a referral to another surgeon, a specialist in Toronto. This was the first of many such trips.

Mom had her second opinion and was told that she had to have another portion of her original tumour site excised. They thought that an insufficient amount of tumour had been removed and that she needed to have another three millimetres taken out from around the former lump. Mom wasn't sure what a millimetre was and informed me that she needed to have three *centimetres* removed. I was so shocked that I did not ask her to clarify! Once off the phone, Brian and I talked about this news bulletin. We decided we had to go to Toronto and support her there. This was a 430-km trip for us; a 250-km trip for my parents.

The year finished, as it always does, with Christmas parties, school concerts, and many family phone calls. I participated in writing project and curriculum planning sessions. It had taken me a long time to feel some sense of confidence in myself as an educator. I had begun to have my writing published and finished my M.Ed, which helped me become a better teacher.

Having developed a reputation and some expertise in delivering technology-based curricula, I began delivering workshops to peers, then colleagues on the school board. I finally felt as if I knew what I was doing as a teacher and as a professional. My self-confidence, always minimal in my youth, began to rise as peers sought me out for advice and adopted my on-line portfolio to use in their teaching practices. Like the phoenix, I underwent a metamorphosis: from struggling single parent in my thirties to confident wife and teacher-leader in my mid-forties. I finally felt that life was good. I felt the security of my position, and we enjoyed Ottawa and our livelihood. Brian's long hours and extensive travel for work and my extracurricular activities were fulfilling, if stressful. We hired a housecleaning firm to allow us more free time.

2003: Mom's Surgeries; Dad's Seizures

Mom's second surgery — January 23, 2003

With the New Year came the second surgery. I had to take time off work. Brian and I travelled to Toronto. We were there to provide some support to Mom immediately following her second surgery. I was grateful that I was able to take time off work. I was happy to be a teacher, as our union's collective agreement included a clause that covered this situation. I was allowed time off in order to get medical care for family members, which included my mother. Dad was unable to care much for Mom. He was confused and bewildered. In hindsight, he was not himself. The arthritis in his knees was bothering him and he wasn't as strong as he had been.

Mom and Dad had driven to Toronto together in their van. My parents had been living in their retirement home in Muskoka, north of Toronto, since 1991. They were not at all sure about checking into the hotel or using valet parking, such simple tasks, but overwhelming when coping with illness. I had to talk Mom into using valet parking, since people of their generation feel they must pinch pennies. The Great Depression was vivid in their childhood memories. These little things made the trips easier.

The surgery had gone well with no difficulty. There were no complications and Mom was quite good at doing her post-surgery routine. She was quite religious about her perineal care, as only a United Church woman could be. After she urinated she had to rinse the surgical area off with a squeeze bottle of water, then dry it with a blow dryer.

Mom was at her best in this situation. In her hospital room she lavished love and attention on each and every nurse and doctor, despite her pain. It was pure theatre, watching her. Mother charmed them all. Each nurse and caregiver was greeted by name, and was queried on developments at home. She knew their stories, asked about loved ones, and remembered when they were about to take a few well-earned days off. She had them laughing and always took an opportunity to build them up. I think it took her mind off of her pain, the food she did not like, and her regular sitz baths, required each time she needed to empty her bladder.

My parents in their living room. Mom liked staying in her pajamas, with their precious Sabre by their side.

Mom was used to having medical issues. She was celiac and couldn't eat wheat. She was lactose intolerant, but took pills if she chose to have milk products. She also had colitis, which resulted in the loss of control over her bowels if she felt any stress. She was a nervous traveller these days and fasted before each trip into town. It made life difficult.

My mother had a great spirit, high standards, and boundless energy. One could be morbid and upset at all life delivers, or carry on and play the cards one was dealt. The wise woman looks for the best in each person she meets. This Mom did with panache. I, in turn, tried to look after Mom's needs. She never admitted to any difficulty and hid her pain from most of us. This went against my nature and we would fight later about it.

The time came for Mom to be discharged and to prepare for the two-hour drive north. I helped Mom as we negotiated with the discharge team. They did not want to send Mom home without proper supports in terms of home care. This took a couple of hours of hovering in hallways, standing at the nursing station. Dad was feeble. He was unable to do a great deal of standing or walking. Hospital staff made contact with people at the Community Care Access Centre (CCAC), our regional health care program, and ensured that someone would be there to provide some primary care: checking Mom's blood pressure and surgical wounds.

My father could barely walk at the time, and was unable to make meals or take care of my mother. My mother, stubbornly, denied that she needed help. Still, she was discharged after the nurse spent two hours on the phone to find CCAC home care for her. We packed up her bag, checked my parents out of the hotel, and had valet parking (hang the expense!) bring up their minivan. I stayed with Mom while Brian helped Dad bring the van around to the hospital. I recall standing on the pavement beside the van, in the barren Toronto cityscape, thinking that I ought to go with them on the two-hour trip north, or drive them home myself. Mom was adamant in her refusal. I was teary and feeling some dread. My students did not necessarily need me, but likely wanted me back in the classroom. We hopped on a plane at Pearson Airport and took off back home to Ottawa and our jobs.

On the way north, Dad had a "bit of a moment," to quote Mom. He had a petit mal seizure while he was driving. Not that they understood this at the time, but Dad had to pull off the road, and he was not sure what had happened. Aunt Irene, Dad's sister, told me much later that Dad was discharged from the army during World War II due to a petit mal seizure. I had not known this—or could not recall. Mom and Dad arrived home stressed and exhausted.

On hindsight, I should have gone with them to get Mom's care on track. Dad was unable to cope with making meals and was in great pain. It would have helped to gain a better insight into their health needs. My stubborn, determined mother was so terribly cheerful at home. I had to respect her independence, but she was fighting to recover, and it did not go well. It broke my heart to hear her talking about sleeping on the first floor since she could not navigate the stairs. Dad was in pain making meals. As much as Mom wanted to be home, it wore them out.

The problems with old age are the aches and pains that ever increase. Coming to terms with each passage of life has led me down an interesting path. It is clear to me that it is important to be able to determine what is or is not a serious health risk. A key part in helping seniors keep their health is in preventing serious issues from occurring. Mom and Dad never really looked their ages and could never accept the aches of old age. Dad's arthritis had always fuelled much anger and grief. At this point, all of their health issues converged and made their life difficult, demeaning, and demanding. They argued and fought over silly things. My daughter, Caitlin, after a stressful visit suggested they should have marriage counselling! They were depressed and suffering from emotional stress.

My parents continued to try to look after themselves at home. The house is on a small lake in Bala, the self-proclaimed Cranberry Capital of Canada. It is built on a rock, where the pink, gray, white, and black of the Precambrian Shield rises up out of the ground, providing a perfectly solid foundation in the basement. The main floor is open concept, with a similar view of the lake and the trees. The wood stove is the main heat in the house, and sits in the one mini-wall of the living room. Off the living room is the TV room, and down the wee hall was a bathroom and what should have been a bedroom. Mom and Dad decided, since it was their retirement home, that they did not need another bedroom, so this was Dad's office, with sliding glass doors that open to the back way and the driveway. The second floor consists of one large bedroom, sixteen by twenty-four feet, with an ensuite bathroom. The sliding glass doors, which frame the south-facing vista, look out over the calm lake and the long walk down to the lakefront.

I found out later that Dad had visited his doctor in December of 2002. It seemed that he was having trouble figuring out which driveway was his after driving home from town. To my knowledge, Dad and his doctor had not pursued this issue. I was not told about the incident and nothing else was done. In hindsight, it was a flashing neon sign and a predictor of things to come. Dementia is a symptom of many diseases and disorders. Organizations such as the Alzheimer's Society have done much research on dementia, activities of daily living (ADL), and instrumental activities of daily living (IADL) concerns; for example, losing your way on a familiar drive home, or having mental confusion, are research-based symptoms of many medical issues.

Dad's grand mal seizure — February 24, 2003

Mom and Dad went home to their remote property. Mom stayed on the couch on the main floor, as she was unable to make her way up the steep stairs to her bedroom. She was sore and was told to limit her activity—as if that would stop her! To ensure that her stitches did not become infected, she continued to follow her post-surgery routines: sitz baths, and the blow dryer after every visit to the toilet, and she continued this mandatory perineal care for months. Even so, she contracted an infection and required antibiotics. Thankfully, the CCAC-provided home care nurse helped her; her doctor had prescribed antibiotics, which irritated her stomach and provided more complications for her already frail health.

On February 24, 2003, before Mom was fully recovered, Dad suffered a grand mal seizure in the kitchen, falling to the hard linoleum floor in convulsions. Mom phoned 911, and the ambulance attendants had to wend their way into the house through the office, the only doorway with decent enough access. They would come to use that doorway a lot! I could not imagine the stress and fear she faced. Dad was taken by ambulance to the hospital in Bracebridge. Mom stayed alone at the house. They decided that tests were warranted, including an MRI and a CAT scan. He was sent home to wait. Mom told me, "I knew in that instant that our lives would never be the same again." If only she had really come to understand this and accept it and to seek home support!

Instrumental activities of daily living (IADL) — Monday, February 17, 2003

Mom was to develop another tumour in her groin every year or so until the end. But, for now, she was coping. They could no longer manage their IADL. Mom had help at home: a neighbour continued to do Mom's and Dad's banking, another picked up the newspaper for them. Yet others put out their garbage can every week and brought the garbage cans back into the garage. They were conscientious caregivers, these neighbours. How they fit all this in with their daily lives, I do not know. The dog was no longer going for walks, but stayed on the property in his dog pen, or drove in the van for shopping trips that Mom attempted. Dad could not walk far.

Dad's driver's licence was rescinded because of his medications and the possibility of a seizure, and this hit his ego hard. This is the law in Ontario. Family physicians have an obligation to report medical issues that affect driving ability. Mom could not travel easily, due to her colitis, and had not driven in many years. I remember her reading up on her driving manual, trying to ace the annual test for seniors. Transportation is an issue that can prove difficult for many seniors. For my Dad, it was shameful to lose this independence, another issue that contributed to his morose demeanour. Unfortunately, my mother passed the driver's test, but required help from neighbours in navigating the minivan in and out of the driveway from time to time. I wish I had been told. This was a major sign that all was not well and that their living circumstances were not ideal for them.

Magnetic Resonance Imaging (MRI): the diagnosis

A diagnosis for Dad meant a long drive to Toronto for the Magnetic Resonance Imaging (MRI) scan. (The MRI is a scan taken to show the structure and functioning of the brain. Once taken, it would be forwarded to the doctor.) A neighbour drove Dad in. This was just one favour in a long line of many favours. After the MRI, Dad and the neighbour simply turned around and went back home. Another appointment had been made for a week later for Dad to go back to Toronto to talk to the oncologist regarding the MRI. I found it so bizarre that things could not happen any more quickly than this. How difficult it was for this man in his late seventies to be dragged down to the city, a two-hour trip at best, sit waiting with a volunteer driver for the scan, which was usually not done at the scheduled time, and then to have to drive home, and then arrange transportation back again in a week to hear the results.

The results told us that Dad had a tumour located in the left, prefrontal lobe, in the prefrontal cortex, which plays an important role in memory, intelligence, concentration, temper, and personality. This is a sophisticated part of our brain that facilitates the setting of goals, the ability to make plans, and judge priorities. It guides our eye and head movements and sense of orientation.

Dad's cancer was said to be *low-grade hemispheric astrocytoma*. He had mixed gliomas classified into oligo-astrocytoma. Of course, he couldn't understand this, could not read the information provided, nor comprehend it. My mother was on information overload and simply did as the oncologists ordered. Treatment usually involves surgery, depending upon the characteristics and numbers of astrocytic cells present. He was to have surgery on March 18, 2003.

Dad's surgery — March 18, 2003

Mom and Dad travelled to Toronto for the surgery. Mom, Dad, and I met at the hospital. This was just at the time that SARS hit this same hospital (March 5, 2003). The administration didn't realize the issues around communication of this dreaded disease. After it was diagnosed, great changes and limits to visitations were made in hospital policies. Families with sick or dying loved ones in hospital could not visit. I am amazed that we missed this crisis.

When we met with the surgeon postoperatively, he forecast that Dad's language would be affected: he had lost his ability to speak, and we were told not to worry about that when we next talked to him. It was "normal," he said. He was unsure which language skills would be affected, but thought that gradually some or all of his language skills would come back. I found out later that the prefrontal cortex, the area above Dad's left eyebrow, affects a great deal of cognitive functioning, as well as language. Once his speech returned, and he could articulate sentences, Dad had trouble retrieving nouns. This proved to be a clue for me, later in 2006.

My mother was quite upset when we saw him. Dad had bruising around his face, caused, I assumed, from falling out of bed. He had always gotten up in the night to go to the bathroom, and now must have been falling when he did so. He refused — or could not remember — to call for a nurse for help, nature calling him rather loudly. His face was terribly bruised. It broke my heart to look at him. I wondered why he would not be restrained or at least given a bedpan. Both cheeks were black and blue. He had these huge staples in a large "U" shape on the left side of his brain. I felt sick to my stomach. It was agony knowing that I could not prevent his pain. But then I found out, after some pain and crying, that the bruising was due to the surgery and not his falling. At the time it was a horrible thing to think about. I wish someone had told me. I still feel terribly sad when I think about it. I felt helpless to prevent my father's pain and suffering.

Dad could not talk at all. It made visits frustrating. We wrote things down on a piece of paper for him. It took a lot of time. Jesse, twenty years old and my middle child, visited on the second day. Jesse was living in Toronto and attending York University, which was not too far away. A genteel, confident, personable, good-looking young man, and an aspiring actor, he brought a larger-than-life presence to our misery. Jesse was clutching a large, family-sized box of cereal he had bought on the way to the hospital. He fiddled with it and we joked about the size of the box while we tried to pretend normalcy and visit with Dad. He was brave to visit. I found the visits excruciating. Dad was disoriented and asking the same questions several times. When he had to go to the bathroom every ten minutes, he would flash his equipment to us, desperate to get to the bathroom in time. This was like an inoculation and prepared me for all that happened later.

Dad's voice was scratchy. All of the hair above his ear was gone. He was talking gibberish. Mom and Dad did not always remember what the doctors explained to them and they did not understand this problem, despite the forewarning. It was the beginning of my frustration that they would not allow me to be part of this process. I should have insisted. At this time, the doctors thought Dad would have to have radiation therapy, but they were unsure. This depended on whether the tumour was benign or not. He was in no condition for radiation therapy, what with his arthritis and depression.

This marked the beginning of my gradual lack of faith in the system and the exacerbation of my own mental health issues and sense of losing control. These two seniors were to be sent home, guided by hospital staff to find neighbours to assist in ADL. It was heart-breaking to find that they could not manage their IADL; their inability to successfully take care of themselves or their pets seemed to me a bizarre way to live.

I went out to the bookstore before getting dinner for Mom, who was back in the hotel room. I had forgotten how great it was living in the middle of a city. I bought the book *Talk, Talk, Talk,* by Jay Ingram. I knew it explained some of the quirks of the brain and language. I read some of it out loud to Mom. It helped us to understand a bit of what was going on in Dad's brain regarding language. By now, Dad could put together smaller sentences, but was unable to retrieve nouns. He could describe "those animals with black rings around their eyes. They eat garbage." The word *raccoon* was somewhere in his brain, but would not come to the surface. The word was as irretrievable as his old life.

Mom wanted chicken from a well-known fast-food place, even though it usually upset her stomach; I bought myself sushi and devoured both dinner and my book, reading parts aloud to Mom.

Discharge routines; onward home — March 20, 2003

Before Dad's discharge, a doctor did a geriatric assessment to assess Dad's motor skills and determine his basic needs. I knew that despite the fact that Dad would receive home care on Friday, it would not be enough. The assessment needs to be done on both family members. Sending him home as ill as he was, with a wife who was also in a fragile state, only set them up for risk. He was very wobbly on his feet. We did not know if this was temporary or permanent. I began having trouble remembering when Dad was normal.

Dad recovered from his surgery at home, and the medical community provided a nurse to check his sutures and to do some blood work. Once this was no longer necessary, the visits stopped. The Local Health Integration Network (LHIN) Unit's Community Care Access Centre (CCAC) took care of this for them. Mom, receiving some similar support, did not have the benefit of anything but nursing care. What they needed was someone to assist with IADL.

I demanded that my Mom give permission for the CCAC case manager to phone me long distance, in Ottawa. This helped me considerably. CCAC's nurse arranged for professionals to go to the house to check on both Mom and Dad and give Dad regular blood tests and ensure that his sutures were healing. Her nurse did not know all of the medical issues they faced. Mom would not admit her extreme needs to anyone but me. I had to speak to CCAC long distance and let them know what was really going on.

Smart geriatric assessment and case managers interview care recipients separately from caregivers in order to get a better perspective on a case. This provides more information than an ailing senior may want to share. Many families and seniors appear to be in denial.

When a senior keeps getting lost on the way home, he or she is putting everyone else on the road at risk. Since a simple driver's test will not necessarily diagnose unsafe driving habits, family doctors, provided with information from family or caseworkers, have the authority to demand that a driver's licence be taken away. Without the option for case managers to inform family members and ask that seniors be taken for medical diagnosis of symptoms such as dementia, the seniors and families are powerless to access more supports. Many seniors are able to exhibit "normal" behaviour and refuse supports as they convince health care professionals that they are fine. CCAC provides only limited care immediately following a hospital stay.

The neighbours continued to ensure that some of my parents' daily needs were being met. They achieved a false sense of security. Dad was feeling better, although he still could not walk without aid, and he needed a diversion. He and Mom missed their old dog, Sabre, a Husky and Malamute mixed-breed dog that had died the previous fall. They had put off getting another puppy for a while, but not for long. Dad desperately wanted a new one. They had not been without a dog and a cat for years. Mom's cat, Snuggles, gave her much affection. They heard of a dog that had had puppies, and off they went to adopt Bandy. Bandy was a Dalmatian/beagle cross. Poor Bandy was an eager, young, undisciplined puppy who loved to jump up on Dad, and anyone else who visited. Dad had such difficulty walking with painful arthritis; his knees were feeble, and life was hard. He had huge issues with keeping his balance as well as the effects of the brain tumour. There were many difficult times as he cursed the dog after it jumped up, yet he loved it so much. This contributed to Dad's anger and maladjustment, and, despite my protests, they tried to care for this young canine. I had never heard Dad swear until now. His anger in not being able to manage himself, his life, and his puppy created a poisoned atmosphere. Visits were demoralizing and frustrating for me as I picked up on Mom's and Dad's frustrations.

Mom never fully accepted her prediction that "life would never be the same again." Dad still was not recovered. Mom ended up being responsible for the dog, as well as all the driving and transportation and IADL issues. She was angry when Dad slept all day. It was not *normal*, and fervently prayed things would go back to the way they were. She would phone and tell me how angry she was with him.

I suggested that if he was tired he *should* sleep. In the meantime, their neighbours continued to provide the assistance Mom and Dad needed to remain in their home.

I carried on working in Ottawa, worrying about my adult children and my dear husband, whose job stress revolved around security and transportation issues. I toddled off to teach school every day. September found me teaching a split-grade class in the same small school. My assignment from the year before had changed from a Grade 6 class to a Grade 4/5 class. I was unhappy having to master two new curricula at the same time. The demand that I move from the freedom of my portable outside, into another classroom, was the last straw.

Khaled Hosseini, in his book *A Thousand Splendid Suns,* speaks of the things that shape a woman. The events in our lives give us substance. It is in the unseen effects of our lives that we develop our minds and our souls and become who we were meant to be. In a woman's life it is our disappointments, our burdens, and our grief, as much as our achievements and joys, that shape us. It is in dealing with adversity that we find our character. I had always told my students that winning was easy; it was the losing that one must worry over and work through.

In education, advancement is not so easy if your principal is not on your side. Keeping your head high is difficult knowing that you will never be going through that glass ceiling. With my sense of failure foreshadowing my depression, I survived a difficult work assignment with little support from a principal who browbeat me. I fought hard for recognition, working on many high-level projects for my school, school board, union, and my profession, all the while questioning my abilities. Fall passed, we made it through our wonderful Remembrance Day ceremony, report cards, and parent-teacher interviews, and the year finally ended.

2004: Stress — And More Stress

March comes in like a lion — Monday, March 24, 2004

March arrived with great excitement for me. I travelled to Atlanta to give a presentation of the work I had been doing with students, staff, and colleagues in the areas of curriculum and technology. With great excitement, I flew to the biggest airport in the United States and navigated my way to the city, to a lovely hotel, and began schmoozing with colleagues similarly interested in integrating technology projects into authentic learning opportunities. Much excitement was generated as I represented my school board, with a large poster and wearing the "Staff Development" t-shirt they gave me, spreading the word about the great work we were doing in Ottawa. I was flying as high as the plane I arrived on as I shared my projects incorporating digital cameras and iMovies, and helping students create on-line portfolios for student-led conferences. I was surfing in a sea of Apple Computers and it was bliss. My head was filled with plans and ideas and I gained some self-confidence as I began to realize how much I knew about pedagogy, despite my principal's misgivings.

The week of March 24 brought me down to earth and began another difficult time for all of us. There was more to come. The personality issues with my principal became worse. I began to do all I could to get out of the classroom. In March, I worked on a writing project for Internet Safety. It resulted in an article I managed to have published in the principal's newsletter. There was stress in travelling to Toronto, but it was a break as well.

On top of all this, my mother developed another lump. It was a scary proposition. It was fortunate that my collective agreement gave me time for family medical issues. Back we had to go to Toronto. There, Mom received more bad news from the doctor. This lump, which she had so casually mentioned, required surgery.

These were stressful times. As always, it involved a long trip south for a cell sample to be taken and sent for analysis, and then a trip back to the city a week or two later to learn the results. It was this time frame that was the most difficult — waiting for the follow-up appointments. Once things started to happen, one could fashion a game plan. I had difficulty making phone calls during the day, as all' of the daytime calls I needed to make were long distance from Ottawa to Muskoka.

Part of the problem, familiar to many seniors, is transportation to and from appointments, adding stress to an already stressful situation. Mom depended upon the Cancer Society volunteers to drive her. One phone call to the coordinator, and she made arrangements for all the appointments. We were so grateful for their help.

My principal, on the other hand, did not demonstrate any understanding, and I had issues at work that would not be resolved. Balancing personal stress had been manageable in the past, because I felt that I was making a difference to my students. My work as shop steward for the union was satisfying, yet it threatened my boss. I think, as a female principal/leader, she was unsure of herself and came across as overbearing and difficult while trying to appear confident and strong. There are women who have trouble working with strong women, and I bore the brunt of this issue, despite working in a school district with a history of strong female leaders and a collaborative approach to teaching and learning. The frustrations mounted as I was not allowed to make long-distance phone calls from the school phone to check on the results of my mother's latest biopsy. It contributed to my worries. Due to these concerns, I took time off work, again, to go to Toronto to help my mom. For help in supporting my parents, I brought in the troops. My daughter, Caitlin, met my mom at the hotel the first day Mom was to be in Toronto.

Caitlin, twenty-five years old at the time, was attending Waterloo University — not too far away from the Toronto hospital. Caitlin is a responsible, stable, strong, young woman. Taller than I am, with blonde hair, the opposite of my dark hair, she spent her youth being shy; this she inherited from me. She had blossomed into a hard-working, bright scientist: a hydrogeologist who understands water and the earth. She loved her science program and eventually earned her bachelor's degree and then her M.Sc. Taking the co-op program, she was either at home working between semesters, or spending a work term in Toronto or closer to home. Caitlin was and is my rock. She helped me make it through those difficult times when our family divided and we left the matrimonial home in the divorce. She continued to be there for me. We met in Toronto to give some help to Mom.

Caitlin and her grandma were very close. They had a special bond. In her high school years, when school finished in May, Caitlin would be welcomed to Bala to spend a pampered week or two with her grandma and grandpa before starting her summer job. In those golden years, before all of these health issues, Caitlin would go to church and play her flute during services and sing in her grandmother's choir. The choir embraced and adored Caitlin.

Mom had her surgery, and Caitlin was there for her; I could not be there that first day, due to school commitments. In the meantime, Dad was at home in Bala with the cat and dog. Neighbours had strict orders to phone, visit, and monitor him, to ensure that all was well with him. We worried that he had what I had come to understand was dementia, but we had not encountered direct experience with any symptoms yet. We phoned Dad, but he could not hear us on the phone and did not want to talk too long. It was hard to tell if the tumour had affected his hearing or if this was old age, stubbornness, or senility.

Caitlin had to leave on the second day to go back to university; Brian could not be there due to projects at work, but my brother had arrived from B.C., where he lives, and he and I shared a hotel room. It was some comfort having him there; so often caregivers are daughters. The burden was less when it was shared. Robin and I visited in the hotel, and I gave him the updates that I could. I had not seen him in years at that point. We trundled over to the hospital to see Mom.

My brother worried about Dad and, after a day, he rented a car to drive north on the weekend to see him. When people phoned Dad, he was not inclined to talk. He wanted his privacy and, I think, to mourn his old life. Dad's left arm was twitching, Robin said. We did not know what that was all about. His blood count was 85 — this they found from the blood work the CCAC nurses did for him — but we did not know what *that* meant, either. We were not allowed to talk to the doctors (he had a family physician in town as well as an oncologist), and for that matter, we did not know how to contact them.

We fumbled in the dark. This was a tragic mistake on my part. Illness in a family had an impact on everyone, especially those who end up as caregivers. My mother thought that I couldn't deal emotionally with all the issues we faced. She did not understand the impact this had on me: worry, fear, frustration, and anxiety that carried over to my family and my work life. Cancer is a disease that strikes the entire family. Mom was trying to protect me, remaining positive and optimistic, but in the end it confounded me.

The rest of 2004 disappeared in a blur. I kept in close contact with Mom. She and Dad seemed to be able to manage their activities of daily living. I continued to work on my precious garden in the heart of the city. My husband's work was high-level, stressful work that involved several ministries and a firm that was going into bankruptcy. I focused on my job at school and on family issues at home. Our plates were full. I began to get the feeling that I was just play-acting at what passed for normal. How could I be worrying about silly issues at school, staff meetings that went haywire, and co-workers who were raised in the Me Generation, when my mother was so ill? I began to feel burned out. Parent-teacher interviews began to hold an agony of their own as I tried to argue with parents who did not think I knew enough to do my job. I did not, of course, allow myself to hear the wonderful parents who supported and encouraged me. One tends to hear the critical comments rather than the kudos. I focused on my failures and battles rather than on my successes.

Jesse, thankfully, survived his first year at York University. He found a summer job. Caitlin worked on her Master's degree. Terry, my youngest, was navigating his way through his first year at Carleton, on scholarship and living in residence; he had a part-time job. A good-looking, tall young man, with the same dark hair that his brother and I shared, he was a brilliant student. Terry was totally engrossed in his Humanities degree and maintaining his scholarship; he spent little time with us and more with his father (my ex-husband). We had had our issues, but we would see Terry from time to time and share some discourse and casual conversation. With a keen interest in history, he and Brian share a depth of knowledge. I learn much every time we speak and learned much about teaching from this bright young man.

My boss continued to ride me. As shop steward, I was responsible to help ensure that the rights and responsibilities of my teacher-peers were maintained. She resented my questions at staff meetings.

When she began correcting my behaviour and questioning my values in public, I began to feel a loss of control. Eventually, in May, I took some time off work to regroup. I sought counselling and the support of the superintendent and the school board safety officer. We had tracked a series of events in which this principal publicly berated teachers. Little was done. The counselling I received confirmed that such behaviour was not uncommon in schools: bosses who had forgotten how to be leaders and bullied in the name of discipline. I finished off the school year by going back to work in June, feeling stronger and better about myself, if a bit shaky.

I had sought and received a minimal amount of help from the school board in my dealings with my principal. Bullying was on the rise in education. I read all I could and continued to practise yoga, exercise regularly, and do my best to relax. Something happened over the summer, and my boss seemed to have developed some civility in her dealings with me. It is a hidden and secret world in the golden towers of the Board office. I applied for a transfer to a middle school, then suddenly rescinded it, as my principal was transferred to another school. I was afraid of ending up there.

September rituals — September 2004

A new school year brought a new principal. At the same time, with our school population diminishing, we lost our half-time vice-principal. This had a huge impact on the school climate. My teaching assignment was a straight Grade 5 class, which demanded a bit less of me than the split-grade class of the year before. It did, however, include a wide array of special needs students. I read, researched, wrote to clarify my curriculum, and found some challenges that I could conquer. The work led to several more workshop presentations, which gave me such joy. It was such a blessing to have learned from my teaching assignments, incorporated new information into my curriculum practices, and adapted this to present it to colleagues. I was quite angry at not being able to teach my favourite Grade sixes, and had to swallow my anger and frustration. I loved the challenge of preparing them for middle school, independent learning, and taking responsibility for their work and their actions. My new principal understood my need for professional development and challenge. However, he was not supportive of my attempts to become a principal; with three of us on staff trying for this competition, he had to spend time and energy to limit his focus. Now it is a moot point, but heart-breaking nevertheless. I had made mistakes that could not be forgiven while dealing with the emotional issues I had faced, and I realized that it was time to think differently.

Thanksgiving and errands — October 2004

The school year took off full swing with Individual Educational Plans (IEPs) for each of my special needs students. I had many meetings for which to prepare and students to test and identify in order to design individual curricula. I had a student I felt was dyslexic. (His previous teacher thought he was fine and an "A" student!) A psychologist's report confirmed my suspicions, yet seemed to infer that I was an inadequate educator and attributed his lack of success in Grade 5 to my shortcomings. I had a student with Marfan's Syndrome, one with neurofibromatosis, one who was a selective mute, five who had learning disabilities, and two who were high-ability learners. Then there was a student with autism, one with ADHD, and another three who were learning English as a second language (ESL) and who required extra support. I was blessed with a teaching assistant, Sue, who was an incredible support to me in my classroom. As a Special Education Specialist, I drew on all my knowledge and experiences and researched all I could about the disabilities of my students in order to better deliver a good program for them. I was making progress and felt more confident than ever before as I worked with a brilliant student teacher and assisted new teachers in developing their curricula and behaviour management strategies.

Report cards and parent-teacher interviews out of the way by now, Brian and I visited Muskoka at Thanksgiving. We knew we needed to check out my parents' health. Mom and Dad worked together to cook their traditional great turkey dinner. It was the last time.

Brian spent much time walking the dog to escape the bickering between my parents. In between, Dad slept a great deal while Mom talked to me. They were frail but determined. Every time Mom and Dad had errands in town, they would drive together. In the past, Dad would load the minivan with the dog and he and his dog would motor on into town. Now, errands had to be carefully planned. Mom would fast, as she did not want to risk eating and having a colitis

Dad wasn't able to stand for long. His knees were giving him much pain and he was short-tempered. This was the last Thanksgiving turkey dinner they ever prepared for us.

attack, and both would pile into the car with the dog. Mom, with her colitis, did not like to leave the house very often, despite adult diapers, which she refused to wear much. I think it put added stress on Dad as much as on her. Dad shopped, leaning heavily on the shopping cart, while Mom stayed put in the car. The glorious town librarian would put together a book bag to allow them to continue with their reading—although Dad never was able to read much after the tumour was removed. He had to give up his precious puzzles, which had kept him busy for hours. This was yet another insult. In hindsight, he would have benefited from talking books.

Transportation

Transportation is a huge issue for seniors with diminishing health. Mom had not driven the car in thirty years, although she passed her licence renewal test when they became mandatory. Dad had been the sole driver and took good care of Mom, and did groceries and errands all the time. Recently, the news has been full of stories of elderly seniors whose adult children must supervise their driving habits. Adult children continue to seek help from the medical profession in having the Ministry of Transportation re-examine their parents' skills and abilities and make a decision whether to take away their driver's licences. It was a scary thought that once I had to be mindful of my teens' driving habits and now had to monitor my parents. There were times that I gripped the seat as I drove with Dad. In hindsight, I should have spoken to his doctor to have his driving skills retested and his licence revoked if necessary.

Back in Ottawa, I submerged myself in work. It wasn't hard, with all the special needs students in my classroom. The challenge, however, was becoming onerous. The difficulties I had with determining my career path and facing the future were draining. I was short-tempered and frustrated. I had a couple of kindred spirits on staff, but some of the young teachers had different work ethics from mine. My practicum project, required for the principals' course Part 1, was met with less than satisfying support. Teachers are hard-pressed to meet the daily requirements of creating exemplary curricula, maintaining classroom discipline, collecting hot dog money, and fulfilling all the other job-related needs. Entertaining students more used to thirty-second sound bytes than time spent reading and writing is a balancing act at best. My project failed to drum up after-school teacher participants, and I wasted precious energy on it. Another failure with which to deal! The year finished with yet another Remembrance Day assembly, December report cards, parent-teacher interviews, and Christmas/ Holiday concerts. I still felt restless.

This was the last time Mom travelled:
Caitlin's and J–L's 2005 wedding. From left to right: Jesse, Brian, Jennifer,
Caitlin, Jean-Luc, Terry, Mom, Robin. (Rami Ibrahim)

2005: Independence Issues

Loss of independence: the car transfer
— March 31, 2005

Mom and Dad continued to sink into the abyss of dependence, anger, and frustration with the ravages of old age. Dad was so very upset with not being able to drive. He had Mom transfer the car ownership to her, an issue that made life difficult after her passing. Often he would state his frustration to me. It was difficult listening to Dad complain. The tumour had robbed him of his independence and any perceived control over his life. He was quite bitter about this insult.

We could not visit over Christmas—I feared the driving conditions; and I wanted to re-energize over the Christmas holidays. Finding new challenges is very important in my field. I applied to teach part-time at the University of Ottawa. There was a sudden job opening for teaching student teachers how to deliver Social Studies curricula in primary and junior classrooms. I had ten days to prepare a curriculum. It was a stressful few months. I had two cohorts of forty student teachers for three hours a day. I was released part-time (Wednesdays), while one of my best friends, a retired Special Education teacher, took my class of Grade 5 students back at the school. It was quite a learning experience.

Of course, student teachers are a difficult crowd: they "know everything there is to know" about teaching, but there were some dear aspiring teachers. There were only three men in the group of eighty or so student teachers. I put together some presentations; in a six-week period, we met a total of eighteen hours. I found that they were weakest in behaviour management—teacher education courses covered little outside of science, technology, literacy, numeracy, and physical education. It so happens that ninety percent of teaching is classroom control—and ninety percent of learning is taking responsibility for the learning process. I encountered some mature and immature learn-ers in these young adults. There was a wide range of personalities, and I elicited some negative reactions as I presented my curriculum.

Translating the Ministry of Education curriculum expectations into effective learning activities depends upon many factors, includ-ing the personality of the educator and learners, the (dis)abilities of the students, effectiveness of the learning environment, and the sup-port provided by those around you. I felt high and dry being a part-time lecturer. While issues have recently emerged in the quality of university education: student disengagement, grade inflation, lack of student effort, and high self-esteem with little output or effort (see *Ivory Tower Blues* for an in-depth analysis), I felt I did the best I could at the time. My evaluations were not very positive. I felt more defeated than ever.

The powers that be at the Board office suggested I try and obtain a transfer. With my high seniority number (I was in the top one-third of the seniority list), I should have a good chance of success. I worked on my resume, continued to do research, read, and write, and began doing work for an international curriculum group, the Ontario Educational Computing Organization (ECOO), and as a result made contacts all over the world.

Travelling to Atlanta brought a bright spot to my career. I felt respect and admiration for the creative work my students continued to produce. I simply followed their lead! I knew I would be an asset to any staff and was hopeful of finding a classroom at the Intermedi-ate Level. I liked working with the older children. I had left a great job in 2001, teaching Grades 7 and 8, in order to work closer to my home in the city. Being demoted from Grade 6 to Grades 4 and 5 in town was humiliating and defeating. I felt sure that I might find another job in a school that would appreciate me more.

House hunting — April 27, 2005

Retirement was good for Brian; with a buy-out package from his employer, he chose the good life and Freedom 55! He made my lunches, did the shopping and housecleaning. In the meantime, I was keen to find a job in Muskoka. Scrutinizing the Web site for job vacancies, I knew that hiring for September began in May and June. I scouted out jobs on-line and looked for anything I could find. There were several. The jobs had been offered to teachers already on staff as a transfer, as was the practice in most bargaining units. The remaining jobs were ones that teachers did not want due to the difficulty of the job, or the location. There was no job for me there. I decided to put in for a transfer to an intermediate position.

Spring passed in the great excitement and buildup to Caitlin's and Jean–Luc's May 22nd wedding. It was a glorious time, a wedding that went without a hitch. The parties and the excitement proved welcome diversions, a blessed break from work and health woes. Jean–Luc, a brilliant encryption engineer, had formed his own company and was working as a consultant at a good job. He was a responsible, fun-loving fiancé, and we were very pleased with this match. Caitlin and Jean–Luc had bought a house. Life was unfolding as it should.

I knew Mom was in pain when she attended Caitlin's wedding in May. She was weak and feeble and fighting ill health, but would not admit it. Out of her element and her home, her condition was quite obvious, and she could not cover it up. My brother had taken time off work, picked Mom up, and driven her down from Bala. I do not know how she managed that trip other than with a determination to attend this special event for a special granddaughter. It was the last time we had such a terrific celebration. Caitlin was beautiful, and her attendants quite a wonderful group of young ladies. My memories were filled with great times and lots of happy visits. Lately my brain was full of the anguish of keeping on top of Mom's and Dad's health care issues.

The responsibility of caring for ailing parents is a daunting task whether they live near or far away. With Caitlin happily married, Jesse off to the University of Alberta, and Terry working towards his degree, I felt that I needed to do, and could do, something more for my parents. It naturally fell to me. They lived in a small town with few human resources. Brian was amenable to moving to Muskoka. We reasoned that my parents could remain in their home if we could help them out once a week. This was my goal: to find a job and a house close enough that we could help them manage. We did not know how truly ill they both were.

I was prepared to work at anything in my field—even teach primary students again! Having completed Part 1 of the principals' course, I refrained from applying for the vice-principal competition in Ottawa, since I anticipated a move to Muskoka. It was sad to abandon the dream of a principalship. It was the first time I had understood that that dream would die. I was tired of the big-city politics in Ottawa anyway and I was ready to move and live in harmony with nature. I was tired of fighting a system that needed improvement and that only rewarded those prepared to work within the system, within the box. I was becoming tired and burned out. I had been presenting work-shops in various areas: special education, technology, and pedagogy, and had spent a term teaching university students. I felt that with my knowledge, education, experience, and training, I had a great deal to offer to an employer. Little did I know that I would end up feeling as if I were "*from away*," like a foreigner in a different country.

The jobs that opened up in the area included an intermediate position in MacTier, about a half hour's drive from Mom and Dad. I applied, but was not granted an interview. It was such a shame. I was angry and frustrated. It seems that in education it is *whom* you know and not necessarily *what* you know that counts. It would have been an ideal job: familiar curriculum and located close to my parents just off a main highway during snowy winters. We kept on house-hunting and scouring **mls.ca** hoping to find a place. We wanted a house that was fairly small—a bungalow, perhaps, and then we could switch houses with my parents when their health demanded it.

It was a pleasure driving all over Muskoka house-hunting (with or without our agent). It was a chance to get out of the house and away from Mom and Dad. Mom and Dad bickered almost constantly. They had hearing issues, anger management issues. They had much displaced anger. Dad was still sleeping for hours and hours during the day and Mom was angry with him for this reason. They were both angry about the way in which their lives had changed. They could not come to terms with the aches and pains of old age. They had been such active members of the community until now. They had spent hours serving at the church bazaar, singing in the choir, or working at the Bala Cranberry Festival in the past. Now they were virtually housebound and limited by how far Mom could drive and how long Dad could stand up with a shopping cart. It was incredibly frustrat-ing for them, but they took it out on each other and it bounced off us. My anxiety did not lessen.

In June, with great joy, I was transferred to a middle school to teach language arts and math to Grade 7 and 8 students. My principal was newly appointed. He had such energy and spirit, and he seemed game for anything. I just adored him. I packed up fifty-three boxes of teaching materials, sold or gave away my junior level posters and curriculum units, and began to prepare my curriculum for the next school year. I felt energy and excitement with a great staff that had a reputation for new, innovative ideas and with specialists in computers, physical education, science, and other disciplines. I began to hone my knowledge and researched intermediate literacy and numeracy strategies. I bought teacher resources and read all I could.

Radiation treatments — July 2005

In the first three weeks of July, anticipating my transfer and hopeful of a more positive and supportive environment, I finished off my education by taking the principals' course. One cannot even contemplate a principalship without the support of one's current principal. I was hopeful, moving to a new school with a fresh start.

In the meantime, Mom had developed two more tumours. Finally, Mom's oncologist decided that she had to have radiation treatments in July. She told me not to worry and that she was confident that this would get rid of the tumours at long last. She never asked questions about mortality rates for her type of cancer. She told me that it was a relatively unique type of cancer (leukoplakia) and they were experimenting with her treatments. My intensive three-week course consumed me. I phoned Mom regularly for updates. In hindsight, I should have helped her out. She was unable, intellectually or emotionally, to ask the oncologists the hard questions.

During the surgical process, Mom also had a lymph node taken from her leg. They wanted to prevent the cancer cells from metastasizing in her body. I managed a visit, but I could not stay, due to my other commitments back in Ottawa. My parents carried on, somehow, with neighbours picking up the slack. Mom had a fierce determination to stay in her own home. Dad was beginning to waver, but we did not know it at the time. He was more realistic about the limitations that the isolation of their lakeside home forced upon them. It was an hour to a hospital, forty-five kilometres to the surgeon, thirty-five kilometres to the nearest big town; they were unable to navigate their way to Toronto for oncologist appointments. Their lives changed immeasurably. They could not walk down to the lakeshore anymore. Dad could not drive. Mom was too weak to drive to the store.

Mom's radiation treatments in Toronto were extremely difficult, except for the socializing. The Cancer Lodge in which she stayed is a wonderful place for folks to live while having treatments. She was driven down by a volunteer on Mondays and stayed weeknights. She was driven home again for the weekend. I failed in trying to convince her to let me drive down with her. She was stubborn, as always. All I could do was to phone and check in on her progress. Neighbours, in the meantime, looked after Dad. He was incapable of doing many IADL. When we visited, we regularly brought him sandwiches.

The radiation wiped Mom out. I had zero contact with her doctors and could not ask about survival rates or a prognosis. I had to rely on her reports, which were confused at best. She could not hear everything they said, and perhaps did not understand it all. She had not looked well for more than a year. It was hard to see as a daughter. You were never prepared for such a thing. I would have liked to ask questions, but I was not permitted to do so. It was a huge mistake not to insist on my attending her appointments. Mom was beyond rational thinking in some ways. A cancer diagnosis and radiation treatments can wipe a healthy person out, and Mom was far from healthy at the time. I did some research on her lymphectomy, and found that she should have had specialized massage therapy for this, but there was no one who would go to her home to do it.

The oncologist: back to Toronto — August 17, 2005

By August, Mom had to go to Toronto for another appointment. It was in regards to her new tumour, number five. She refused to let me go along. By now my course was finished and, being a teacher, I was available if needed. She was adamant. I should have been stronger and fought this. She could not hear properly and was under stress. At age seventy-nine, she had an unfailing trust in doctors, who tended to gloss over details and use acronyms that only they understood; they treated elderly patients as if they were younger and had perfect hearing and cognition. The truth was that radiation and chemo has a profound effect on seniors who are already frail, and Mom was not offered statistics that took her age and condition into consideration. I should have been there to ask the questions that burned in my brain. One cannot really move forward without all of the information.

The doctor told Mom that he was not sure that the chemo he suggested would work. She wanted to give it a try. I should had gone in with her and asked the questions we all had: treatment rates, survival rates with and without the invasive treatments, survival rates based on age and stage of life. Many people facing "the big C" cannot and do not process much of the information presented at the time it is delivered. They have information overload and need an advocate to keep information straight, take notes, and provide help in understanding the information. I ensured that I took notes when Mom phoned me with information. I kept diaries all the time, as did Brian. I kept on doing research on my own, but could not find anything on *leukoplatia* (I learned later, in 2008, that it was *leukoplakia*). "Cancer in the groin" was covered, but it did not seem to apply to her situation.

Dad's MRI checkup — August 24, 2005

Dad had another MRI in August; they were scheduled once every six months post-surgery. How disturbing to be juggling the illnesses of both my parents. I felt as if I were barely able to keep my head above water. I had a meeting to attend in the city of Toronto and that made it easy to pop in to see Dad and his doctor. Mom was in favour of my presence there this time. She knew Dad couldn't hear much. Dad and his volunteer driver were to meet me at the oncologist's office. I did not know how I convinced them to let me go in, but I was concerned, and I think Mom knew that someone else ought to be there with him, not being sure how aware he was of his reality. In such a situation, people tend to shut out extraneous or indigestible information and take in only what they can face at the time. I knew Dad was not processing information all that well, and I was glad that I met him there. The tumour had not grown, and the five-hour trip finished without further incident.

Back to school — September 2005

The school year ended and began again. That September ritual consumed me: creating curricula, bulletin boards, seating plans, class lists, and attending staff meetings. Another school year ended, with yet another change in program for me. I had applied for and won a seniority-based transfer to another school. I was ecstatic to be teaching my favourite Grade 7 and 8 students again. I was excited to be working with an exemplary Special Education Resource teacher with whom I shared a philosophy of teaching that respected the individual as well as the class of students and the staff. We worked hard to integrate special needs students in various classrooms. We worked hard with one young lady who was afraid of attending school and developed migraines. We tested and worked with some needy kids and developed behaviour management programs that showed improvements in our young charges. It was an exciting time.

The principal in my new school, Dave, did everything with an enduring calmness that inspired and generated calm in all of us. This principal was a kind man, a caring leader who had gone through similar caregiving issues to mine with his late parents and understood the importance of family. The "sandwich generation" is not an easy one. A kind man who listened to me often as I barged into his office, the door was almost always open, and we would talk about the health issues my family was facing. He has a caring heart and an affable disposition, as well as a huge amount of empathy. He knew the ins and outs of this kind of ordeal. It did not matter what was going on — he would listen. We were both in early, so as to get work done, and I felt bad about interrupting, but I would often darken his door. Dave helped me and my husband carry boxes into my classroom. "Salt of the earth" he was. I decided that if ever I became a principal, I would want to incorporate his style into my repertoire.

As I fit into my new school with a keen, young staff, I tried to share my expertise with Special Needs students and worked hard to advocate for my students. My Grade 8 homeroom class was challenging. My small Grade 7 special needs class was equally, if not more, demanding. I worked hard to identify their learning needs and styles. I taught them many lessons and we created a classroom community of eager learners.

I participated in the training and development of a new computer system for a special needs student that incorporated software and peripherals that allowed for voice-to-text and text-to-speech capabilities. The system scanned and then read aloud grade-level texts for the weak reader. It was cutting-edge technology and very exciting. Unfortunately, the computer had to be locked down due to board policy, and we could not configure it easily. It was frustrating for me, my student, and his family, as we could not adapt it to enable its use at home. It totally defeated the purpose of this expensive unit. I argued with our IT people and made no progress.

As I juggled my home life and my school life, I came to terms with monitoring my mother from a distance while keeping in touch with my now adult children. Caitlin was into her first full-time job, gainfully employed by a respected firm of ground engineering and environmental services. This was her field of study and most reward-ing to her. She had great benefits including (shudder) maternity leave. When did I get old enough to be a grandmother? I was barely coping as a daughter with ailing parents! My son Jesse was working hard in his intensive drama program at the University of Alberta. Terry was attending Carleton University, working as a teaching assistant, and living with his father. It was great that they made few demands of me—I had little to give at this point. Brian, my rock and pillow, kept me organized and helped me deal with the inevitable stress around report cards, Remembrance Day ceremonies, parent-teacher inter-views, and school activities.

The stress of managing a new curriculum, new students, and a new classroom, resulted in frightful hot flushes and some measure of depression, and I fought to figure out who I was, where I fit in, and where my career should now go. My students were funny and fun and continued to challenge me. I loved walking around the school on yard duty. We had great chats as I informally counselled some of them. I liked working with this age group. They could discuss issues. We could work our way through inappropriate behaviour. My favou-rite memory was of our integrated math activity as we cleaned up the schoolyard and then graphed the garbage we found. It gave us a purpose to work with numbers and we incorporated digital camera technology,[3] creating a Web page of information, sorting and select-ing data.

We spent much time sharing and exploring holiday traditions in the classroom. I had a wide range of students with various back-grounds, and we visited all of the fall religious celebrations: Hanuk-

---

3   For more information, please see **www.jilks.com/portfolio/photos/ photos.html**.

kah, Ramadan, Festival of Lights, and so on, from various traditions such as the Jewish, Muslim, Buddhist, and Hindu religions—we were one big happy family. With students reading between a Grade 3 level in Grade 8 and others reading and writing at a level far beyond high school, I was challenged to create individual projects that met their literacy and numeracy needs. My creative juices flowed and I enjoyed rising to this new challenge. They inspired me and filled me with hope for the future. Their interests in a wide range of people from Rosa Parks to Martin Luther King to various Olympic athletes and local politicians running in the upcoming federal 2006 election led us to explore many issues. They raced in to be first to update the bulletin boards with new information or medal wins. I felt confident that I had created a classroom community in which learning was lauded and integrated with the real world. We began participating in an experimental blogging project with Ontario Ministry of Education funding. It was not too successful, but that is another story!

In the meantime, the sleepless nights, with my throwing off the covers and becoming drenched in sweat, were very difficult for me. I had to resort to sleeping pills on occasions such as the night before parent-teacher interviews. There were times when I simply needed to sleep. My personal life coloured my world so darkly that I began to suffer more and more.

To combat the stress, I continued to sing in the Ottawa Choral Society and to exercise regularly. I tried various homeopathic menopause remedies such as Black Cohosh. None of them worked. But we celebrated Christmas with the kids, as they fit us in between parents, step-parents, and in-laws. We sent care packages back and forth from Ottawa to Muskoka and I talked to my parents quite regularly. We had fun with a new kitten, intended to be mine. Eventually it adopted Brian, who was home full time. It was fun having a kitten around, with her antics lightening the atmosphere. We had a great holiday and I began to breathe again.

2006: Mom's Passing

This was an exciting time in my career. In our classroom we had followed the municipal fall 2005 election. On January 23rd, 2006, the federal election was also fun to watch. We recorded data and created reflective reports on the election, tabulated results, and compared campaign materials. We scoured newspapers to keep informed. I was quickly creating curricula to reflect the events of the day and I had to keep on my toes. It was tiring, but exciting. The students read biographies of exemplary athletes. We integrated math, language arts, and research-based activities. The kids were quite keen, but I was getting somewhat stressed with my personal life. Juggling the concerns about my mother's and father's ill health was a burden, with me a five-hour drive away. The phone calls continued to worry me.

The bizarre thing about contacting my parents was that they went upstairs to bed at exactly 8:00 p.m. Dad had pills to take at that time, and they both seemed adamant about taking them no sooner or later. Once they were upstairs in bed, they would watch a ball game, or other sports, but without their hearing aids turned on. They would meticulously remove them and put the aids in their respective cases. They could not hear the phone ringing. Many times I could not contact them and realized that they were simply in bed. I worried and felt upset about this until I realized this fact. Then I had to let it go. I could not convince them that it was a concern. What if the fire alarm went off? When we moved into the house much later on, I found that they had turned off the breakers for the fire alarms. I need not have worried they wouldn't hear them!

A dreaded phone call — more lumps
— February 9, 2006

Mom called again with the news that she had two more lumps. She went to Toronto and had a CAT scan to see what it was all about. She had had five surgeries by this time, and this did not sound like good news. She was quite optimistic, despite having had one tumour per year over the past four years. It was decided she would have chemotherapy. I am not sure who made this decision, nor the information on which it was based. She was a bit vague about the details, the timing, and what they expected this treatment to do for her. I went to the computer to do some research. It did not help. I had no specific information from Mom, who still remained positive. Chemotherapy was a difficult treatment, not necessarily indicated for older seniors. She was going to have chemotherapy every three weeks for six months. That was what "they" thought would be best. She would get the Cancer Society volunteer to drive her to the therapy, just as with the radiation, and would be able to stay at the Cancer Lodge in Toronto. All was taken care of. I was told later that the purpose of radiation is to reduce a tumour to prepare it for chemotherapy. If the radiation does not work, chances are the chemotherapy would not work, either. I wish I had asked the questions of her oncologist. But I was forbidden to do so. When I asked Mom for details, she was vague and did not know the answers, nor would she question her doctors. I had to ride the wave and look after myself. It was all I could do.

To further my career, I had just begun to take Part II of the principals' course, the final requirement to become a principal. It ran every other weekend in Ottawa, five minutes from my home, from February to April. I knew that if I managed to secure a transfer to Muskoka, it would be good to have this under my belt. It would help me with any job aspirations I might have in a new school board. As it happens, that was not to be, due to burnout, but it was an interesting course with like-minded individuals. It really helped me to keep up friendships and outside interests. It took my mind off my individual concerns and let me see the bigger picture: the management of an entire school.

Meanwhile, the February 2006 Winter Olympics in Tofino began. I prepared materials for the students to read, write, and reflect upon. They created PowerPoint slide shows, from my template, about various Olympic events. I worked hard on these projects to get my mind off my mother's cancer issues. The work in the classroom was a welcome break to my stress. All of us were quite happy with our independent projects. We would rush to the computer lab to find more information; we plotted Tofino on the map; the kids rushed in to update the medal standings every day. There was an energy and a synergy in this project. I barely had to teach, only facilitate, as the kids took ownership of their work. They helped each other find information and shared findings with each other. I worked on information and continued with our blogging projects. We took digital photos, compared notes, and had lively debates. It was a rewarding class of students. We worked so very hard.

March break visit — March 11, 2006

Brian and I made the five-hour drive to visit my parents during March break. It was difficult. I was feeling pretty worried about Mom's cancer, but mostly her proposed treatment. She insisted on making us lunch when we visited. She leaned heavily on the counter to support herself. That simple project set her back for days—she was simply too tired to stand up and cook. I asked her to save her energy to fight the cancer, but would she listen to me? A resounding NO! I had heard that many daughters go through this with their parents. Just getting up every day took a great deal of effort for her. It broke my heart to watch her, working at the sink. Mom had adamantly refused all help at home. Dad could barely walk; he shuffled with a heavy step and arthritic pain in his knees. Mom still made his lunch, leaning heavily on the counter for support and obviously in pain. It was agony to watch during visits.

How on earth she would tolerate chemotherapy was beyond me. She could barely eat and keep meals down with her colitis. She was tired and angry and in denial. In my mind's eye I had prepared for this eventuality. My mother, with a strong sense of family and a psychic mind, knew that my grandmother and aunts and uncles would be there on the other side. I saw this as a time to reflect on a life that had given much to the community in terms of her working life, her career with the Rotary Club, as well as her numerous volunteer activities. It was heartbreaking that we could not celebrate these accomplishments. She was beyond any sensible reflection or conversation about her life. I wanted reminders of family stories. I wanted to recall her early years growing up in Toronto and be able to tell these stories to my children. It was not to be. She spent time worrying about her impending treatments, about my father, about the pets, and it was the first time I realized that I was going to be the matriarch. I began to feel that I had lost my mother as I knew her. She had changed as she turned inward to fight her cancer. She had no energy left to worry about much else.

The interview — March 24, 2006

I scoured the electronic job postings in Muskoka. With great excitement and trepidation, I applied for a job in Parry Sound — a forty-five-minute drive from Bala. I read what I could about "Section 20" classes. I found that they were classes of behavioural problem students, students with anger management issues. We drove right through from Ottawa up to Parry Sound for the interview, 430 km. I was asked probing questions about my capabilities, skills, knowledge, and educational philosophy. I had dealt with enough kids with behavioural problems that I was confident I could do the job — if they wanted me. This might be my only chance for a transfer. It was a far cry from the Ottawa city schools in which I had worked. It was even more distant, in terms of philosophy, from schools in the south of Ottawa. I had worked in three small towns: Manotick, North Gower, and Nepean. How much different could it be? Little did I know!

There were four people interviewing me. I have had many interviews and did not feel too upset by this panel. I had worked with a number of different kinds of student exceptionalities and had experience teaching all grades up through Grade 8. They asked me questions about behaviour management that I had little trouble answering. I had dealt with students of various physical, social, and emotional backgrounds, as well as many disabilities. One of the interviewers (a retired superintendent) asked, on my behalf, what would happen if the special funding disappeared for this job? I would be last hired and first fired, should they be in a position to lay off staff. I had a foreshadowing of what was to come, which did not worry me too much at that point. I felt sure that I would find a job somewhere, as I would be on the seniority list. Fortunately, attrition had meant that most school boards have not had to let teachers go for many years. I was not worried.

Due to time constraints, and my wish to avoid the negativity between Mom and Dad, we did not stop in to see my parents this trip. Mom phoned after we arrived home, questioning my goals and plans. She wondered if it was a good idea to change jobs and school boards and move from the thriving, exciting city of Ottawa, very friendly for families, to a small town. She seemed not to want me there. I was devastated at her apparent rejection of my goal: to move closer to help them. I had promised her, during one of our heart-to-heart talks, that I would help them stay in their home as long as they could. In hindsight, that was a major mistake. I was shaken that she was not unconditionally supporting me as she always had done. The events were now unfolding as they would, I was committed, and I knew I needed to be nearer to them.

Mom dropped another bomb: she told me that what she thought was her first chemo treatment was merely an appointment for a discussion and CAT scan. I had my principals' course that weekend, which thankfully kept me busy. However, it did not keep my mind off all my mother's issues. Once you have a diagnosis and a treatment plan, you just want to get on with it. As I sat for five hours in class with my colleagues, learning about being a good principal, I worried over being a good daughter. During the breaks, I talked to my friends, which eased the pain. I was grateful for having a focus, group presentations, and projects, and I only cried a bit during that day! This was only the beginning as the treatments and Mom's cancer ramped up its invasion of her body.

Giving notice — moving — March 30, 2006

I was awarded the job in Parry Sound, to start on April 3rd, if I was able. I phoned everyone who needed to be phoned: my family, principal, and friends, and began making lists. We booked appointments with the real estate agent, the plumber/handyman, the painter, etc., to make repairs to put our Ottawa house on the market. Brian, bless him, would be home alone with the cats, cleaning the house and arranging with many service people required to get the house into shape to be sold.

My new principal wanted me to start creating a new classroom right away, with only one week's notice; he supported my work as a special education teacher, and I felt he believed in me. My new class did not yet exist. I would be starting from scratch.

I talked to my principal, Dave, right away. He assured me that leaving so soon would be no problem, despite an industry standard of two weeks. He understood how much my family life affected my work life, since he, too, had dealt with ailing parents. I was torn between my work and my family. What a dear man he is!

I was sad to leave Ottawa, but happy to be able to help my family. I could be replaced! Already emotionally exhausted from caring for my parents, I now worked hard physically to pack up all my teaching materials and move them home. I spent hours after school, and a professional development day, March 31st, putting my things into boxes. The boxes from LCBO are terrific, small and sturdy, and I packed as much as I could in them. I would leave a lot of materials for my supply teacher; she could use some of these things. My students helped me carry boxes to the car at lunchtime. They were great Grade 8 kids. It was an interesting class with a wide range of learners. They had various needs in terms of cognitive ability, culture, language, and learning abilities.

They quickly replaced me with an eager, capable supply teacher and a mother of teens; how fitting, since managing the adolescent is a tricky business. My oversized farewell card from the students was touching. Decorated with a large happy face, I took it with me as a memento of good times.

I felt bad leaving my students, but knew I needed to be closer to my parents. As an adoptee, I had been loved and welcomed as a chosen child. It was my turn to provide some care. There was no one else who could provide this care and advocate for them.

On March 31st, I packed up the last of my teaching materials. We were supposed to go and see Jesse in his last show at his university in Edmonton, but I knew I could not manage it. Caitlin, Jean–Luc, and Brian would fly to Edmonton, and I would drive to Parry Sound alone. I left right after my course finished on the Sunday afternoon. The car was packed to the gills.

April 1, 2006

April entered like a lion. I was quite sad to miss the trip to see Jesse's final performance as a Bachelor of Fine Arts student. He had a big part in a great play. It broke my heart having to make these kinds of choices. I knew that Jesse would have many more acting roles, and I did not know how long my mother had left to live. And I was starting a new job at a pretty crucial time.

I arrived in Parry Sound on a Sunday afternoon, driving 430 km west from Ottawa, Ontario, in beautiful weather. Navigating around the town, I found places to eat and where to get coffee and emergency toiletry supplies. I had found a Bed & Breakfast that took off-season boarders and safely settled in there. I nestled in and got used to the new sounds and new setting. I was worried about sharing a bathroom with young people who were rooming there; I had never lived away from home before.

The Parry Sound community is beautiful. Trees and hills line the roads and highways that I discovered as I drove about exploring. Lakes peeked out around the next bend at every turn. I felt I had come home.

I worked on my entry plan and tried to piece together all the parts of a classroom puzzle. Curriculum is made up of an instructional repertoire of instructional skills, pedagogies, tactics, and strategies, but a classroom community consists of integrating one's philosophy with that of the students and marrying that to the school community. I eagerly awaited the integration of my new students. I sat in a meeting with my new principal, the absence manager, and my special education supervisor. The room was dirty and cluttered, and I had to figure out how to make it liveable.

Mom's 81st birthday — April 4, 2006

After a day spent cleaning, sorting, and trying to get my head around my new classroom, I drove to Bala for a visit and dinner on Mom's birthday. As usual, with Mom's obsession with perfection, everything was preplanned. All of Mom's parties were done with panache and grace. She very clearly had an agenda. Two neighbours were invited, and probably had bought the groceries, and they were there when I arrived. They were terrific family friends, helpful women, both widows, who had done a great deal to help Mom and Dad continue to live in their home. One of them picked up the family newspaper, retrieved the mail, and picked up miscellaneous items from town, and another cleaned the kitty litter box every day and brought mom homemade soup, amongst other chores.

We made the meal, and the three of us worked at it while Mom barked orders from the couch. She was tiring out as she directed the work from where she lay. She wanted a particular green dish for a particular food item. We could not quite figure out which one she meant or where it was. Were we ever stressed! I told her that we could not find the right green bowl for the chutney; another bowl would have to do. She was angry and said, "It's my birthday. I can do it my way." Absolutely adamant! Mom wanted to remain in control of the small things, since she had lost control of the big ones. We announced dinner and gathered round the table, even Mom. Mom managed a few mouthfuls and feebly went back to lie down on the couch. It was shocking how ill she had truly become.

April 8, 2006

It was very difficult coping with my parents' illnesses. There was no place really to call home and no phone. I was a stranger, a guest in the B & B. I could not figure out the rules around the use of the kitchen, dining area, living room. One boarder was more like a daughter, while the other two of us were strangers. Three of us shared a bathroom. You never knew when you could get into it.

I put voice mail on my mother's phone, after convincing Bell that I had authority. I explained to Mom that I needed to know when Brian called, since we were apart, and we were selling the house. She was reluctant to permit this. I spent days trying to phone Bell Telephone, during breaks, to make the arrangements.

My job, as a teacher in a new school, was very difficult in this situation. I had to leave an old job, move, find a place to live, figure out the town, find a way to feed myself, and fit into a new household, as well as a new community, with no friends around. It was culture shock. I still did not have Internet access at the Bed & Breakfast where I was staying. This meant I could only access the Internet at school, and that was slow and cumbersome. It was a Local Area Network (LAN) computer connection that was like molasses.

I had moved from a city of 840,000 to work in a town of 8,000. Many people knew each other; only a few did not. The school had a clientele that consisted of a wide range of socioeconomic levels (e.g., the School Council chair was one of the town's pharmacists), lifestyles (one staff member is off-grid), and geographic locations (we served the region with several day treatment/system classes). There was much that needed to be done in the way of parenting support, as well as student support.

On Friday afternoon I drove home to Ottawa, my husband, and my cats. What a joy to be back in my own house and my own space! As I drove up the familiar drive, I felt homesick. Spring was coming, and my lovingly created gardens would have to do without me. I attended the principals' course from 8:00 a.m. to 3:00 p.m. on Saturday and Sunday. I felt so bad for my husband—a feeling that lasts to this day. He never seemed to get a fair deal: a home, a wife, and security. He was holding up more than his fair share of the home front, keeping the house clean for potential buyers.

Our old (1969) house had been de-cluttered, spruced up, and made ready to go to a new family. It was in a great neighbourhood, with trees and large lots. Even located as it was in the heart of the city, it was a peaceful spot. It was only a short distance to work. Just a few weeks before, I had driven four kilometres to work and had to navigate through fifteen stoplights. Now I was driving sixty-two kilometres, leaving in the early hours of the morning to get there on time. What was I thinking?

When I returned to Muskoka, I moved in with a neighbour of my mother's. Mom seemed perturbed that I was living so close by. It was a mystery. In hindsight, as long as I was at a distance, she could fool me regarding her condition as she did everyone else. She did not want me nearby to witness the means by which she manipulated people into allowing her to live at home. She drew in all favours from all people. It was part of her denial: All she needed to do was to get through the next little while and she would get better and all would be well with the world.

This new living arrangement lasted a week. I simply could not manage living in someone else's home. I was a middle-aged woman with no control left! We had issues, mostly related to her long history and intimate knowledge of my family. My aunts and uncles had built and owned cottages on either side of her. She knew the family's dirty laundry and liked to bring it out on a regular basis. It was demeaning and diminishing.

I still did not have a paycheque, and needed to spend as little money as possible and still try to look after myself. I had asked to borrow money from Mom until my first paycheque came through, but she refused and further questioned my decision to move here and accept this new job. I was demoralized. Where had my mother gone? It seemed like aliens had come and taken her away—or maybe it was the cancer—and replaced her with a stranger I no longer knew, respected, or recognized. Where was the loving, caring woman who had listened as I worked my way through a difficult divorce and helped me set up the home they helped me buy? My parents' cottage, where I ended up staying, was cold, Mom wouldn't let me turn the water on (in case we had a freeze), and I had to work hard to keep warm with a fire and wood stove that later proved not to meet the safety code.

First chemo treatment—April 10, 2006

We carried on. Mom's leg was incredibly swollen. Without the lymph node draining her system properly, the fluid built up. I did research on massage-type lymph node drainage on the Internet, but no one performs this specialized treatment to a patient in her home here. She was too ill to go anywhere for it. Treatments include elevation of the body part affected, compression, and manual lymph drainage. Mom's case manager arranged for a compression wrap that supposedly kept the water down. She was to massage her leg daily. It did not help. It was uncomfortable on top of her other pain, but she refused pain medications. She was too tired to do this herself, and I was afraid to massage her leg for fear I would hurt her. This condition was a result of treatment, and is called lymphedema, but we had been given no information on the risks involved in taking out the lymph nodes. There was no proof that the cancer would enter into her lymph nodes; it was a precautionary measure that proved to be contraindicated.

A Canadian Cancer Society volunteer drove Mom to Soldier's Memorial Hospital for her first chemo treatment. She refused to let me accompany her. It would have felt good being useful, and being able to listen, ask questions, and learn. I am sure she feared that I would tell them how ill she really was and in no condition to have chemotherapy. They did a CAT scan to look for embolisms (blood clots), which would have meant no chemo treatment, but her leg appeared all right that day.

Mom did not feel too sick after the first day of treatment. She felt that all had gone well. She was glad to get back home to eat, since she had fasted before the trip, as always, to prevent a colitis attack. She had stopped wearing her adult diapers, as they were uncomfortable and were chafing her sensitive skin. The carpets were getting filthy. She felt that this was the dog's fault—the only way she could deal with this reality. She would have diarrhea and not make it to the toilet in time. The dog was, in fact, accidentally urinating on the carpet, as was the cat in the back room office, but neither of my parents could deal with these issues. The house was a mess and I had no energy to clean it. I had moved into the cottage by this time, but with only a small heater, and still no water, so I would come into the house to shower. I ate out a lot and gained a lot of weight. I was lonely and upset all the time. My hands began to shake.

Mom began to have a few more chemotherapy reactions later in the week. I visited her every day, and she began to get worse. She had to go back to Orillia for blood tests to check the amount of radiation in her system. As always, since Dad could not drive, and I was busy working, she had a Cancer Society volunteer drive her. Mom felt the worst around the second week and began to feel better in week three. This was typical. She was optimistic, as always, but in three weeks, treatment number two would reduce her to lying on the couch.

She remained positive and optimistic and lied about her well-being to any and all who asked. It wasn't until the end of the week that her energy flagged. Her hair began falling out. She asked her neighbour over during the day to cut it all short. She told a cousin that her hair had gotten all tangled. She continued to tell the cousins that she was "fine." Mom did not want visitors. She looked horrible: gaunt, frail, no hair, and the house was filthy. Several people asked to visit, and she refused. She was tired and the house was not up to her usual standards. She was not dealing well with the physical demands of living, and the chemo did her in. I was a basket case: juggling a new job, creating a new classroom from scratch, and managing a long-distance marriage.

I had been in contact with the Community Care Access (CCAC) people again to give them a heads-up. They had been helpful in informing me of possibilities for extra home care. I worried leaving Mom alone at the house during the day. She was reluctant to accept more help. I had to work hard to lobby for this. I did not succeed until the last two weeks of her life. Family members must have a say in the type and level of care a senior receives. The work often falls to us and the stress can be debilitating and can impact the entire family.

The drive to and from work continued to inspire me. It was wonderful passing all of the trees and the pink, white, and grey Precambrian Shield rock. The roads were cut out of the rock and water dripped through the fissures, collecting and forming giant icicles the size of my leg. They were like exclamation points demonstrating the amalgamation of earth, water, and land. As the weather warms up and the rock absorbs the fire of the sun, the exclamation points fall from the rock and embed themselves in the huge piles of soft snow. Then they resembled daggers that punctuated the end of winter and the beginning of the new season.

I absorbed the energy and the spirit of nature—destiny unfolding as it should. Each day, as I drove by deep forests, I noticed that the buds on the trees were getting larger and larger. It looked like an artist had gone out in the night and painted more buds. The maple trees had bright red buds. The greens and yellows of the other hardwoods began to hide the homes of permanent residents, as if they were protecting them from the tourists who would soon arrive from the big city. Eventually the homes would be no longer visible. The pine trees were becoming bright green in contrast to the brown of the dead grasses. The colours were beautiful. The deep ruts on the pavement slowed me down. The snow melted and froze and made driving difficult with the spring thaw. I simply absorbed the scenery.

Travelling 430 km home every other weekend, sitting in a classroom for five hours on both Saturday and Sunday for my course, having only a brief amount of time with my husband and children, then driving back to Muskoka, took a toll on me. Monitoring Mom as best I could was difficult. Communication with my children was spotty at best. With no phone and no Internet where I was living, and no time to sit at a computer at school, I began to feel very removed from my children. They continued to e-mail me when they could. Mom made me remove voice mail from the phone. I made arrangements to have a phone installed in the cottage. For anyone who has dealt with Bell telephone, you know how difficult this is. But I squeezed in an appointment and took time off work to be there when Bell arrived. More time off work, but necessary.

Dad's MRI in Toronto — April 12, 2006

In the meantime, in a parallel universe, Dad had been having MRIs every six months to ensure that the tumour was not coming back. This MRI showed that one tumour had begun to grow, while another remained dormant, and the *cure* was radiation treatments. I was not sure what we were to gain by the treatments. No one asked pertinent questions. Survival rates and treatment options were not discussed, since my mother was ill herself, and none of us accompanied Dad to his appointments. The continuum of treatment versus palliative care was one that had not been examined. We never discussed quality of life over treatment options. Mom was fighting for her life and demanded chemo treatment for herself, as well as for Dad. I had little control, no one was looking at the big picture, and Mom wanted to handle this in her own way. The thought was that the radiation would reduce the tumour, but they did not know for sure, nor at what cost to his quality of life. The side effects were not discussed; Mom had little idea, or had forgotten, or not heard whether the benefits or risks outweighed the quality of life. I was helpless and becoming increasingly agitated.

Mom called and desperately asked my brother, Robin, to take time off work and come and drive Dad to appointments in Toronto. Robin took five weeks off from work to do this for them.

I would pop in and visit with my mother for a half hour, then would go to the cottage by myself and to do other things. In an attempt to balance the stress with Mind, Body, and Spiritual practices, I was jogging regularly. I tried to garden for an hour or so on days I did not jog. The nights were bordering on zero-degree weather, and the one baseboard heater managed to keep the temperature up to five degrees or so in the cold cottage. I had the heating blanket on the bed, and that made the difference between freezing and managing to sleep.

Communication was the most important thing I needed right then. As the voice mail I put on my parents' phone had not gone over well with Mom, I felt helpless being away from my home with no means of making or taking calls and had arranged for a phone line to the cottage.

We bought Dad a new phone that brought the decibel level up to ten times that of a regular phone. We had realized that this was why Dad never wanted to talk to us via the phone. After his tumour was removed in 2003, he could not hear much. Brian did a great deal of research to find this phone. Dad's "superphone" blinked when there was voice mail, and it upset him terribly. The problem was that when there was a phone message waiting, the huge, bright red light flashed and Dad could not figure out how to get access to the messages. My only option was to order a new phone line for the cottage where I was living.

I was not sleeping well and often had to get up at night and try to read and clear my head. The stress was beginning to build. Arguments ensued with my mother. Mom became angry when I asked her to think about moving into a retirement home in town. She insisted that Dad wanted to stay here in their house in Bala. She wanted my brother to accompany Dad to Toronto, but did not want him to drive. She wanted to rely on the Cancer Society volunteers, which was totally unnecessary. As it happens, she was wrong about Dad's wanting to remain in a house he could not manage, but we could not convince her of that. Robin and Dad would speak of this when in Toronto.

My cousin had been in touch with my mom. She spoke about the head scarves I had gotten for her. She told my cousin that she was going to go with a friend to get a wig in the future. She told her how appreciative she was of family and church friends who had given them so much support. She was emphatic that she and Dad had no desire to move out of their home at this stage, despite their inability to handle their ADL or IADL. This cousin asked if she could get help with cooking and cleaning, and Mom told her she was "looking into this." As if! My cousin commented, "She is amazing in her attempt to be positive." I spelled that D E N I A L, myself. My cousin encouraged her to accept the help and suggested we get a live-in caregiver in to help with ADL. Unfortunately, there was no room for someone to live in.

The CCAC health nurse would pop in from time to time, but Mom never told her the real story—her pain and incontinence; her inability to manage ADL, to carry wood to fuel the wood stove (they thought the baseboard heaters did not work), cook, bring food up from the overfilled basement freezer. We were sent one weekend to buy meat from the butcher. When we went to put it in the freezer, we found meat that was more than a year old. Mom had forgotten it was there. She had begun to put in duplicate supplies of many household goods. Another sign of dementia.

Another cousin explained that Mom had inherited her stubbornness from her family. He said, "Stubborn is a good servant but a poor master." This made it extremely trying for the family, and I wondered how much her behaviour stemmed from the organic disease, the toxic effects of the tumour or treatment. We did not know. Apparently it is a typical pattern of behaviour amongst aging, frail seniors. Denial, pride, control, fear, and a desire for face-saving, all compound to create intensely negative family relations. I knew we were not atypical, or even extraordinary, but my happy childhood and family life had not prepared me for this situation.

We had an argument and Mom did not talk to me for a whole day. I kept to myself in the cottage. I finally wrote her a long letter. It was like an intervention letter. I told her that I was there if she wanted help, but that I was tired of fighting and tired of trying to give her care that she would not accept. She was angry with me, continually questioning everything I suggested and refusing help. I was suffering seeing her suffer, and she needed to figure out how to graciously accept help. I could not cope this way anymore. We talked after this. She began to realize how ill she really was and how much it affected me. She looked horrible: gaunt, her hair all gone, deep, dark hollows in her cheeks; basically, she was resting most of the day.

It was a turning point for us. We had a hug and a good cry together. I asked Mom's case manager to get us some more home care. Our relationship changed at this point from daughter to caregiver. I began to grieve even more.

Anger, honesty, the phone, and head scarves — April 15, 2006

It was time for me to go back to Ottawa for the weekend. As I drove, I saw a large, tawny deer by the side of the road. She carefully navigated her way across the highway; a car in front of me slowed down and she seemed to know it was all right to cross. As I passed her, she stopped and looked backwards at the car travelling down the road. She was large — probably as tall as me. Her white tail flicked behind her as she bolted off into the forest. There was a great peace that settled upon me. My daughter's animal totem was the deer. I always think of her when I see one. I knew someone was watching over me. The drive was beautiful in the early dawn. I knew I had given up my home, my work, and my friends for a purpose. Nature had the power to heal and I breathed deeply.

Brian and I had visited the Ottawa office of the Canadian Cancer Society the previous weekend. They have volunteers who hand-sew head scarves for women who have lost their hair. Knowing my mother's concern about her appearance, I thought she might appreciate something like this. It was time to give some scarves to Mom. She seemed to like the idea, as her hair was now all gone and her scalp cold and bald. Coincidentally, the woman working there was the mother of one of my former students. It was good to chat.

Mom admitted to hospital — Monday, April 17, 2006

Nearly three weeks in Muskoka had zipped by. Mom was to have her second chemo treatment. She was optimistic that morning. Her steadfast faith, her stubbornness, and the necessity of staying in control drove her. She refused to let me go with her. She phoned for a Cancer Society volunteer driver.

I toddled off to work to try and keep my mind off of things. Work certainly did that. School was becoming increasingly difficult. My students were demanding, needy, Grade 7 and 8 boys who had had little success in their lives. They kept me on my toes. I knew that with enough time, support, patience, counselling, discipline, and remedial work, I could have helped them achieve some academic success and produce some good effort. Unfortunately, I had little of any of these things. They were vulgar, selfish, hormonal boys, with little respect for women, growing into men's bodies. I had no means by which to maintain control, despite my stabs at behaviour modification programs; it was a difficult battle. I loved my work, I knew I was good at what I did, but every day I had a knot in my stomach as I began to anticipate failure. The only time I felt peace was when on the highway driving between home and school. With the sun roof open, the heater on, and the wind in my hair, I could stay in the present.

This month my favourite music was Josh Groban's beautiful tunes from his CD *Awake*. I didn't understand the Italian songs, but hummed my way across Central Ontario with them. I sang "You Are Loved (Don't Give Up)" with him over and over, trying to will myself to be positive.

Mom began her day in Orillia with a CAT scan. It told the health care staff that she had an embolism, a blood clot, in her leg. Instead of having a treatment, Mom was admitted to hospital. She was furious and frustrated. Without her overnight bag, no phone book, no forewarning (Mom could plan her way through a World War), she phoned and gave all of us sundry orders! Beside herself with stress, Mom called several neighbours to make arrangements. She said they *"whisked me off the street and admitted me,"* and she was beyond any comprehension of the seriousness of her health issues. Had she not been warned of this potential side effect? Was there no explanation of the risks of removing the lymph node? She was not in control—she could handle anything if she had time to plan and take charge of it.

I navigated my way home from work, oblivious to the furor at home. Along the highway, I passed sparkling lakes and shadowy forests; I turned the heat on in the car and opened up the sunroof. It was good to feel the sun.

Then I arrived home and checked in on Dad. It was stressful to say the least. It was a shock to find out the latest news about Mom. One of Mom's friends, given the task of finding Dad a ride to his dental appointment the next day, was swamped with things she had to do. Dad and I had a great moment when Mom phoned from Soldier's Memorial Hospital to give orders. Dad felt he was too stressed with worrying about Mom to go to the dentist the next day. He grinned as he held the phone away from his ear—I could hear her giving the Orders of the Day. Dad rolled his eyes as she gave him heck for not wanting to go to the dentist.

Mom never told Dad how ill she was. They never spoke of it. It angered him, he told me later, as she did not give him a say in their treatment plans. He harboured his stress internally. Mom could not let go and let me handle these arrangements. I think I was still perceived as a little girl. My mother was no longer looking after me, but neither was she giving me any credit or responsibility, and I had to look after myself. Dad wasn't hungry, so I went into town to do errands and to have a well-earned yet solitary dinner.

Picking up Robin — April 18, 2006

I was quite happy to pick up my brother, Robin, from the bus station on April 18th. He was coming to town to drive Dad to his radiation treatment appointments in Toronto. Dad and Robin went to Toronto on Thursday and Friday, and stayed at the Cancer Society Lodge, where Dad was an outpatient. They drove home Friday afternoon. Mom was discharged and sent home that day as well.

What a lovely drive into work. I felt a sense of peace in the drive. This was when I depressurized. The scene changed every day. I saw two large turkey vultures at the side of the road. They eyed me as I passed. On another day, there was a fox trotting perkily along the side of the road. She seemed happy that humans had made her a nice trail. It sure made hunting easier! I drove by these gorgeous lakes and trees, noticing the snow and ice slowly melting, as I followed my daily route to work. Each day, nature painted a few more dabs of colour on the trees. They were red, yellow, and dark brown buds of promise and they looked beautiful. Then, in the night, nature painted the buds a little more and a little more until I could no longer see the trees and homes behind. Soon enough, the leaves burst into beautiful green, and the tiny, isolated cottages became invisible behind them once more.

It was Robin's birthday, but I abandoned ship to drive back to Ottawa for the weekend. I still had to go back every two weeks to take the principals' course. I felt a mixture of guilt and relief to escape the health issues that weighed so heavily over everyone's head. It was a palpable pressure, as the roof seemed to be caving in. It was good to get home to familiar surroundings. I drove directly from work to Ottawa, relieved to see Brian.

Mom and I spent some lovely, quiet, peaceful times together during her final months, in between arguments. Mom knew that they needed new carpets and she did not know if she should get them in green for her or blue for me! In March, Terry phoned her to thank her for his birthday cheque and she admitted to him that she wasn't "very well." She was nakedly honest with him. She knew he would not like any guff! There were good times in between the stress, but they were few and far between.

Things were not looking good; it is hard sharing a small cottage without heat or water. I was glad Robin had a brief visit with me, and happier that he was able to share some of the burden. Many families cannot agree on appropriate care, treatment, or other issues. Robin was totally supportive of all I had done. We talked quite a bit as I informed him of all that was going on. I was not in charge, but we developed a plan, kept mum from Mom. Rob would drive Dad to Toronto in the van. Mom didn't trust him, but this was a result of her cancer, which coloured her perceptions and reframed her view on life. Robin is a capable man, with big responsibilities in the mine in which he works, such as blowing up dynamite. I figured he could manage to drive my dad to have his radiation treatments. I could not figure Mom out at all.

In Mom's fight against cancer, her life was framed by survival. She had continually fought my suggestions and interventions. I was powerless. She asked close friends not to visit. I think, in retrospect, that she was ashamed of the state of her home and her inability to keep up the meticulous housecleaning practices she was used to maintaining. She refused to wear her adult diaper except when I nagged her. There were spots all over the house where she had soiled the carpet. I mentioned it, but she informed me it was the dog. It was not.

The previous week, Mom was using the vacuum cleaner, and I had repeatedly asked her not to do it. I thought she should save her strength to fight for her life. She was so very tired. But Mom was always so particular with keeping the house up. She could not let it go. I tried to balance schoolwork with caring for her. She would have special dietary requests, and I would strive to get her whatever she needed. There was much pressure.

Aunty visits — May 9, 2006

By the time I made it to May 9, I had decided to take Tuesday and Wednesday off from work. I had found out that funding for my classroom would not continue for next year, and I could anticipate more change in classroom, programs, or schools. Feeling defeated and alone, I was at home on a sick day, as I was in shock, feeling sick, tired, depressed, and fighting for my health. No longer could I count on my mother to look after me, or to be there when I called. She was fighting for her life and had lost her perspective. Our relationship had changed forever. I wondered how I could continue to cope with working full-time while juggling these battles—hers and mine. When I phoned in sick, I had forgotten that my aunty was coming for a visit.

This "aunty" was actually one of the 200 teenaged foster girls my grandmother took in after her husband died in 1940. My grandmother, a widow whom we grandkids called "Nanny," needed the money to care for her four children. She kept in touch with many of these foster girls. It extended our immediate family. She helped the girls to find their place in life. My grandmother was featured in an article in the Toronto paper. I found it in my mother's files. She was a dear soul, my nanny, and we spoke of her often.

Aunty, who likes baking, brought a lemon meringue pie and some potato salad. I greeted her and took the food, putting it in the refrigerator. She was a strong woman, as stubborn as my mom, and they always competed when bragging about their respective children. I had not seen her in years. Aunty spent about ten minutes visiting until Mom, obviously fatigued, fell asleep. I was working on report cards outdoors on my laptop. I asked Aunty to come outside with me and let Mom sleep. It was a lovely spring day. I wanted Mom to sleep.

I tell this story because I know that cancer patients need rest, and disagreements about caregiving standards are rife, even in the most well-adjusted families. Family members seldom agree on appropriate daily care, the proper placements for ailing seniors, and who should be in charge. It is the duty of caregivers to understand the needs of their patients.

I was the mother bear and tried protect Mom. It was draining for my mother to try to remain awake. Mom could not tolerate visitors being here, her house was filthy. I had to be vigilant.

Aunty and I sat talking outside, while Mom slept, and I could feel my stress levels increase. I was unable to be a good host, but had nowhere else to go. The cottage was cool. I had no patience left; I was tired of defending to various relations what I was doing and how we were coping. I was so very stressed. Finally, I asked Aunty to leave. She was furious. She stormed off home complaining about my ill treatment of her. Aunty still has not forgiven me for this and we do not speak anymore, even though I asked her forgiveness. We make the best decisions we can at the time.

Mom, ill as she was, thought visiting from Aunty was okay. My neighbour made sure later that I knew my mother was upset that I had asked Aunty to leave. It was just one more sweet gift for me to ruminate over; one in a long list of mistakes. As is typical, the caregiver is the one who lacks care and support. I felt lost and bereft.

In hindsight, I realize that I wanted to spend time alone with my mother while I still could. Someone had to look after me, though. I simply could not handle a visitor.

Make a joyful noise — May 10, 2006

"Make a joyful noise unto the Lord" is the motto that drove our family. I had sung in choirs since I was in my early teens. During my long drive to work, I found solace in music. I played various CDs and sang out, sunroof open, at the top of my lungs to the animals and trees and small lakes I passed on the long drive to work. There is peace either in singing or listening to music. I played Meatloaf, lots of vocal music, Christmas music, and I cranked through *Messiah* several times. Colm Wilkinson's album *Some of My Best Friends Are Songs* (2004) struck a chord for me. From "We Are One": "The slower you move; the faster you go."

These words resonated with me. I needed to be positive and work from my inner strength and access the strength of my family. I used to feel that we were a family and that I was not alone. I memorized the entire CD. I tried to go slowly, feeling burned-out and stressed beyond belief. My work was destroying my confidence in myself as a teacher. My inability to look after my mother very well was destroying my self-esteem. She would accept little outside support and would rebel vigorously against suggestions that we bring in caregivers or find her another place to live. We did have a nurse, Christine (she did not have any choice about the nurse). I rather liked Christine, and we talked about Mom's case.

Mom did accept help, finally. We had had an argument; I wrote her a letter articulating my frustrations, and we made peace. I knew then that she was *really* ill. It took me ages to convince her to accept the wonderful services the health agency provided. It turned out that all of her caregivers were terrific people. Although many of her friends had worked hard to help my parents meet their needs in the past few months, and most of them understood and respected Mom's need to do it her way, the time had come for expert assistance.

A cousin visits — May 11, 2006

My cousin who lived thirty-five kilometres away came to visit. She stayed a reasonable ten minutes. The problem with someone in palliative care was having outsiders understand that conversation drains a patient. I was out at work when she came. My cousin signed Mom's visitation book, which I had prepared. I had found it hard figuring out who had visited while I was at work and wanted to keep a record of care and visitors. Brenda, Mom's personal support worker (PSW) from Community Care Access Centre (CCAC), came to do a bit of vacuuming and meal preparation. Jean, a friend, came and dropped off some cookies. The communication book really helped, partly because they wrote down what they did for Mom and it gave us something to talk about. It was good to see that someone still cared, despite my perceptions to the contrary.

School was becoming increasingly difficult and more of a burden than a relief. To my mind, the discipline in the school was not strong enough. Perhaps it was the philosophy of the place: "Just love them enough and they will be fine." I was on my toes every minute of the day. The revamped school day, with the new "nutrition breaks" of twenty minutes twice a day rather than the energy-rebuilding forty-minute breaks, was hard for me to deal with. My stress levels were high, as I could never find a moment to depressurize, trying to fit bathroom breaks and phone calls into this short period of time. And there were few available phones.

It was too late for my students, this late in the school year. They needed a modified curriculum. It was way too late for them to buy into my program. I was treated more like a supply teacher than a homeroom teacher. They were rude and swore constantly, and I had to put them on a token system for swearing. I took a baseline count of how often they swore and gave them ten free swear tokens. If they could accumulate enough tokens between them (I think it was forty!), I would take them out to play basketball. Mostly these four boys needed to be able to understand their limits, and this dragged me down. My students needed much discipline and constant supervision. This plan worked.

I was informed that I was to teach Grade 3 the next year. I was not amused. I found some relief and managed to switch jobs, schools, and locations for the following September with a teacher who wanted to teach in Parry Sound. This new school was about twenty kilometres closer to home.

In the meantime, the school climate was tough. There were bargaining issues with the occasional teachers. The school board ended up locking us all out. I was to go and present three workshops in Toronto on Friday and Saturday. With the lockout, the school board did not want me or the other two Parry Sound conference participants to go to Toronto. Late in the day, we found out that the lockout had ended. I was relieved that I could go to Toronto for a break.

Mom became weaker each day. She was eating about a tablespoon of food a few times a day. I picked up potato salad from the corner store, at Mom's request. I ordered it specially, as this was not tourist season, and they did not have much in the store. They were most amenable to helping me out. She ate a mouthful and then she slept. I was to leave for Toronto for the conference. I phoned the Community Care Access (CCAC) people yesterday and asked them to send someone to look after Mom. Rob and Dad were expected back from Toronto at around noon. I had two workshops to present on Friday, one in the afternoon and one in the evening. Then I had another one to present on Saturday.

Jennifer gets out of town — Friday, May 12

I checked in on Mom at 7:45 a.m., and she could not physically get up. When we spoke, she said she felt pressure on her lung. She could not breathe very easily and when she sat up, she got dizzy. I told her to lie down. She was coughing up small amounts of dark mucus. She had a sip of water, and then I phoned her doctor. I asked Mom if she wanted to go to the hospital, and she said, "No, let's wait for Doctor to arrive. He may have a solution." She sent me out of the room. I knew I was stronger than she thought I was. She was trying to protect me. It was a peculiar situation for me. I had seen all the shows where the family gathers around a bedside. They get back as much as they receive in being with ailing family members. I did as I was told and went downstairs. I clearly felt pushed away.

By eight a.m., the cat was pacing and the dog was upset. They seemed to sense impending doom. I had lost perspective and did not know how short a time there was left. I cleaned the basement out, since they were coming to install a propane furnace to replace the wood stove. It took me two hours to sort through the years of junk. The dust was incredible. It felt good to do something worthwhile. It was pouring rain. It cleared, but another weather front was moving in. The water pond pump was off in Mom's and Dad's beloved goldfish pond, likely broken, and I had another phone call to make to arrange for repairs. The rain had lasted all night and the pond had overflowed. Maybe it was just a circuit.

By nine-fifteen a.m., Mom needed her adult diaper changed, and I had to change it for her. She was unable to move her body well enough to lift it out from under herself. It was humbling to help her this way. Finally the doctor arrived. He told me that there was thrombosis in her right leg—blood clotting. He said the tumour was pushing up on her lung, and this was the reason she could not breathe. I didn't know there was a tumour in her lung. This had never been mentioned. Why she was sent for chemotherapy with a tumour racking her frail body, I do not know. She was now palliative, the doctor said. We had to keep her comfortable and that was all we could do for her. At last someone had finally said it. I had come to terms with this. He asked me what her wishes were and I told him that Mom wanted to stay at home. There was nothing else they could do. Dying was hard. It was comfortable here and the same things would be done here as in hospital. He told me he would order oxygen to help ease her breathing.

Mom's doctor was about her age. He had been practising in our town forever, and I was grateful he could visit. I had no idea that there were palliative care teams around, or hospice organizations. I was alone fighting this battle of wills with Mom.

Upstairs, in private, I am not sure what the doctor told her. I did not know what they discussed, or even if Mom was honest about her situation. I wondered if she still thought he "would find a solution." Mom did not bother having her morphine pill prescription filled a few days ago (after the failed second chemo visit, this is what they sent her home with: no care arrangements, just a prescription). I had to make all of the calls. Mom could have had the prescription filled in town, but she stubbornly thought she would not need it. Poor Robin would have to take care of this later. This was a big mistake, as "town" was thirty kilometres away. Rob and Dad were due about noon. I had to leave for the trip to Toronto, just before then, to make my conference.

Another caregiver, someone who had never been here before, was coming for the 11:00 a.m. to 2:00 p.m. shift. I met her at the front door and explained the situation once again. She was sent by the Red Cross, through the CCAC, and gave Mom a half glass of SoyNice, a soy-based drink with no lactose. Since Mom had problems with milk tolerance, this was a terrific meal replacement and easy to drink. Christine, the CCAC nurse, came by to check in later and she left a note. I know that these health care providers knew that death was imminent, but no one thought to let me know what was going on or what to expect. It angered me later. After I left, a company delivered oxygen: a mask and a tank, which they took upstairs to Mom. This would help her breathe.

I bought Mom some flowers before I left for my conference. She always liked large flowerpots on the deck. I do not know if she ever saw them. I bought a small bud vase for the table, with a carnation and a little bear that said, "#1 Mom!" on it. I had filled the plant containers the week before with her favourite impatiens. I'd bought some big planters and put flowers in there, as well. I was so glad I did. I would be back the day before Mother's day, the 14th, but I knew I had to act quickly. Who knew what I would have time for later?

I took off in the car, mentally preparing for the three workshops I would conduct. It was a pensive drive. I had spent a career developing my practice. I had delivered workshops to my peers, demonstrating exemplary teaching strategies that incorporated technology into curricula. How relieved I was to get a break and take my mind off the stress of caring for Mom. This was my field and my profession and I felt like an adult again. I knew I had created three strong Power-Point presentations and was excited to be able to share my ideas. In Ottawa, I had developed a reputation for incorporating technology into my work. I was quite excited to go to the big city and share my expertise to an all-female group of attendees.

It was bizarre how incompetent I had felt for the past month as I attempted to deliver home care to my mother. Our lives had been framed by my mother's cancer diagnosis, and subsequent invasive treatments, for the past number of years. Out of my element, living in the country, I was beginning to feel a sense of helplessness.

Such an independent, fiercely private woman, Mom hid her ill-health from everyone. I continually asked relatives for help, but Mom baldly denied that she needed anything from them. I was exhausted, but for the first time in my life my mother was not keeping my needs uppermost in her mind. Far from my husband and children, I dreaded the day.

Navigating in the big city, Toronto, I checked into my hotel, found the University of Toronto, and presented two of my three workshops. I felt energized and enthusiastic. I felt like a whole person again. I had not had to go into school that week, since the school board had locked out the teachers. I had spent a few days lobbying to be able to attend the conference, in between looking after Mom. The superintendent had forbidden the teachers to attend, and couldn't make up her mind if I was to be allowed to go to present my workshops. Commitments had been made; I was determined. Brian was going to meet me at the hotel in Toronto this afternoon. I was so happy. It was a much-needed break. It was easy for him to fly to Toronto from Ottawa. I did not phone home, as I knew Robin would be busy and would certainly call if things changed. Little did I know.

Mom's passing — Saturday, May 13, 2006

I took off for the university early in the morning to prepare and deliver my remaining workshop. I had heard no word from Bala and hesitated to phone them. The buzz was exciting. The conference was aimed at helping female teachers to take risks and incorporate technology into their curricula.

My well-earned break was to be short-lived. While I was out presenting my workshop, Robin had phoned the hotel and left a message to for me to call. Brian, arriving at the hotel before I finished my presentation, returned the call to Robin. As I walked into the hotel room, Brian gave me the news that Mom had passed away.

I never felt grief, just a giant sucking in of breath. I focused on what needed to be done next. We took a moment in Toronto to have a good lunch, make plans, and draw up checklists of things that needed to be done. It was surreal.

Apparently, on Friday, Robin had taken Mom to the hospital in the evening. A couple of neighbours had gone with them but came home later that night to check in on Dad. The hospital could not do anything for Mom, and Robin brought her home at about three-thirty a.m. on Saturday. They went back to sleep in their exhaustion, Mom and Robin sleeping on respective couches. They woke around seven a.m. and talked a bit about grandkids, and so on. They had good conversations, in between Mom's naps, and laughed over good times. I missed that opportunity. I have to learn to let this go and deal in the present.

Mom's breathing got more and more shallow. Eventually, around nine a.m., Robin looked over at her and saw that she had stopped breathing. Dad, on prescriptions for infections, was quite out of any concept of reality. He became very upset and told Robin to get her body out of the house. Poor Rob had to hustle, with the aid of his cousins, to find an undertaker to remove Mom's body. Dad was emotionally distraught, Rob said, and could not deal with all of the things he needed to deal with. He did not recognize Mom's body as his dearly beloved late wife. (Dad was suffering from prostatitis, which we did not know at the time. He was incoherent much of the time and was having difficulties getting to the bathroom.)

I must go back in time to explain this next problem. In their will, Mom and Dad named my cousins (husband and wife) as executors. We are not sure why, since the will was redone in 1998, and Robin and I were adults at the time. These cousins live in Southern Ontario, and it is a fair distance to visit here, especially since they have a farm. Fortunately, they happened to be visiting in the area at the time. Robin and the cousins made arrangements to send Mom's body to the funeral home and to have her body cremated.

Once at the funeral home, they signed the agreement with the funeral home. My cousins declared my father unfit to be in charge and took ownership of the problems. Dad certainly was in no condition to take care of these things. In hindsight, my brother and I should have simply signed the agreement with the funeral home and taken control. We had *power of attorney* for both medical and financial affairs. In the meantime, my cousins began acting as executors and, once they had done so, since Dad could not at the time, they had complete signing authority for all matters. This became a problem later when trying to remove Mom's name from documents and put them solely in Dad's name.

All of the arrangements had to be done between my cousins and the funeral home from this point on. We could not even take her remains out of the funeral home for the memorial service, as we were not executors. Our cousins had to sign a letter later, as executors, giving us permission.

By the time Brian and I arrived from Toronto, the funeral arrangements were made and the contract signed. My cousins and my brother had begun writing Mom's funeral announcement, but they did not know some of the names. The obituary left out Mom's dear adoptive sister in Lethbridge, whom I had not seen in more than twenty-five years. I felt bad — another mistake for my hindsight list. I had to take over this job. The next day was Mother's day, and I had an obituary to write. In hindsight, we should have postponed the small family funeral until a later date, rather than having it a week later.

Radiation side effects
— Sunday, May 14, Mother's Day

I created a list of things I knew needed doing. I had to write a eulogy, arrange and create a funeral service, clean up Mom's clothes, give them to charity, and make the phone calls to friends and relatives. Robin and I talked for a long time, figuring out what we should do with our father, still fighting his undiagnosed and untreated infections. Dad was unable to make it to the bathroom all of the time. He was incoherent and could not keep his pills straight. He had thirteen to take in all: some in the morning, some at noon, and others at night. This is called "polypharmacy." It is a huge predictor of ill health in seniors. There were many complications possible with pills prescribed by his doctor as well as his oncologist, and neither talking to the other.

We ended up hiding the pills and giving them to Dad at the appointed times. This inability to manage this self-care task was a huge predictor of dementia and future problems. Dad's radiation treatments — he had been having five a week — made his forehead raw and red. Dad ended up putting his powerful topical arthritis salve on his forehead, making it even more inflamed. Robin labelled the jars to help him. He ended up just hiding them, as Dad could not understand what to do. Dad fretted over the pills almost hourly, trying to get them straight in his mind (a sign of dementia). We attributed this to the radiation treatments. It was a heck of a few days.

Funeral arrangements and phone calls
— Monday, May 15

I was granted bereavement leave from work. Did I mention I was a mess? I could only function by sticking to the to-do list. There was so much to do, and we had to ensure that Dad's needs were being met. Robin took Dad to Toronto for the penultimate week of his radiation treatment. Brian was to leave later in the day for Ottawa, leaving me alone at the cottage. He had to remember to bring back my black dress for the private family funeral later in the week.

Mom had put her bra, slip, and panties at the foot of their bed, ready for the morning, the night before she died. She never got dressed again. I had not cleared them up. I could not bear to touch them. When Dad got up in the morning, I went in to help him get dressed for the radiation treatment and the two-hour trek to Toronto. He still had his sense of humour as he said, "I hope you aren't going to make me wear those clothes!" I was not sure how much he understood about what was going on. His humour was something I loved about him and such a surprise at the time. We had a good laugh over that one.

I phoned every person in Mom's phone book whose name I knew. There were names of people there that I vaguely recalled and many more that I thought I knew, but I was not sure. There were some people I needed to call, but Mom had not written their phone numbers down. Mom knew those numbers off by heart! It was a tough task. I had to cancel appointments I noted in her calendar. I phoned Mom's first surgeon to let them know she had passed over. I spoke to someone on the phone and felt comforted. She gave me comforting words and told me how much they had liked Mom. She'd had such a compassionate spirit when she was healthy, and they would miss her.

Another hard thing to do was to clean out the clothes closets. I could not imagine Dad doing this chore. It had to be the most difficult thing I faced at the time. Mom's jewellery I packed up for the storage locker we rented. I ended up taking the clothes far away to another town. I imagined seeing people walk around town in her clothes, and it spooked me! I kept a few sweaters, but cleaned out the entire closet immediately. Hanging long dresses wrapped with dry cleaning plastic bags, I recalled a different time when Mom and I used to have nice clothes to wear for work in the city! Country life for both of us was different. I had eschewed my high heels for clogs. It felt like a demotion.

It had taken me years to feel like a competent, capable, well-dressed city girl and professional. As a stay-at-home Mom, I had gone from a frumpy housewife to taking care about my appearance, watching all the "What Not to Wear" shows to try and take better care of myself. In Muskoka, I had had to modify my stylish wardrobe and had difficulty getting a decent haircut. I had to force myself to put on makeup, and seldom made side trips to the big towns to replenish my makeup cabinet. I had begun to neglect my appearance. I was sad and lonely. All of my friends were far away in Ottawa. Robin and Dad went to Toronto for more radiation therapy. Brian went home to look after the cats. Our house was still on the market, and we needed to keep it in pristine condition. It was just me and Bandy, Dad's dog, who was still peeing on the carpets.

More paperwork — Tuesday, May 16, 2006

Today I had another list of chores: Copy Dad's birth certificate for the lawyer, pay the furnace bill, arrange to be around when the new goldfish pond pump was installed, phone my cousins (the executors) to clear up details, get the bank book updated, go to the funeral home to pay the deposit, gather up photos for the Visitation Room later that week, invite relatives, including cousins, to the private family service on Saturday, order flowers (I forgot to order some on Dad's behalf), find the family tree I had created, book a veterinarian visit for the pets, and check into why Dad's bank account was frozen. (This was the first, but not the last, time this happened.) It was great being busy. After a death there is much to do. It is the aftermath, when everyone goes home, that is the most difficult.

I received a couple of phone calls; the town knew Mom had passed away. Things were quite quiet, but I was not too lonely. There was much to do. I was numb. I went into the liquor store for wine, and the cashier, a wonderfully kind woman, spoke comforting words.

It was her son, an ambulance driver, who helped take Mom to hospital the last time. He was devastated; I was coming to terms with it. We made Mom happier by keeping her at home to pass on. She had her way to the very end.

Then a cousin called. She had noticed during her last visit that Mom's bathroom needed cleaning and thought I should get going on that chore. I was exhausted. She said that perhaps I could call Molly Maid to have it done. I could not face this task. I could not drum up the time and energy to book an appointment. I certainly did not have the cash. Her next suggestion was that I should now move back to Ottawa and try to get my old job back. I was too tired and stressed beyond belief to argue, discuss, or explain my life to her. We argued ("Don't you get snippy with me, young lady!" she said), and she hung up on me. I was not in the best of moods when communicating with anyone. All I wanted was someone to give me some help, not to give me more orders. I did not know whom to ask for help, even that being too much of a task to figure out. Any people skills I possessed disappeared in my depression and grief. I wanted to hear comforting words, and mention of the good things my mom did, or experience a kind gesture, such as someone bringing me food (like Dick and Beth, Dad's friends, dropping off sandwiches for us) or helping me with errands. I was alone and feeling hopeless.

Cleaning up MORE paperwork — Wednesday, May 17

Mom had handled her cancer treatments and her battle with this disease with a strong determination. During her last month alive, she had asked me to take care of a bit of correspondence and guided me to her snail mail file box. It contained her address book, envelopes, and a plethora of multi-occasion cards for her extensive correspondence list. I found a datebook with everyone's birthdays and anniversaries. As I sorted through this box, I spotted a folder of quotes she had collected over the years. I think it was her way of directing me, without admitting she was ill and dying. It contained poems such as "Miss Me, but Let Me Go." And "Do Not Stand at My Grave and Weep." These she clearly wanted read by those who remained; yet we never spoke of her looming death.

Mom knew what was happening, but kept her pain hidden from all but a few. I thought over how Mom never came to terms with her situation. She continued to attempt to maintain her house, made Dad's lunches, vacuumed and dusted on a good day. I did not think she denied what was happening to herself, just to the rest of the North American continent. Most people I phoned upon her passing were in shock. This task was one of the hardest to complete.

As Mom's condition worsened in her last year, she said goodbye in her own way by phoning to speak with friends. She contacted a few people with whom she had lost touch or had not spoken to in a long time. Still, nobody knew. In early spring, Mom had phoned our family friend, Rev. Dr. Jean, in Toronto, and asked her to conduct her funeral when it happened. Jean was amenable. I was unaware of this. Mostly, Mom protected people from her pain. Mom would tell everyone she spoke to here in town and friends in the United States that she was "Just fine!"

Brian and I had to look at this with amusement. In Muskoka, when you jump into the chilly water, everyone would ask you how it feels. The proper Muskoka response is, "Once you get in, it's just fine!" Brian and I called Mom's health "Muskoka fine." We decided that "Muskoka fine" meant you were upright and breathing.

2006: The Writing on the Wall

The first funeral — Saturday, May 20, 2006

Our three adult children, Terry, Jesse, and Caitlin, as well as our son-in-law, Jean–Luc, came to town for the funeral. It was good to have family around us. It is a shame that we seemed only to meet for hatching, matching, and dispatching (baptisms, weddings and funerals!). Jean–Luc and Caitlin had driven Terry in from Ottawa. To get Jesse here we had to arrange for him to fly in from summer work in Connecticut. If Dad had not been so ill, it would have been fun. As it was, we were preoccupied with caring for Dad, as well as ourselves. Everyone was great pitching in with meals. The boys all hung out together, Robin, my late forties brother, Jesse (twenty-three years old), Terry (twenty-one), and Jean–Luc (twenty-eight).

Preparing for the funeral and visitation demanded a great deal of me.
It was therapeutic, however, to look back on Mom's life and her life's work.
On the left is her urn, with a few artifacts that represented her to me.

Caitlin met me at the funeral home, and the men went to the house to prepare dinner while we girls set up the visitation room with photos and artifacts. That evening, the men had a grand time getting to know one another again. It wasn't since Caitlin's May 2005 wedding that we had all been together. My sons were masters of ceremony at their wedding, so they hadn't had much time to visit, and Caitlin and Jean–Luc had been rather preoccupied with numerous friends, family, in-laws and outlaws! The wedding was a fine time for the rest of us to visit with my mother, who was in pain but was pleased to attend the ceremony and reception. I prepared a slide show, which included many shots of the kids at the cottage with Mom and Dad. It was lovely to honour those early years. After the speeches, Mom was taken home early by my devoted brother, where she could rest. I had never seen her so weak and was grateful to be focusing on my speech and the joyful occasion.

But time marches on. We all age, and the cycles of life are certain. The boys had cigars and port outdoors under the stars; a fitting tribute in the place Mom loved so much. Up at the house, we visited, made plans, and talked over the old times. Robin spoke, finally, about his work in the mine. He had kept much information to himself, Mom being the worrier she was. Terry was incredibly impressed with Rob's tasks. "How come no one told me my uncle blows things up for a living?"

The private family funeral was planned and ready to go. I was not prepared emotionally or physically for the kind of funeral I knew Mom would have wanted: choir, Toronto friends and family invited, including many *Hymns and Hers* (to quote another favourite album by the late Oliver Schroer). The visitation the previous evening had gone well. A few neighbourhood friends popped in. They asked where Dad was, and I had to explain that he was quite ill. He actually refused to attend. For a week Dad was up at night, lighting the wood stove all alone, urinating on the carpet, and falling asleep on the floor. He could not get to the bathroom due to physical, emotional, or locomotor issues. He left taps running and still couldn't figure out his medications. When we found him in the morning he was there on the floor in a puddle of urine. Dad was so ill we decided that Robin had to take Dad to the hospital. The rest of us—Brian, Caitlin, Jean–Luc, Jesse, Terry, and I—took off to attend the funeral.

Now, in hindsight, I know that Dad was delirious (see the final section of this book for more information), from either the radiation, his urinary tract infection, or the multiple drugs he was taking.

My brother missed his mother's funeral. At the funeral home everyone asked about Dad and Rob, and I had to explain the turn of events. Dad was incoherent. Everyone said that the last time they saw him he was "just fine." We did not know that his incontinence was not normal after radiation treatments, and that he was susceptible to infections as a result of this treatment. We did not know if it was the tumour affecting him or the numerous pharmaceuticals. More lack of communication and information—there should be a pamphlet or something that can be given to family members. Mom and Dad were beyond comprehension of the effect and the potential side effects of radiation. Again, they did not ask questions.

After the funeral, my boys, Jesse and Terry, helped Brian and Robin bring Dad home, still undiagnosed and unmedicated. Caitlin and I delivered some flowers to the church and then prepared lunch at home. Robin could not lift Dad alone, nor get him in and out of our car or Dad's minivan. This was an awful chore after a funeral. Medical staff could not find anything wrong with Dad that they could fix. He was sent home. Later we found out he had a urinary tract infection; urinating on the floor was not normal.

That night, all the boys but Brian went out to the rock concert in town, had a number of drinks, and had their own wake. It was great for them to bond and get away. They had rented rooms in the motel and there were some drunks raising hell, but the boys slept soundly.

No more radiation—Sunday, May 21, 2006

By Sunday, Robin and I had decided that we would not take Dad in for more radiation treatments. He was too ill and could not sit up. He was urinating every ten minutes. He was leaving the tap on and letting the water run all night—when he remembered to wash his hands. Dad was both delirious, having symptoms of dementia, and fighting the brain tumour. It was time to revise the treatment plan, if there was one. We phoned the oncologist's office and let them know, then cancelled the reservations in the Cancer Lodge.

The next day, the kids went back to work in their respective cities, while Robin hung around for a week. We spent a lot of time planning for Dad's care and figuring out what to do next. Brian and I agreed that we would move into the house and buy out Robin's share. Dad we would move into long-term care (LTC). We couldn't see any other options. It was heartbreaking after hearing about Dad's time in Toronto visiting with people in the Cancer Lodge. He had had a grand time there with Rob. He explained to Rob that his mother wouldn't let them move into more sensible living arrangements. Now was the time, and Dad was not pleased, but realized that he would have to live where he could be looked after. He needed help with many ADL and all of his IADL. He was unable to do any shopping or errands, he couldn't keep his pills straight, he could not walk well, nor could he stand long enough to make himself a meal.

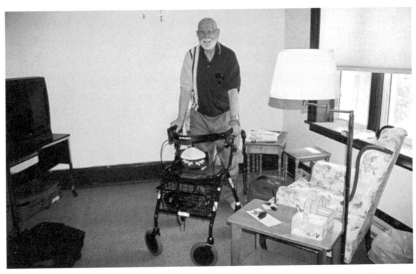

We had to place Dad in a retirement home, and he was amazingly happy there until the brain tumour began interfering with his cognitive functioning.

Retirement home vs. long-term care — May 29, 2006

Robin and Brian did the research on the retirement and LTC homes. They toured several in the area and spoke to staff. The decision was to put Dad into Gravenhurst Manor. A private retirement home, the Manor is a beautiful, small, and well-run profit-making residence with a brilliant manager named Gay. Brian, with his experience in finding various living arrangements for his mother, was a big help. With a variety of placements in the city — from supportive living in private apartments, to retirement homes with meals and laundry, to LTC with full nursing support—we thought that the Manor was the best choice. But first, we had to get him well enough to manage there, and worried that his urinary infection might not clear up in time.

Fortunately, it did. We chose a large room for Dad, with room for his bed, dresser, and large TV. We talked about which furniture to take, worried that we might overcrowd the room. I packed up Dad's things. Dad had not visited, but he was not sentient enough to understand. We simply could not care for him at home. I had to work and Robin had to go home.

As it was, Dad's room was crowded. Many of his pants did not fit him, and I was unsure what to bring. I was overwhelmed. I took far too many clothes in for him. There were things in his room he had not worn in years, but I had no way of knowing this. I would regret this considerably when he had to move, yet again, into the LTC home in late August.

I booked a local handyman, Paul, to move Dad's things for us. He had a trailer and had helped me clear out the basement of thirty- and forty-year-old things the month before. Paul was terrific. Paul and his friend "Old Burt" begin the chore. (Burt was nicknamed "Old Burt" because while on a job, a client asked where "the old guy" was. Burt was actually younger than Paul. We kept up the moniker for a long time. We found humour where we could.) I kept Dad busy in the living room while my brother helped carry things out to the trailer.

I drove Dad in his van to Gravenhurst Manor. We made it into the Manor with no trouble. We had done most of the paperwork beforehand. They had one bedroom available, a big private room. It was too bad Dad could not have gone there earlier, with Mom. They would have enjoyed the atmosphere and the conviviality. We asked Dad where he wanted his bed. He wanted to face the window and his precious outdoors.

We loved the atmosphere of The Manor. It was a well-appointed facility with a variety of private single and double rooms. The furniture consisted mostly of antiques, with period knick-knacks meant to make the residents feel at home. The panelling on the walls complemented the polished mahogany pieces, with all the little nooks and crannies that were popular in their day. Antique doll carriages and dolls decorated the corners. The local florist donates an arrangement weekly. The sunroom was bright and cheery, with new curtains and comfy furniture. There were wide hallways to accommodate the inevitable walkers that made life easier for residents.

Located on a main street, there was much local traffic. Parades and other regular events drew crowds; garage sales and summer festivals provided entertainment. The annual garage sale was orchestrated to coordinate with the town street sale. Residents were primarily able-minded, with some locomotion issues. This is the difference between long-term care and a retirement home. Residents could walk across the street to the various churches, go to Stedman's for coffee with friends, or be picked up by family for celebratory dinners and special occasions. Happy Hour was a fun time to visit. Some residents moved in there for the winter, moving back to cottages for the summer. I was glad that Dad had the money to stay there. It made life so much easier.

We saw that the previous tenant had had pictures on the walls. Rob and I talked about this. We thought we should have one of the cottage or the lake. Rob, Dad, and I were trying to decide which paintings to hang in his new room. When I went back to the cottage, a painting of our cottage frontage had fallen off of the wall. I figured that was a sign from Mom that that was the one I ought to take in to Dad.

"Nice place" — May 31, 2006

Life carried on. Brian went back home to Ottawa. I went back to work. Dad was quite lucid on the phone. He told me he had cleaned up the place, his one room, and proceeded to tell me all about the set-up of the room. I had been in the room with him and had helped set it up, but I listened patiently as Dad described his room. "When you come in the door and look there — does it ever look beautiful: the chair and the lamp. I wanted to get the place looking pretty good." He told me he had a "freezing machine," which I took to be his air conditioner. He told me that he would "kid some of the girls along"; he was always a terrible flirt. He had just had his hair cut and he was feeling tired from that, but he was happy.

It took me three trips to the motor vehicle licensing bureau to have the vehicle transferred to my dad's name. The first time, I went in with power of attorney and the death certificate and my dad's information. It was during my limited lunchtime, and I had little success. I had to get Dad to sign the form, and they were a bit confused by the whole situation. The peculiar thing is that Dad was not allowed to drive, since the doctor had rightly taken away his driver's licence after his seizures. Back in 2003, he made Mom transfer the vehicle to her name, since he was quite upset with not being able to drive it anymore.

The vehicle licensing bureau would accept only my Dad's signature or the executor's. I had to go trucking back to Dad, find his paperwork, and figure out what to do. He could not walk to the motor vehicle bureau down the street from the Manor, so I ended up taking the papers to him to sign, returning to the bureau three times before it was all done. In the end, we had a car licensed to a man who did not possess a driver's licence.

His inability to retrieve nouns was worrisome. Obviously the tumour was back, as this was a symptom of his 2003 surgery. We had to remember to use short, clear sentences, as we were unsure as to what kind of cognitive impairment there might be. In the meantime, I was emotionally distraught. Thinking all was resolved, I had gone back to work, fighting with students who were unwilling to work and had huge behaviour management issues; the days were long. My stress level kept getting worse. I regularly drove from work in Parry Sound straight south to Gravenhurst to see my father. It was a 100-kilometre trek and very difficult after a long day with my students. I would go out to dinner alone a lot, or I simply made popcorn. I did not feel like cooking. With Robin home in B.C. and Brian back in Ottawa, I was alone. I missed my children and their emotional support. With Mom gone, there was no one here on my side.

The cottage was cramped, but, to be positive, it was warmer in May. I was not sleeping well. The sun rose early, I would wake, and inhale the fresh, clean air. After work, if I did not go in and see Dad, I would garden for an hour with a glass of wine in my hand. No one was around for most of the week. It was good therapy getting my hands into the soil. The plumbers graciously came when I called them, desperate to have the water in the cottage turned on, and now I could shower in the warm cottage rather than tramping into the deathly quiet house.

Taking care of pets — June 3, 2006

I was in charge of Dad's dog. Poor Bandy was either urinating or leaking some liquid on the carpets all over the house. Bandy, a cute little white and brown terrier mix, was a bouncy, happy dog, but more than I could manage. Brian would walk Bandy twice and sometimes three times a day when we had visited in the past. If Mom and Dad were seriously arguing, both being ill and out of sorts, it was a good break for him. The stains on the carpet were terrible. I had told Mom a year ago, but they had not been able to rise above their ill health to do anything about it. This was another symptom of the inability to manage IADL. Brian, after driving 430 km to see me, offered to take the dog to the vet forty-five kilometres away. We had to get her well enough for a new home.

As I was considering taking her to the Humane Society to find a new home, I knew Dad would be most upset about this. Robin and I kept discussing the issue, with Brian's support. The vet thought that she could have a urinary tract infection, but, since she wasn't urinating where we could see—in fact I had never seen her go outdoors and do it—it could be something else. She was constantly licking her hindquarters, and they felt that she could have a hormone deficiency. The problem was that Brian needed to gather some urine in order for them to test it to rule out an infection.

Brian came home, reported on events, and we found a margarine container for the urine sample. Brian walked the dog around and around the block but she wouldn't produce anything after the first time. The first time, you see, he tried to sneak up behind her and put the container under her. It did not work and it spooked her. He gave up. He drove back to the vet's office. They had an assistant help walk the dog, similarly following with a container. Eventually it worked. Within a few days, they phoned to tell us that she did not have an infection and to have the prescription filled for hormone tablets.

These seemed to do the trick. After three days, we could see her urinating outdoors. Success! Brian now had to go back home to Ottawa, but this success left me with a happier dog. It made me so sad, though, knowing we had to give her up. Every day when I spoke to my father, he would come up with a new idea so that we could keep Bandy. Eventually we had a solution. One of Dad's Red Cross workers agreed to take the dog. She came and picked her up that night.

It was a blessed relief. I was doing as much as I could to look after myself, never mind my dad and the dog. I did not have a doctor at that point, and was not very healthy. I was eating poorly, eating out a lot, and drinking too much. I was clearly feeling my bereavement issues; I did not recognize the huge stresses from all the other factors: moving, living alone, not having support. Supporting Dad was quite difficult. I was not emotionally prepared to visit him daily, although I felt guilty about this, and tried to visit twice a week. An attempt to find a counsellor through work was singularly unsuccessful. Suffice it to say that there were no counsellors in my local area. A phone counselling session, at the end of which she suggested I didn't need any further help and would be fine, infuriated me. I dropped the whole idea — a really bad move at the time.

Dad still had an infection despite medication. He needed much care. He was continuing to urinate frequently, almost every ten minutes. He was becoming increasingly difficult. We did not realize how ill he was. I continued to do his bills, collect his mail, and to try to look after his affairs. He could not write cheques, so I would fill in his cheques and get them ready. He had just enough energy to sign them, but that would soon cease. In a surreal attempt at normal life, we sat and talked about what needed doing. His banker asked him to sign authority over to me to take care of his financial affairs, but in one last desperate bid to keep control, he refused.

I picked up the mail today. This was to prove the most difficult and long-lasting issue of the grieving process. My parents continually received mail from organizations to which they had made donations. Soon I would receive a letter from my mother's best friend since childhood, Betty. This woman had moved to the United States and they hadn't visited in many, many years. I did not recognize her name in Mom's address book. She wrote to Mom asking what was going on, as she had phoned twice and hadn't heard from her. I had no idea that Mom had kept up contact with her, nor did I know her married name or recognize the foreign address.

I found her phone number in Mom's obtuse address book and made the call. There was no answer. I left a message saying that I was Joan's daughter and wanted to talk to her. After a couple of days, she still had not phoned, and I phoned back. This time Betty was at home. I explained to her what had happened and felt so very sick at heart. Having gotten in touch with a couple of bereaved spouses in trying to contact all of Mom's friends, I was reluctant to do so again. We spoke for a half hour. Mom had phoned her way back in the spring and said her good-byes, although Betty did not know it at the time. This is a story I heard several times over.

June 7, 2006

I had dinner with Dad. It had a lovely décor, the Manor. Dark wood, antique china pieces with doilies, other period pieces. The large whiteboard revealed the menu for the day. It included special events: birthdays, outings, and general reminders. Dad forgot to tell them I was coming. Well, not exactly forgot. He told them I would visit the next day. When family members visited, usually the staff would create a lovely table setting in the sunroom, where there was some privacy and a chance to talk over family matters and have a good visit.

It was spaghetti and meatballs and salad. The seniors do not eat much. Perhaps, approaching fifty, I ought to slow down, too. I sat at Dad's table with his four tablemates. They had their various medical issues, hence their presence in a retirement home. One of them insisted on telling me jokes that he believed I did not know. I was rather tired and I asked him to stop. The strain of the past few months showed. Another lady at the table asked Dad where Mom was. He really did not know, aside from knowing she had passed away.

Lana, a Red Cross support worker, signed Dad's book today and wrote that she would be there to visit with Dad every Thursday. This is comforting. Dad liked his room tidied and needed company. I wrote in his guest book that Brian and I would bring Dad fish and chips next Sunday, Father's Day.

Visitors — June 14, 2006

One issue that concerned me was knowing who was visiting Dad, and keeping track of his caregivers. We were promised, by CCAC, that he would continue to receive extra care. I bought a guest book, in a silver (manly!) book cover with a silver fine-point pen for Dad's room. Some people were most kind in signing it for us. It frustrated him no end when he could not recall the names of visitors. It was a great investment.

Two of Dad's good friends, Dick and Beth, visited him in the Manor. They asked if he wanted anything. He was anxious to have some music. The call went out. Later another choir couple brought him in some hymn books. He would happily sing for anyone who asked (even for those who did not). A chorister all of his youth and adult life, his voice remained strong, even as he forgot the words. We visited that day, too. Dad asked about having photos of Bandy. I asked the front desk and they said sure. Robin and I talked about it for a bit. I went back to the house to select some. We brought Dad some roses from his garden. Mom used to go out and "steal" them, putting them in one of her many crystal vases in the living room.

The literature suggests that appropriate gifts for seniors in retirement homes or long-term care facilities include toiletries, greeting cards, costume jewellery, washable housecoats or sweaters, non-slip slippers, jogging suits, leg warmers, candies, fruit, or cookies in containers. Bringing them recent newspapers, photos of home and the "old days," a thermos of tea to share, and talk about the old days were called for and quite welcomed. I found that people were reluctant to visit. It is difficult seeing someone dear to you in such a condition. Dad was exhibiting more signs of dementia and was hard to talk to.

Father's Day — June 18, 2006

We brought Dad fish and chips from BJ's, his favourite restaurant. His favourite takeout meal is from a local burger joint. He complained that they weren't hot enough. We had brought it in a cool chest that kept it quite warm. He wasn't hungry and had lost his appetite. We had been so excited, planning this event.

For such a long time, he had been too stiff to walk, the arthritis giving him much pain, so Mom would phone the restaurant and preorder their meals. They would drive the two kilometres to town, and Wally Sr. would bring their meal out to the minivan. They liked to support small businesses in town. Wally and his family had shown them a lot of concern, which was returned in kind. The townsfolk all knew when folks were ill. They commiserated and demonstrated their concern.

I decided to take some trees down back at the house. The lakefront we remembered as kids had disappeared behind the new growth. Dad and Mom had spent many hours with pruners and clippers reclaiming land. But since they had become more infirm, Rob postulated that they seemed to want to feel enclosed. He thought that they must feel safer with the comforting arms of the trees surrounding them and their property.

I consulted with Dad, explaining that some of the trees are obviously dying, and that neighbours had had trees fall on their house in windstorms. I felt enclosed, too, and needed to see the lakefront, for which we paid dearly in taxes. I phoned a man who would come and do the job.

My brother promised to phone Dad later at six o'clock. Unfortunately, Dad's hearing was pretty bad, even with his supersonic phone. I hoped Robin would be able to have a conversation with the father that he adored. I noted this in the guest book, just in case Dad would read it.

Aunty returns — Monday, June 19, 2006

Some of my cousins visited Dad at the Manor. They wrote, "Ray is in fine spirits. Loves his new home. So happy to chat with him." It seemed so positive and optimistic.

My aunty came to the house while I was out at school. She seemed to be looking for trouble. She was invited to my cousin's cottage (four doors down) for lunch. Aunty went in to visit my dad after, I must presume, peering in the back windows of our home. The house was in bad shape. The back room carpet, visible from the back door, had been terribly stained by the cat's urinating on it. Mom did not have a sense of smell, due to a childhood fever, and Dad was too ill to be aware of it. My brother figured it out when he visited a year ago. He had duly cleaned the carpet, as had Mom and Dad. The smell was still there; likely the cat had been staining the carpet for a couple of years. Mom and Dad did not have the wherewithal to clean it, nor to realize how foul the odour was.

Robin and I had torn out the foul carpet, taken the blankets and sheets that had been in the closet and similarly urine stained, and had it all taken away to the dump. We had to clean out the room. I washed the floor with ammonia and hoped we could re-carpet it without further odour issues. I began moving boxes into the room.

It was a mess, but we knew we had to replace the carpets. It was the first step in a long process to make the house habitable again. Of course, no one but us knew this. I had had boxes of old junk taken away: rusty old tools, papers, and years of accumulated belongings that neither of my parents had been able to throw out. I vowed to learn this lesson and not visit this same issue on my children when our time came!

Aunty drove the thirty kilometres from home to Gravenhurst to visit Dad. Afterwards, he complained. He told me that she had torn into him and told him that Jenn had "destroyed the house." Dad complained to me that she had bothered him. He just wanted some peace with visitors who could chat and not pressure him or arrogantly tell him what to do. Nobody understood what was really going on or how much we were fighting pressure and stress from everyone who seemed to know what we should do, when, where, and how.

Family memories — June 24, 2006

The literature suggests that autobiographies (Jilks, 2007), with the use of photographs, are a wonderful way to come to terms with your life. It allows for reflection and a time when family members can share the past, something uppermost in many seniors' minds. I wish I had created something more concrete than this, but Brian and I chose four photos of Dad's precious dog, Bandy. I put them all into a frame. It really pleased Dad. They were fine photos showing Bandy in the frog pond hunting frogs, as I had taught her to do! She had never spotted frogs until that first spring. I had taught my kids to catch frogs. I thought it only right to teach this puppy, too. She spent many hours frog hunting. We hung the pictures together. Dad and I debated which could go where. I enjoyed such tasks. It was good to be able to do something positive for him. He was happy with the efforts. He never asked for a picture of Mom—that would come later. Dad sat there trying not to cry as he gazed fondly at his beautiful, spirited doggie. We made a decision and I got out my hammer and nails. I had to take the frame down, however, as he wanted to take the photos and pop them into his walker basket to take into the dining room to show his new friends.

He had difficulty with his new friends. His hearing aids whistled to torment those not hearing impaired. He would turn them up too loud, as he did not find them effective, and then the whistling would start. Some of his tablemates asked that he be moved. He was quite insulted.

It took awhile before we would speak of Mom. I let him take the lead, but I never lied. He knew she was gone. Eventually his friends in the Manor asked about her. He asked me about her death one day, on one of our nicer visits. He said he could not answer questions about her and he was curious. He had no memory of the weekend she died. He was angry, he told me, that my brother had not told him anything. We did not realize how off-kilter he was at the time, emotionally and physically; we did not realize he could not remember the whole event. I shared the saga with him.

As I cleaned up the house, I discovered old photos and found pictures of Dad in his garden. In Dad's handwriting I spotted the meticulous organizational skills that allowed a man with only a Grade 10 education to build, renovate, and plan his life and his daily work. The paperwork shows a sketch of a long-gone garden and the plans for the vegetables that only ever seemed to ripen after we had left for Toronto for the winter. I realized how meticulous they both were, not just Mom. I began to uncover hidden diamonds as I rediscovered parts of Dad's personality forgotten and overshadowed by my mother's strength and illnesses.

School was over for the summer, and I settled into a routine. Brian visited every few days each week from Ottawa. The summer brought its hope and promise. Swims in the healing water of the lake and more gardening helped to pass the time. I ordered four cubic yards of garden soil. I shovelled it into the wheelbarrow and dumped it on my father's precious gardens. Getting my hands in the dirt, I could get in touch with my true nature again. The smell of the rich earth and the gratitude of the plants healed my soul as I placed blankets of peat-rich earth around my dad's garden.

Furniture and carpets — July 5, 2006

New carpets were ordered—finally. All Mom's and Dad's possessions, furniture, etc., had to go into the locker with Mom's jewellery and Dad's tools. We got possession of the locker on July 3rd. We booked movers for the Thursday to move their things out of the house. The plan was to sell some, give some to my sons, and move our things in. There was no way Dad would have been able to live here alone. The movers took all of the remaining furniture to the storage locker. They were beautiful mahogany pieces and we could not lift them. It cost us $300. But it is only money, as I told my second husband the accountant. It was the energy that cost me more than I could know or understand. There were many details, all requiring much emotional energy, to look after, and many decisions I had to make on behalf of my dad.

We had carpet and tile installed in the upstairs bathroom. What a treat. I brought in a mattress and slept on the floor upstairs, rather than in the cottage, susceptible as it was to the vagaries of weather. How great to have a hot shower, too. It was beginning to feel like home. Stretching back and getting that hot water on my sore back was bliss. I spent much of the day gardening. It is lovely therapy.

Rude awakening — Tuesday, July 11, 2006

Dad had to vent when I spoke to him next. He told me that a cousin had popped in and woke him up. He was so very angry. I did not know what to say to him. I listened and tried to commiserate. Dad always had his door locked when he slept. Staff checked in on him using their master keys, especially if he chose not to go to a meal, but otherwise they would let him sleep. I realized I ought to talk to the manager and ask her to give an order not to let visitors into Dad's room if the door was locked.

Staff made announcements when meals were ready, and if someone didn't show up, they would go and find out why. Sometimes residents would be out for a meal, although they did have to sign out of the building, and sometimes they could be sleeping. It was such a great way to ensure their safety.

It was clear that Dad's physical health was going to be a big issue. He was a tall man and hard to lift. Staff phoned me to let me know that he had fallen in the dining room. In hindsight, I believe that it was the tumour controlling either his reactions or his ability to navigate around the room. Two young women on staff picked him up and took him back to his room. He refused to stay in the dining room and eat his dinner. I believe that he was embarrassed. I did not know it at the time, but this was the beginning of Dad's mobility issues. I hoped Dad's doctor would come in and see him, although he hadn't seen Dad since May, as Dad's GP was housebound with his own health issues. Partly retired, he kept his older patients. They trusted him.

Funeral home — Friday, July 14, 2006

Again, back I went to the funeral home. I had to set up the room for the visitation scheduled for the 15th. I chose some flowers from the florist. The flowers were delivered the three blocks to the funeral home on the Friday. I forgot to order flowers from Dad. I had to scramble and phone the florist again.

I booked a haircut with a new hairdresser; I was hoping she would do better than the previous two people. It just was not quite what I wanted. I looked and felt frumpy. I had been so busy that I hadn't been able to truly research this problem and find someone I liked. Brian and I were in a restaurant and I spotted a young woman with a smashing hairdo. I asked her where she had had it done. That's where I went. I had been without a hairdresser I could trust since April!

Caitlin and J–L—daughter and son-in-law—and Rob and his son, Keegan, arrived on Friday. We were a bit crowded, but Jesse and Terry could not attend due to work commitments. That night we unexpectedly got an offer to buy our house in Ottawa. We raced into town to get the fax and sign the papers. Any offer would do at this point: long-distance marriages are tough. Despite issues with real estate agents' leaving doors locked and cats unable to get to the litter box and a carpet being replaced, it all worked out. The deal fell through the next day, but it worked out later. What stress?

Mom's memorial service — July 15, 2006

We scheduled a big Celebration of Life for Mom. In hindsight, I should have skipped the first private funeral and concentrated on this one. Two funerals were one too many. Writing Mom's eulogy was a cathartic yet difficult process. It forced me to go back and find all the great things that made Mom who she was. The recent life that was framed by cancer was dispelled by her activities and a youth that included music and much church involvement.

I went with a Christmas theme for Mom's service. I am sure that anyone who knew our Joanie understood why I went with this theme! Christmas was Mom's favourite time of year. I remember the joyful choir rehearsals in Toronto at Lawrence Park United Church; candlelight service, midnight Christmas Eve communion service, which was preceded by an open house at her best friend's house; a glorious time of year for music. Mom invented *Christmas in July*—here in Bala, the Bala Trek, Mom's open houses, with Dad charming one and all and serving as wine steward. There were some terrific photos, the four of us, current dog in tow, driving with the Scythes family, amongst others, to chop down Christmas trees, with hot chocolate and marshmallows to follow. (Caitlin has perpetuated that tradition with her dear husband, Jean–Luc.) Mom set up the house *just so* at Christmastime. She always began playing Christmas carols in August, when she came home from the summer at the cottage.

After Mom's memorial service, we had a reception. The caterer did a great job. I knew Mom wanted a fine splash. I did not want church folks worrying about baking for the service, as her dear church friends were in mourning almost as much as we were. It is a shock when your peers begin to get ill and pass away.

Summer was a busy time in cottage country, with folks entertaining loved ones. I felt healthier, happier, and began to get accustomed to my new life.

MRI appointment in Toronto—July 18, 2006

Dad's lawyer had to evaluate Dad to see whether or not he was competent. He did an assessment of Dad's capacity. Apparently, if it is not done correctly it can be challenged. If it could be shown that Robin and I were exerting undue influence on Dad vis-à-vis his finances, a public guardian could be assigned. How bizarre! I *had* to take control of Dad's financial matters, since Dad could not even write a cheque. We had power of attorney for this. Dad had been violently opposed to this in June. He thought he could still keep track of things. We had to check out and renew insurance: life, car, home. As boarders in Dad's house, Brian and I had tenant insurance.

I went back to Ottawa to clean up and sign papers to finally sell the house. It was good to get home to familiar surroundings and civilization. Poor Dad had to go all the way to Toronto for his MRI. The manager of the retirement home said that she could book an agency worker to accompany Dad to his appointment. It made good sense, since my relatives refused to help out with this chore. Toronto was a long drive for a fifteen-minute MRI, but it was important, they all told me, to give us some concrete data about his condition. This person, hired from a seniors' support service, accompanied Dad in my stead. She sat up in front with the driver while the other ambulance attendant sat at the back with Dad. It was well worth the expense.

Most of July was spent in visiting Dad, ensuring that the house was taken care of, and shovelling my four cubic yards of soil. It was good to get outdoors. The sun, wind, and rain were healing. More often than not, Dad would be sleeping when I went into town to visit. I would not wake him. If I had errands, I would do them and then pop back in to visit. Some nights he stayed up late and then would sleep all day. Staff were kind enough to bring him snacks when he woke up. Although it was a relief not to have to worry about chatting and having conversations, this new "normal" was unnerving.

Cats move to Bala — July 23, 2006

Back I went, home to Ottawa. This time it was to bring the cats back to Bala. We had an issue moving them, as they were not amenable to being picked up, both having been feral at some point in their past. It was a lesson in planning and preparation. After many discussions with the veterinarian, he prescribed Valium for old Mitz. She is a tri-colour long-haired cat. My plan was to put Sady, the young tabby, into her carrier, drug Mitz, and then pop her into the carrier. Funny how often one has to go to plan B. I caught Sady, the agile one. I popped her easily into the carrier, but it was not shut properly after I popped her into it, and she fell out on the way to the van, which was packed with the things I needed to take back to Bala. It took me a long time trying to catch her, and I finally gave up. We tried tempting her with treats, but she wouldn't take the bait for a long time. She knew something was up. Brian, my cat whisperer, finally coaxed her. I could not believe it.

Mitz did not seem phased by half of a Valium tablet. It was supposed to knock her out. I simply herded her — or perhaps, more like a bullfighter, scared her — into a basement corner and wrapped her in a blanket. She was easier than the wee kitten, Sady, to corral. The drive back to Bala was easy, and we had no further mishaps. They quite liked the new house and settled in after a while. They both arrived none the worse for wear, and adjusted to their new home. I set up the litter boxes and put out food. They ate readily. Sady was anxious to explore and eat. Fraidy-cat Mitz needed a bed under which to hide. This was where she was the most comfortable.

July 24, 2006

Meanwhile, at the retirement home, Dad just did not want to do anything. We respected this. I would find his glasses for him and help him get dressed. By now, staff were letting him sleep in until after everyone else had eaten. It was less stressful for all. They would bring him a muffin, coffee, and juice on a tray. They did not have the staff for such personal care, but they kept it up for a while.

Dad called his room his "home." He would tell me that he wanted to go home if he was in the hall. His stomach was giving him problems, too. He told me he was "grindy in his stomach." He made it to supper alone some days, and after a meal he would feel better.

The doctor had been in to see him. Dad's GP was ill himself, but no amount of talking could convince him of that; he was incorrigible. Dad wouldn't speak to the doctor. He hadn't seen him since Mom had died in May. Dad had infections in both of his ears, and had prostate and urinary tract infections. No wonder he had to urinate constantly. He wanted the pee bottle, rather than going the four feet from his bed to his bathroom. I could not understand how he could get this ill. I guess the infection he had had last month had not been cleared up.

We ended up putting oil in his ears weekly and washing them out with a syringe and bulb. He was on more meds than I could keep track of. I was so glad I did not have to worry about it. The retirement home manager was a nurse and managed ably.

Two days before the furniture arrived at the house (what panic!), they started installing the main floor carpets. It was crazy with noise and uproar. It really bothered me. I was juggling the house renovations with my father's problems. In the meantime, Dad's knees kept buckling and he had many falls, simply tipping over sideways as he tried to make it from a standing position to the bed or the chair. He was using the walker irregularly and everyone worried he would break something. The worry was frightful. It was a sign that the tumour was affecting his mobility and balance.

With our house sold, we were happy to wrap things up and stop the weekly commutes. I was happy to have a husband around again.

Oncologist in Toronto: the final diagnosis — July 26, 2006

A week later, Dad and I went to a follow-up appointment with his Toronto oncologist. Dad had a 2:30 p.m. appointment. I made arrangements to take him to the city in an ambulance, as he could not walk, and I could not assist him. I knew I could not manage him alone. Dad was ready a couple of hours before our estimated departure time. He loathed being late. I made it to the residence about a half hour before the ambulance was due. The problem with conveying patients like Dad to such appointments, aside from the distance, was booking an ambulance to get him there. The ambulance was delayed an hour and a half due to an emergency in another town. Dad was quite upset with the delay. Eventually they arrived. I sat up in front with one attendant, whose name was Steve; we chatted as he drove. The other—Steve #2—stayed in the back with Dad. Dad needed to urinate every ten to fifteen minutes or so. This became a problem fairly quickly, as Dad was unable to pee in the bottle when horizontal.

We arrived at the hospital for our appointment and checked in. They took us into a back hallway, where the doctors' offices were located. We waited about half an hour, after I sent Steve 1 and Steve 2 for a coffee. As we waited, I attempted to chat with Dad. I could hear another man in the hallway complaining that he had driven in from out of town for this appointment and had been waiting three hours. I felt somewhat guilty, since we got in quite quickly to see the doctor, who was now behind in her appointments by a long shot. We were paying for the ambulance by the hour, and I kept my mouth shut. Wait times for appointments were one thing, but waiting times, when you were scheduled for a particular time, was another issue.

In retrospect, I wonder why on earth we had to drive 250 km, taking up the time and energy of two paramedics and an ambulance, in order for the oncologist to tell Dad that they could do nothing more for him. It was a distressing meeting. The radiation did not work, the tumour was back, and, therefore, chemo would not do anything for him either. It was Mom who had decided that they would go ahead with the radiation in the first place. I truly question it now. If only I had read the statistics and asked a few more questions. If only I had been able to talk to their doctors all through this medical journey!

Dad's oncology treatment was over and it was going to be a matter of time. Why was there no follow-up? Why did not someone phone to see how Dad was reacting to the radiation? He had horrible symptoms. I wonder why they did not tell Mom and Dad about the statistics. Was there anything to learn from all this? For example, what was the impact of the radiation? Was there justification for giving an eighty-one-year-old person radiation treatment? What was the prognosis? The odds of success were not high, I found out later. Tumours tend to come back in the elderly. Treatment does not have much chance of success in this situation.

The oncologist's "bedside manner" was most empathetic; pregnant, she was going on maternity leave soon. She was visibly dismayed by having to deliver this kind of news. Once the doctor had yelled loudly enough for him to hear, she managed to let Dad know that they could do nothing further. He seemed to understand this; later conversations told me so. The doctor told us that Dad had two tumours in his brain right now, according to the MRI done last week. One was inactive, but the other was growing. I suspected this all along. Dad's difficulties with language had begun back in the spring. They were similar to his original problems when they removed the tumour in 2003. He was totally aphasic at that time. His communication difficulties told me that there was something brewing.

The doctor indicated that tumours that did not respond to radiation would not respond to chemotherapy. So there was nothing to be done. I wondered why my mother had had chemotherapy after her radiation. But that was in the past. In younger people they could try giving chemo, but in older people there was toxicity that did them in. We had to manage Dad's health care needs and assess possible treatment as we encountered each barrier. They said there would be pressure and headaches, as well as increased irritability. I wish I could have gone back and asked more questions.

I asked for a time frame, and the doctor told me that when he started to sleep half of the time, he likely had a month left. I was not sure that this was an adequate gauge for us, as Dad slept a lot and had insomnia the rest of the time.

Dealing with mortality — July 27, 2006

Planning began regarding Dad's needs. I had to talk to Gay, the Manor's manager, to discuss Dad's prognosis. Gay is an angel. Slim, beautiful inside and out, tall and blonde, and a bit younger than myself, she ministers to her various residents with the patience of Job—despite Dad's wandering the halls at night and creating havoc. I continued to worry. Just when I thought I was beginning to heal from my bereavement, we had to go to a whole new level.

In the following days, Dad began to reflect upon and demonstrate that he understood his prognosis. We spent some time getting used to it. This was something my mother would not let me do. I found some healing power in discussing what was happening, bringing it out into the light and recognizing it. He said, "You know what's going to happen to me. I'm just going to go." I wished that were the case. "*Do not go gently into that good night*"[4] did not really work for me. I would prefer that he went gently. He was anxious and upset many times.

He was angry, agitated, irritable, and totally belied the myth of the benign senior living in his golden years. I hurt for him. I hurt for me. My children were not getting the attention they deserved. Our family had been broken and bent, as had the path I thought I would follow. I was mystified with the process of aging and death and felt helpless most of the time. There was no one there for me. As advocate, I was responsible for Dad and had to be on my toes at all times to ensure that his needs were being met. There was an egregious lack of coordination of care.

Furniture arrives — July 27, 2006

Our furniture arrived at the house. What a relief to be able to try and settle in. It did not take us long. What a nice sense of familiarity for me. I still could picture Mom lying on her couch, which was now gone, wasting away each day. I was glad to be able to replace that image with our furniture and a brand-new start. *She* had a new house

---

4   From a poem by Dylan Thomas.

and a new place to live. I was sure she wanted us to be happy here. Many years ago, she had asked if we would want to live here, and I had assured her we did.

Planning began regarding Dad's needs. I talked to Gay, and we discussed Dad's prognosis. Since he had been declared palliative, we needed to prepare for that. Gay told me that they had had another resident who stayed there during her palliative care, but it depended upon Dad's needs. I continued to worry. I was dubious.

In the following days, Dad began to reflect upon his prognosis. He said, "I'm not going to last long."

"Dad, you have a tumour. There is nothing they can do."

I recalled my brother's words to Dad in the summer: "You had a good run, and there is a time for everyone." Mom and Dad both seemed to think that their time was unlimited and that once they got over this difficult bit, things would be back to normal. You cannot choose the way you will die, but at least he had time to prepare for it and come to terms with it if he wished. But that was not to be. He raged until the end. He lost so much of his cognitive functioning that he could not comprehend some things.

Dad, despite balking at using the walker for a long, long time, now began using the wheelchair regularly to go to dinner. This was a big hurdle crossed. He kept falling using the walker, and I worried a lot about this. I was wondering when they would tell us that they could no longer manage his physical infirmities and that we had to find alternate care for him. Despite being adopted, I worried as much as Mom did! I guess this blows the nature versus nurture notion. Every day was a trial.

I brought in a plant arrangement with a yellow bow. In his guest book I wrote, "Hope you like the flowers, Dad. I will water them—not too much!" As I looked through his photos and thought about what meant a great deal to him, I knew it was nature and his animals. I knew he needed some greenery in his room. I enjoyed doing these small things, as I had no control over the big ones.

Hurricane and power outage—August 2, 2006

My friend Eileen came to visit from Ottawa this weekend. It was her birthday this week, and she had combined a visit to Peterborough with a bit of a side trip to see me. I missed my dear friend very much.

Brian was in Ottawa, and Eileen and I were merrily preparing to have our second day of our girl's visit. We were down at the water, swimming, when we saw the clouds rapidly approaching. I knew we were in for a storm—but what a storm! We casually cleaned up our swimming accoutrements and headed up to the house. We opened a bottle of wine and sat on the sofa visiting, watching the winds pick up. I had planned on barbecuing steak later, a fine end to a fine day. The winds picked up and then slowly changed from wind, to gusts, to a torrent of water. The leaves on the trees were blowing in directions that did not make sense. There were down-thrusts of wind, common in the area, as I found out later. The wind snapped off branches and surprised both of us with its ferocity.

The phone rang, and it was my father. He was very upset. He had his good days and bad days. Today he was most upset, as the TV wasn't working. He had been such a go-to-it kind of man. If anything broke, he would be able to fix it and make it right. With the advent of technology, some things began to be beyond his ken, and this made life more difficult. At the time, I really did not understand how severe this storm would be, and I tried to calm Dad down. Our power had gone out as well, but he really could not empathize; TV and his sports shows were much of his life nowadays. He was quite upset that I could not help him fix his TV. I felt as if I had let him down in some way, but could not see myself driving the thirty kilometres to see him, even if I could do something about this situation.

By the time we finished our conversation, the winds had abated somewhat, and I began to get the barbecue going. I had never barbecued in the dark, the deck lights being quite efficient. I did my best without power, and we had a salad with our meal. The candlelight was quite lovely. Eileen and I had shared many meals in the past, as we had gone out every couple of months on a regular basis to the theatre when we lived in Ottawa. I missed my old life.

We did not have any media access, no radios with batteries. Eileen and I took a long walk into town to survey the damage. I took photos of trees down, branches across roadways. It was a horrific sight. As we walked, we could hear the telltale sound of chain saws. It was a bit rustic, entertaining a guest without hydro. We again went for a walk the next day. There were trees down all over town. Almost all of our neighbours had been affected by the storm; we seemed to have been the least affected. The wind swept past us below the house. None of us had power, of course. Our good neighbour came by to see if we were all right. I assured him we were. He told me tales of homes with huge trees leaning on roofs. Branches were down across power lines at the end of our road, and we scooted under them on our walk, fearing for our safety. Eileen and I made our morning ablutions—thank goodness for town water and sewer. Coffee was made in the glass carafe I had seen Mom use many times before dripolators had been invented. Bless her for keeping it around! I fired up the barbecue and sat the carafe on the burner. It worked with a small upside-down funnel. As the water boiled at the bottom of the pot, it forced the heated, expanding water up the tube into the coffee reservoir. It was the best coffee ever!

We took a trip into town. I had to see Dad, and Eileen and I wanted to get some groceries. I went in to see Dad while Eileen went off to shop. We did not know how bad the damage was in town. Many stores were out of power and did not get it back for days.

After visiting with Dad in the hall, I thought it time to go. He hadn't been all that clear with me: complaining about one thing and another. I went out to the car and asked Eileen if she wanted to see Dad. She did and came in. He was quite happy to see her, although they'd never met. She is quite attractive, and my dad was quite perky after being morose with me. He had been begging me to stay longer, but after talking to her, apparently faking normal, he told us to go off and enjoy ourselves. He was a different man. I just could not understand it!

Let sleeping dogs lie — August 4, 2006

Eileen drove home to her family. It was great having a friend over. Brian arrived from his trip to Ottawa. He was tired. Today I let him sleep in the afternoon. He regularly took a nap, due partly to his blood pressure medications. I tried to protect him during those times and hovered by the phone. I usually went outside to work in the garden, taking the phone to ensure I could pick up on the first ring. Sometimes I simply sat and read on the deck outside, letting him sleep in peace. He was a light sleeper.

When I returned to the kitchen, Brian having awoken from slumber on the couch, I noticed that the fridge magnet that says,

"Sometimes I wake up Grumpy, other times I let him sleep" had fallen off of the fridge and was lying on the floor. I think it was Mom's sense of humour, an indication that she was watching and approved. She took such good care of Dad. I was often told, as a young woman, that it is the responsibility of a wife to put hubby first, even before the kids. I understood and agreed. I adore my husband, who has been incredibly supportive to my kids and me. He is such a loving, kind, caring man who does so much for all of us. I knew that this was Mom's stamp of approval.

Phone calls and lifelines — August 5, 2006

One issue for seniors and their families includes communication patterns. I have heard many stories of ailing or frail parents whose communication with adult children borders on the pathological. Seniors facing the transfer to a care facility feel isolated, powerless, and alone. Anxiety and fears of illness manifest in repeated phone calls as seniors, in their confusion, forget about social niceties in a desperate bid to manage their fears. Dad called us over and over again at 10:30, 10:34, 10:38, 10:40, and 10:50 p.m. and simply dialed over and over again. He was confused. He said, "I couldn't get the thing right." (We don't know if he meant the TV or the hearing aids.) I took a couple of Dad's calls, but eventually Brian took over. Finally, Brian patiently talked him down and promised to do something in the morning. Dad had lost all understanding of the function of objects, and it could have been the TV or the phone that he could not get to work. We never really knew.

The next day, Dad phoned me at seven a.m. to complain that he was having trouble breathing. I asked if there was pain anywhere. I called the desk and talked to Sophie. He had called for Patty four times, another caregiver on staff. Now he said his throat was hurting. He said, "Nobody cares." He couldn't get enough attention. He was perseverating about his health. Complaints like, "You don't care about me!" escalated. He was clearing his throat a lot. They gave him some cough medicine to help him. He was physically and mentally bothered. We attributed all this to the progress of the brain tumour. There was much confusion. These were clear signs of dementia, which we did not know at the time.

I phoned his doctor and asked if there were meds he could give my father. Dr. K. said that it was a question of knowing if Dad had anxiety or confusion. If we gave him a tranquillizer we could screw him up. Another dead end. I called and spoke to Sophie. She said Patty had tried to feed him breakfast, and he wouldn't eat. He stared at the food and refused his pills. Sophie went in later and he still refused his pills. By this point he was on pills for tumour reduction, as well as the original pills to prevent high blood pressure. The third time Sophie went in, he had a muffin and coffee and they chatted. Gay felt bad, since they were stretched thin for people to help. If Dad slept at night, things were good, but if he slept in the day, they were hooped, because then he wouldn't sleep later. I recall taking one of my children as a toddler off of naptime since he wouldn't go to bed until ten p.m. if he napped in the afternoon. Reversal, methinks.

A good day — August 7, 2006

Today I went in to see my father and he wasn't quite so depressed. What a relief! It was the holiday weekend, and there were fewer staff on duty. He was mixing things up and phoned me four times today. Dolly, his Manor neighbour, said he had had a bad few days. He was having a problem remembering my phone number. I cheered up the worker who was in puttering about. I asked how she was doing, and we chatted. I told her about Dad's being a gardener and raising African violets.

Gay said that we needed more help. She offered to arrange more care in the evening, at our expense, when their staff was hard-pressed to give folks their meds and get them to bed. Most of the other residents were okay, but Dad drained their resources. We agreed to get someone in at 7:30 every evening. This proved quite practical. I asked them to write in his "guest book" what they had done for him. This gave us something to converse about with my father, as well as an idea of what they could do for him. The notes were full of gentle, quiet times; the support workers would massage his feet, help him tidy his room, or talk with him.

The wallet — August 8, 9:30 a.m.

We had been looking for Dad's wallet for days. I had looked in every drawer, under the bed, and in his walker basket, but it was nowhere to be found. I visited a bit, gave him some candies, and talked to the staff. Gay had a good idea and went into his closet and looked in the pocket of his robe. Sure enough: he had not gotten dressed one day for breakfast and had put the wallet in his robe pocket. Even while he was being miserable and crotchety, Dad had his rituals. He would put his wallet in his pocket, hankie in the other pocket, and always made sure he locked his door.

He was distressed about something else, too. Gay was the one who told me he always kept his change in his pocket in a Kleenex, all wrapped up. He was very agitated that he did not have these things together. He could not articulate that this was what was wrong. Blessings to Gay.

He was in a relatively good mood. Not as depressed as the other days. I got him dressed and helped him get breakfast. He couldn't tell the time. He knew the clock by his bedside was wrong. For fifteen minutes he kept trying to get the time right—looking at his watch, and so forth. I gave help. I could not stand seeing him getting so frustrated. This was another sign of the loss of cognitive functioning and dementia.

I found out from the staff that Bandy, Dad's dog, and her new daddy had been in to visit. I had kept in touch and given Dad reports from the new dog owners. They had originally offered to take her in for a visit, and I made this request. Bandy and her new daddy had a walk every day in the forest. Bandy must have been in heaven, figuratively speaking. Dad had totally forgotten the event, aside from the fact that he verbally mourned Bandy every time I visited, sometimes several times.

Bandy's new mummy told me that she had had a hard time getting Bandy to eat in the kitchen. I explained that Bandy is a one-trick pony. The only discipline she had ever had was to stay out of the kitchen. She would sit on the edge of the rug but wouldn't set foot in it. The new owners wanted to feed her in the kitchen and they worked for weeks on deprogramming her, even sometimes hand-feeding her! It is a humorous story in a sad chain of events.

Last week, Dad had had to give a urine sample. I am not sure for whom or why, but I had seen the container there. There were several people coming and going. I never really knew who was there to see him if they did not sign his guest book. The sample container was gone from his bathroom sink, and he had urinated into a vase. I cannot imagine why. I liked to take flowers in to Dad from his rose garden. I would put them in a vase. When the flowers died, I threw them away. He must have decided that the empty vase made a good urine bottle!

Long-term care (LTC) home — August 11, 2006

We visited Dad today, and he was in a pissy mood. He was morose and depressed. He had phoned the night before (seven times) asking for one thing or another. He called at one a.m. and I spoke to him to calm him. The staff said he was also calling their front desk, where the care staff sits while on duty. He confused their number with some sort of agency that would help him.

Brian and I went to visit him. He was sitting in the sunroom. There were a few ladies there, too. He complained again about being cold. He could not hear well, and most conversations with him had to be at many decibels. The story of the benign old folks in these retirement homes is a myth. One old lady, a few seats away, made a point of asking someone if she was cold and commenting to another that *she* did not find it cold. It is quite hurtful, these kinds of conversations. I guess there isn't a lot to talk about. It reminds me of small-town life.

There was a Bible study group scheduled for the sunroom. I began to tell Dad that we had to leave, as the shouting that masqueraded as conversation would distract them. This group met every Friday at 10:00 a.m. The lovely woman that led the group said we could stay, but I knew Dad could not hear them. He was quite angry with me. One just has to do what is best.

We went back to his room. He kept asking for help with the TV. He asked everyone to get the TV remote to work. His conversation was so bizarre: "When am I going to get that?" in relation to nothing I knew of. And later, "That it's all broken down to is the other one's calling me later." I figured out that this meant that the staff member on duty said she'd come by to see him later. He phoned them at the front desk. They would come and see him. He did not understand that they came by and did not associate that person with the number he had phoned. This proved to be just the beginning of this issue.

He complained about "grade missiles" while trying to get in touch with us. He said there was a meeting and "we are changing the dial thing." He was so distressed and could not figure out how to work the remote. Gay had put large numbers on it to help him figure out which buttons to push to change channels. It was not really his fault, as at home they'd had to figure out the more complicated satellite menu, and now he was back to basic cable. He could not make the connection, so to speak.

We went and looked around and had a tour through a long-term care home in Gravenhurst. I did not think that there would be much difference between these government-subsidized institutions, and we were pleased with the Gravenhurst location. I did not realize that some were profit-making centres and others were non-profit. We wanted to find a location that suited us, since we knew we'd be visiting a lot. I filled in the forms and took power of attorney for him. Dad was no longer able to make decisions. His cognitive functions were quite limited. He could not even keep track of his pills anymore, and telling time was beyond him. His attention and memory were gone, but he wasn't a risk for running away—he simply needed twenty-four-hour nursing care in his state of dementia.

There were many booklets explaining the facility and their philosophy. I duly read all the information. Brian was incredibly helpful in sorting through it with me. He had placed his mother into such care several years ago. I was numb when we visited—seeing all the seriously ill patients. The Alzheimer's floor was the most difficult. Brian's stepfather had had Alzheimer's, and he knew what to expect. Brian asked all the right questions for me. This would work for us.

The client, or alternate decision-maker, should the client be deemed unable to make decisions, can take advantage of a long-term care placement and must sign a series of documents. The case manager has permission forms—such as permission for CCAC to gain access to information from the doctor, and a facility choice list, which is reviewed by the case manager. Sometimes, if the client has dementia issues and behaviours that are beyond the coping ability of a regular placement, then he/she must be moved to a secure wing. Clients are deemed ineligible for this more intensive care if they can drive or manage their own needs. Then they are advised to go to a retirement home. Files are shared with the long-term care homes on their facility choice list, and names will go on a waiting list until a bed is available. Clients request the type of accommodation they desire on their facility choice list, such as whether or not it will be a private room. The client must choose no more than three homes, based on location and physical requirements. (We made this choice for my father based on proximity to our home.)

As spaces become available, that facility will contact either the case manager or the client. When a bed offer comes, you have a few days to accept the offer. It is pointed out that should a resident be admitted to the hospital, the bed could be kept reserved for medical leave for twenty-one days. Otherwise, the resident loses the bed placement and is discharged from the long-term care home. If a resident requires a psychiatric assessment, he/she might stay away for as long as forty-five days; this is the only exception to the rule.

One a.m. call — August 12, 2006

When we got a call in the wee hours, it was usually either an emergency, the Manor needed to talk to me, or it was some nutbar. But this time it was Dad again. It was bittersweet relief. Brian took the call for me. The first time, Dad grunted "Uh," and hung up. The second time, he managed to say, "There is something wrong in the upper or lower part of the house." Fire is a big concern up here. We wondered what was up. But he did not think we could do anything, so we convinced him to hang up and go to bed. The third call was something about the "burners." Fortunately, the duty staff took the phone and said there was no problem — no fire — no worries — he just could not sleep or make the TV work. She told us he was agitated and confused but not afraid. I called the Manor in the morning and they said he'd been up until two a.m. and then had gone to bed. He then got up at seven-thirty and went down to breakfast.

Of course, Dolly, Dad's neighbour, did not like Dad's watching TV in the wee hours, since he had to crank the volume up so loud it sounded like fight night next door to her. Poor woman.

It seemed as if it was after dinner that the panic always started. Was this Sundowner's Syndrome or a foreshadowing? Many elderly adults miss spouses and they become very sad and agitated in the evening. By the time we managed to get in to visit with him, he told us, "I don't even know what to think about."

"We're taking care of you, Dad. You need not worry."

"It doesn't get a good thing on here."

"It's the best they can do, Dad."

"I asked three girls to help me and they wouldn't do it."

"Dad, they don't know what to do for you."

"It's all wrong now anyway."

"Yes, Dad. It's the brain tumour coming back."

"They're not taking care of me." These wonderful women who tried to help him simply could not. What he wanted was to be back to normal. This would never get better, I began to understand.

"Lord, give me strength," I prayed.

He was terribly confused. He kept telling me how mixed up it was in his head. This started back during the time he had a bladder infection. He just could not get things straight and he knew it. This was profoundly difficult for all of us. How much worse would this get?

"It's not mine" — August 14, 2006, 7:30 p.m.

On our drive into Gravenhurst, I spotted a black road-kill squirrel. It rested on the double line in the centre of the road. Its little tail fluttered in the breeze. From across the road, we spotted turkey vultures. There was a mother and her hatchlings. They are the natural garbage collectors that keep our Muskoka clean. They flew across our path and almost hit the car in their efforts to find food in this dry August month. One never knows what kind of wildlife will fly out of the forest.

When we went in to visit Dad, it was noon and he was sleeping. We did errands, casually puttering around the town. What a relief not to have to work. It was incredibly stressful working in April and May and looking after Mom. Thank goodness the memorial service was over. I began working on Dad's obituary and announcement. It was good to prepare. I found it lovely looking through papers and uncovering the facets that made up my father while he was still a sentient human being. I had forgotten much and came across a great deal more I had not known. The grieving process is complex, but necessary.

Today was a really bad day. When we returned, Dad was awake and in a foul mood. He adamantly refused to put in his hearing aids, put on his eyeglasses or pants, eat his breakfast, or take his meds.

At each request he would say, "It's not mine. It's nothing to do with me." He refused to use his walker. He knew he had lost all control of everything around him and in a juvenile temper tantrum he decided he would not co-operate with anyone. He sat on the edge of his bed repeating his mantra, "It's not mine. It's nothing to do with me." It was a clever statement and we still use it often when angry and frustrated.

As his agitation increased, it became increasingly difficult to work with him. He understood little. His hearing aids were not working. We thought it was the swelling of the ear canals. We were flushing his ears out weekly, but the wax damaged the hearing aids. He could not figure out how they worked. He would fiddle with them and turn them up so loud they squeaked. It drove people nuts at his dinner table. One person complained and so they changed his table to a more amenable group. It broke Dad's heart. He was very angry that someone had complained. Mom and Dad had spent much of their lives looking after others; my older aunts and uncles, acquaintances—as they became unable to do things for themselves, my parents pitched in.

Dad would often wander around after nine p.m. and later after most of the residents were in bed. Dolly called for a staff member to come and look after him. Bless her, for her help. He had gotten up and was in the hall in his undershirt and boxers—without his walker. He must have used the railing on the wall for support. He got himself into the sitting area at the end of the hall and was in a chair, unable to get up. Dolly said it isn't the worst thing she'd seen. She had found another resident in the same sitting area wearing only a shawl. Dolly sent her back to bed. Dolly was such a good person looking after some of these lost souls. His insomnia was having a bad effect on his routines and the ability of the retirement home to take care of his needs. I constantly racked my brain to figure out how to resolve these issues.

We had been scheduled to go to PEI to see my actor-son in his latest production, *Anne and Gilbert: the Musical*. I could not go and leave Dad alone. Yet again my parents' ill health made me choose caring for one of them over seeing to my children's needs. It was too far away if something happened to Dad. I had to advocate for many issues for my father. This was not the time for me to be away, but we hadn't had a real holiday in two years. I should have taken the break.

I was stressed beyond understanding. I was hoping that my family understood. Brian remained steadfast at my side.

Declaring dad incapable — August 15, 2006

By August, it was time for Dad to be placed in another care centre, with 24/7 nursing care. I spoke to Gay and I spoke to Dad's case manager at CCAC, who said that we would have to put him on a waiting list. She said it was best to get him on a list soon, before it became an emergency to get him from a hospital into a long-term care home, as he could be placed anywhere up to 150 km away.

I did some research. In order to be able to take responsibility for Dad, we had to sign official papers for power of attorney. This represented a huge change to our relationship, primarily in the eyes of the law and the medical health system. He was now a candidate for a bed in an LTC facility. The CCAC nurse made this call and evaluated him, finding him incapable. Dad's doctor, now feeling better, made another brief visit. Dad refused to talk to him. He could not understand why his doctor had not been in to see him all this time. Still fighting for adequate health care for him, we were wondering if he was suffering from a urinary tract infection again. He seemed to need to urinate every ten minutes or so. His hearing seemed all right today and he ate his muffin in his room as I watched. His knees and feet were bad — so swollen.

We had bought him special socks to keep the swelling down. It was hard getting them on — but he had two pair he wore only in the day. The staff rinsed them out every day. The socks seemed to help, but they phoned the doctor for more suggestions, and he prescribed diuretics. This meant that instead of Dad's urinating every ten minutes, it was now every five minutes. We never managed to reduce the swelling in his legs despite massage, and despite the socks. Getting old sucks! The alternative was worse, however, and we kept on trying to do the best we could. It broke my heart to see his painfully swollen feet.

Phone calls — August 16, 2006

I left a note for Dad in his guest book: "Caitlin is 27 today! Her wedding photos are here. Very sleepy, Dad. I brought you four packages of Werther's candy! I only put two in your container. We'll save two for tomorrow." This was really a message for his caregivers, but I liked to pretend that he could understand all this.

I could say he was eating them like candy, but he practically inhaled them. This was a blast from the past. Mom and Dad would sit on the TV room couch and watch a ball game, sharing a container of Werther's. It was a lovely remembrance for him. It seemed to ease him physically and emotionally. It gave him something to do, as well. Unfortunately, he would eat too many and have no idea how many he had eaten.

At 4:40 p.m., Dad called me again. He began phoning at all hours for many unfathomable reasons. "I'm dialing to get the place in town." He knew he wanted help but did not know where to get it.

"I had someone to talk to."

"Who did you want to talk to, Dad?"

"I'm trying to get the papers . . . here comes a nice little girl with a buggy." This was the nurse with meds for him. I could picture her. They had a trolley with a binder containing information about each resident's medications, and juice or water to help the medicine go down. They did these rounds three times a day for each person requiring it. I imagined this was who had popped in to see him.

Dad was becomingly increasingly agitated. He could not retrieve nouns and knew there was something wrong. He knew "buggy" wasn't right, but desperately tried to keep up communication efforts.

At 10:50 p.m. Dad called again. He said, "I'm trying to do things and I can't get them done." Having cleaned up the basement and his papers, I knew how meticulous he was. Thankfully Brian took this call. Dad said, "I wanted someone to get Band-Aids in the jar."

Brian spoke calmly to him. He explained that we could not do anything tonight and that we would take care of it in the morning. After fifteen minutes of conversation, we realized he meant that the candies in the can were gone and he wanted more. If only I had known that; he had more in his basket — I'd hidden them away. Brian was being so wonderful. There we were, sitting up and trying to figure out my Dad's concerns. We were thrilled when we put the pieces of the puzzle together.

Happy anniversary — August 22, 2006

Finally, I managed to put my husband first. It was time to look after my dear husband, who never complained about this huge disruption in our lives. Caregiver burdens are huge issues in the literature. Research abounds on this topic, yet our needs were going unmet. With great relief, and many discussions, Brian and I decided to go away for a few days to Stratford, a short drive south, to a show. It was our fourth wedding anniversary. I had neglected Brian, including our living apart for days on end all summer. He had travelled back and forth from Ottawa to ensure that our house was neat and tidy and was sold.

We had to leave lots of phone numbers; our daughter's contact information was left with the Manor, as well as our Bed and Breakfast contact information. I was terribly worried that something might happen while we were away, remembering what had happened with Mom. It was a foolish concern. Dad wasn't going to pass away so suddenly, but I had no way of knowing this. Nor did I know if he would get into more trouble. I crossed my fingers.

We had a great time and were pampered in our B&B. I felt I could breathe again. Nothing untoward had happened while we were away, and we popped in to see Dad on the way home. All was well with the world, except that Gay had to take Dad's Werthers away, since he had diarrhea, and she thought his eating a bag of candies a day had a negative impact on him. Dad was grouchy: "Helluva life!"

An outdoor fall — August 23, 2006

My feeling was that we could not protect our parents from doing certain things and we could not limit their activities to a great extent. Dad was given a bracelet with a monitor and a buzzer. If he was in trouble he could press the button and help would soon arrive. I tried to encourage Dad to go out for walks, knowing how much he enjoyed the outdoors. Until today, he was not inclined to do so. After this day, he never ventured out again.

His walker was a sturdy machine with a seat, in case he became tired. It was a cranberry colour, with a large basket. Later he told me his story about his trip around the building. As he came around the corner and tried to navigate a driveway, there was a car parked, blocking the sidewalk. Able-bodied folks do not understand the hazards that face the less able. Dad, with his failing eyesight, man-handled his walker, and with his feeble knees, he fell off of the sidewalk and he and his walker ended up in the street. Several folks, sitting in the sun porch, spotted his mishap and called for help. They got out there and helped him up quite quickly.

I talked to Dad's doctor about his condition. His GP told us that the tumour was growing in the frontal lobes and affecting his personality; this was the seat of inhibitions, and that Dad, after a life of goodness, had suddenly been released from doing all the proper things. This was quite a shock.

Gay continued to worry about Dad's falls. He slept in late and they would bring him a tray. On the days he insisted on moving about, his right knee seemed to give way and he would fall over sideways. I had no idea if it was his knees and the arthritis, or the brain tumour. It was so hard to face this every day.

Poor Dolly—her patience was waning. She said that he was still up at night and very, very loud. I phoned the placement officer and asked again about a waiting list. With great relief, I learned that Dad had been accepted into the long-term care home. This time, a miracle, they assessed Dad, and all of the people involved in the decision had come to the conclusion that he would fit into an empty private room on the second floor of the LTC home. I was quite relieved, since I had wondered if he would be placed on the third floor with the patients who are flight risks. He did not need a secure bed, there are codes and security measures on all of the floors, and only those with enough means to cognitively figure these out can get out. What a load off.

Visitors — August 25, 2006

My Aunt Irene (Dad's sister) and my cousin had been weekly visitors to Dad for a month. My aunt is a couple of years older than Dad and has breathing problems, but they made the trip north to see him regularly. Today they visited and he was pouting. He knew change was in the air again and it was upsetting to him.

Dad's best friend, Dick, was in. He and Dad were often mistaken for each other, and Dad did not appear to recognize him. Sometimes

I thought this was one way Dad did not have to be embarrassed, but it is hard to tell. Dear Beth, his wife, told me that I was "doing a good job" and that we were wise to move Dad into an LTC home. She told us to keep in touch. Simple words that meant a great deal. We were isolated, friendless, and lonely. So many folks had been so involved in my parents' lives. Everyone knew what we should do for Mom and Dad and were quite eager to tell us. It was nice to hear kind, comforting words.

We knew what we had to do, and it was tiring having to explain our actions and our plans. Passing by, a neighbour asked how Dad was doing in the new place, and I had to say that he had not yet been moved. It was peculiar and distressing.

More phone calls — August 25, 2006

Dad's phone calls kept up. Poor Dad. He did not know who I was on the phone, but had managed to either use speed dial or phone us. There we were: ten p.m., tired and reading in bed. It was Dad on the phone. We felt a mixture of relief and worry. Was it Dad, or someone telling me he was sick? He said, "I'm trying to contact Walker Ave. [our old street name in Toronto] or the Manor." He could not figure out whom he had phoned. He could not hear us on the other end; his hearing was bad even on his Superphone. "I guess you can't help me," he declared and hung up. He could not dial properly, but the phone number remained his lifeline in his mind. He used to chant "762" all the time, the first three digits of his phone number. On a good day he remembered the entire number, but many days he did not.

Dad goes into long-term care — August 28, 2006

Today was the day. We went over to the Manor and packed up his things. I had made the mistake of taking in suitcases on Friday. It disturbed him so much that the Manor staff had to take them and hide them. Lord knew he was agitated enough. We managed to get Dad into the car with some difficulty. He was a tall man and, although he had lost weight, he still was a significant size. Brian drove the minivan with Dad's chair and luggage. I drove Dad in the car.

The foyer was a lovely place. With a couple of couches and chairs, and many flowers donated by local florists or grieving families, it was always bright and cheery. He could not manage his walker, and we had to find a wheelchair. He could barely lift his profoundly swollen feet, and we had difficulties with the footrests. I wheeled him by the front desk, where I had previously completed almost all of the paperwork. We passed the central courtyard. Filled with patio furniture, trees, and mature plantings, it was quite nice. They had barbecues there in good weather. It was a peaceful place to visit.

Upstairs we went, to Dad's room. It was pretty stark. It was definitely a hospital-like setting: bare floors, a simple hospital bed, pine-laminated wardrobe, and two two-drawer dressers with a few nails in the walls for pictures. I wrote down a list of pictures to bring and hang up. They encourage families to help make the resident more at home. The window overlooked the front parking area and courtyard. I would later spend many hours gazing out. The curtains were a neutral brown colour, with a window that, thankfully, could be opened in good weather. The sun shone into the room, making it bright and giving more hope than we had a right to look forward to. I wisely did not take too many clothes in for Dad. He would never be outdoors again and never again require a winter coat. We left those things in our rental locker.

He was not hopeful, nor optimistic, nor particularly pleased with being there. I took him on a brief tour of the dining room. There were two big dining rooms per floor, with an adjoining cafeteria for food preparation.

Today, Monday, was the regular day for the doctor's visit. There was one doctor for this floor. He usually did rounds with the charge nurse, visiting briefly with each resident and noting his/her needs. The charge nurse could phone the doctor at any time and usually had a standing order for meds as required. The charge nurse and the doctor needed to do an initial assessment of Dad and they asked me to leave Dad's room. I stood in the hall.

Each resident had a framed plaque screwed to the wall outside the room and beside his or her door. In this enclosure, staff put a brief biography of the room's resident. It humanizes the person, who was often unrecognizable as the person he/she used to be. I read some of them as I waited for the doctor and nurse to finish. I prepared one for Dad, not as succinct as the others. (I am usually accused of being too wordy in my writing.)

We declined to stay much longer, even though we were offered a meal. I thought it best he get used to the routine, the room, and the requirements of the institution. We left him at dinnertime, hoping for the best.

Time for a wheelchair — August 30, 2006

The rules of the Long-Term Care Act say that whenever there is a significant incident, the institution must phone the family. Since Dad's phone calls had ceased with the removal of the phone that he could not understand anymore, my stomach no longer churned into knots at the ring. It turned out that Dad had fallen again. I had to explain that he had fallen five times in two days in the past while, and that it was to be expected. His balance was off and his strength was going. There was little we could do. Unfortunately, he continued to get up in the night. He either refused — or did not know — to push the call button to get help. He would get out of bed and then fall to the floor. The staff wisely put his bed down as low as it could go and placed two mats on the floor. Eventually, he would not be able to raise himself out of the bed. In the meantime, this assuaged all of our concerns.

It was now time for a rented wheelchair. Brian and I could not support him enough to help him move about. His balance had disappeared. We had to find one somewhere. There were places that rented them, which was what we needed to do, since we didn't know how much longer Dad would be with us. Since he was slumping over so much, I worried about him. He seemed to lose his balance just sitting and would fall over to the side. He had been using the nursing home's wheelchair, but he still had the walker, which cluttered the room. There was little enough space, what with the pads they had on the floor. I found it difficult remembering what I needed to do for Dad. I made notes for a frame of reference. I could not focus much of the time. This was the difficulty: balancing home, work, and Dad's care. It was already time to gear up for September and a new classroom of eager kids.

2006: I, Caregiver

The last vestiges of summer
—September 1–2, 2006

This was a time for family to rally round. How nice to have the young people visit this weekend. Caitlin and Jean–Luc came all the way from Ottawa, and we received them with big hugs and great joy. Jean–Luc helped with the cooking, which was a relief; Caitlin and I went into Gravenhurst, while Jean–Luc took care of supper. J–L also helped me by putting up a shelf in our bathroom. He is such a good man. I am so glad he is Caitlin's husband. It was fun showing them how we had renovated the house. I had missed them.

The drive into town never ceased to amaze me with its beauty. Three deer crossed the road ahead of us. They delicately tiptoed across the road, one at a time, checking both ways for threats—just the way I had taught Caitlin to watch as she crossed the street. It was a lovely moment. There were lessons in nature.

We arrived at the long-term care home with some trepidation. We never knew how Dad would be feeling or acting each day. There was a keypad with a code for entering and exiting the facility. This protected those residents who were at risk for flight or those who might get lost outside.

Visitors must sign in to the LTC—a strict safety protocol. (We protect both our children and our parents from strangers!) There was one register for volunteers and external professional staff (e.g., massage therapists or physiotherapists) and one for visitors. It let staff know, in case of emergency, who was in the building. Caitlin and I went to the desk and I signed our names, the time of our visit, the resident we were visiting, and the floor. It became automatic over time, Ray Jilks, 2nd floor, and the date. We put on our badges and went upstairs, using the anti-bacterial agent on our hands.

SARS protocol has had a profound influence on germ warfare in such institutions. LTC home residents, with deteriorating bodies and weary immune systems, are susceptible to hidden dangers like influenza and other infections, just like in classrooms. Any group situation puts people at risk for both infections and infestations.

Dad recognized Caitlin and he was clearly happy to see her. I had been worried. We got him organized, having dropped off our coats in his room, and followed Dad's regular dinner routine, wheeling him into the Muskoka Room, where he had to eat when we visited him at mealtimes, getting his bib, cutlery, and coffee. Caitlin helped me feed him, taking the spoon from me while I left the room to get the rest of his meal. Either personal support workers or kitchen staff would deliver Dad's food, or I would fetch it from the cafeteria across the hall. I felt good assisting, as this gave them more time with other needy residents unable to feed themselves.

Caitlin carefully held the cup to her grandfather's mouth. Dad's hands shook so much some days that he could not hold the cup without spilling. I had to be careful not to interfere too much. This diminished his self-esteem and made him angry. If I showed him that

Dad's hands shook as he held his coffee cup.
I would gently steady him.

I did not trust him to hold something and he wanted to do it himself, he would protest.

Dad could not hear Caitlin—she has a very soft voice—but he knew she was trying to take care of him. He graciously accepted her tender ministrations. He tended to grow tired of me, be angry with me on a daily basis, and it was a blessed relief to have support and a young, fresh, and familiar face. I remembered that our cat, angered at being cooped up for the night, would turn her anger onto the other cat. I was grateful for that lesson now. This displaced anger was something I found hard to deal with emotionally, as a daughter, but I could understand it intellectually. It was a hard concept to negotiate with my ego, however!

Caitlin and I were discussing Dad's gradual decline on the way home. Not as shocking as it might have been, since she saw him at his worst in May during Mom's funeral; but it was difficult for her to see the change in this strong, capable grandfather-figure she adored. At home, we anticipated a delicious meal and some family time. Our precious Jean–Luc had been cooking up a storm. He had marinated shrimp and was ready to tempt our palates. It was wonderful to break bread together and speak of old times. To everything there is a season, and I was now the matriarch, but I had learned to let go and let the kids look after us. There is giving in the receiving.

Back to school — Wednesday, September 6, 2006

As faithfully as autumn follows summer, it was time to go back to school. As a teacher, my life began in September, and this was the first day of school. Bulletin boards had been prepared, shelves cleaned, desks arranged, class lists printed. As always, it was a sleepless night, even after twenty-five years. My placement exchange from a Grade 3 classroom assignment in Parry Sound to a small school, where I would be in charge of a Grade 8 classroom twenty kilometres closer to home, was welcome. I was quite encouraged to be using my knowledge of my new school board gleaned from my previous school assignment. My White Pines[5] classroom work had been tough. A regular Grade 8 class would be a welcome assignment, despite having changed classrooms or schools eleven times in twelve years. The only thing teachers can depend upon is change. Each new principal brought a

---

5   My Anger Management class curriculum: **www.jilks.com/WhitePines**

new assignment or a move to a new classroom as they rearranged their school. Such was life.

The peace and quiet of my classroom had been replaced with the fearful murmurs of students wondering about me, a stranger to the community. These fresh faces were exciting, ready for their last year of elementary school. It was a brand-new start, and I looked forward to sharing my knowledge, skills, and expertise in practising my craft. The principal seemed a bit doubtful of my knowledge, skills, and expertise, but I knew how to do my work. I felt that I understood the Grade 8 curriculum and could integrate this with my work in digital photography and technology. I remembered who I was as an educator. It was just that the stress of being responsible and advocating for my dad was overwhelming and impossible some days. Sometimes I would draw into myself, barely able to cope.

Brian had taken responsibility for checking in on Dad. He cared for my dad as if he had been his own. Brian's father had passed away before his second birthday. With his dad's service medals in a mahogany display case in our home, we honoured both the present and the past. Being an only child, with much experience in caring for his late mother and stepfather, he blessed me and shared his knowledge, understanding, and physical and emotional support in this role reversal. Brian would report to me from the LTC home on his daily visits, and I would write all of it down. Inability to hear had become one of the worst of Dad's issues.

While I had met the LTC residence's doctor on Dad's intake day, he visited only weekly and did not have enough time to see each patient during this visit. This would later prove a difficult obstacle. Right now it wasn't too much of an issue. It was the nursing staff who determined his needs, along with our advice, support, and guidance. In a way, it was a relief to have it out of my hands right now.

My tune soon changed.

Brian took Dad's hearing aids to have them cleaned at the store. It cost a bit of money, but worth it. Dad's ear was raw from scratching his outer ear canal. Everyone said that they had never seen such wax buildup and so small an ear canal. It must have been due both to his physiology and the brain tumour. (I wonder if Dad perseverated on this problem with his ears since he could not face his other issues: grieving over his wife, dog, old life, and lost home.)

Routines: confusion and agitation
— Saturday, September 9, 2006

Our routines continued. I tried to visit Dad three times per week. It was a long haul on a workday. It was a 100-km trek after work. As the stress increased, I realized that I might not be able to cope with teaching. My new assignment involved taking the students on a three-day camping trip the second week of school. For a cottage girl who had never been camping, I knew I could draw knowledge from my experienced student campers. This is the difference between a teacher and a learning facilitator. We had been writing a five-paragraph essay on "How to Start a Campfire," a logical writing assignment based in reality and practical experiences. We had brainstormed information and ideas, and the kids were well on their way to producing some excellent pieces of writing. We'd planned materials and supplies, figured out who would bring kindling, food, and tents. I learned a lot from these kids.

I had spent Friday outdoors on an unexpected field trip to a park in the Sound. The kids needed to have a swimming test in order to swim at the campgrounds next week. The sun on their shining faces, the wind, the incredible Parry Sound Precambrian Shield that felt so solid and secure under my feet . . . it was good to be outdoors.

Brian reported that Dad's dementia, anorexia, confusion, and agitation were increasing. Dad wore these symptoms like Joseph's technicoloured coat; protection against his reality and intolerable situation. This barrier between his situation and reality was more than he could bear. The staff told me he was walking around in his underwear the other day. Perhaps the better analogy is the Emperor who had no clothes. They found him urinating on the floor in the hall another time. I did not know what to make of this. Dad did not seem to understand where he was, but that could have been a defence mechanism. (I recall my grandmother's going into an LTC home and perceiving the caregiving staff as spies.) Staff would write notes to him, since he could not hear them, and communication was difficult. He would ask about my visiting him, and staff would attempt to explain that I would be in to visit later; but he did not understand. He was very upset with being in a new place. His charge nurse thought this a behavioural reaction to his internment, rather than a result of the tumour. I was really concerned and did not know for sure. At this rate, he would not last long. I began to foresee the end.

Dad's aimless wandering, combined with his ability to navigate the institution's halls in his wheelchair, was distressing. It was rather like a pilot who couldn't read maps but knew how to fly the plane. With his new wings, he was free to fly down the halls.

Those who were unable to take showers or baths on their own would get a weekly bath. There was a mechanical lift that put them into a giant bathtub in the shower room. In one reported incident, Dad was sitting outside the shower room, saying: "762" over and over again. I knew what he needed. He was trying to remember his home phone number. He knew if he could call us we could help him. I was sure the amygdala, in the deeper and older part of the brain that stored old emotions, was still working. The tumour had no effect on some of his affective reactions. The tumour ate away particular reasoning skills and left other abilities in place. He was connecting his emotional association with home and his old phone number with safety. (ET phone home!) He associated "762" with safety and well-being, despite years of being ill at home, trapped in his own home and unable to navigate his way to familiar lakefronts, his gardens, or local stores.

At one point, Dad was found in another resident's room. The other resident was very angry with Dad. They yelled at each other some. Brian had to remind me that the other folks on this floor were not all cognizant of their own situations, let alone Dad's mindset. The appearance of some LTC residents is deceiving. They might look fairly healthy but the plaque build-up in their brains was diminishing them like an invisible artist painting over brain cell receptors and transmitters. They had lost their ability to feel compassion, had regressed to juvenile behaviour (e.g., fistfights from their wheelchair seats), and many had pretty much lost their inhibitions. The myth of the benign senior is a falsehood. This was not true of all of them, however, as I would soon find out.

The fire alarm; chronic and persistent pain — Monday, September 11, 2006

On the anniversary of 9/11, I toddled off to school for a second week to spend the day with my wonderful Grade 8 students, a new homeroom class of fresh-faced young people. They were ready for anything, with their whole lives ahead of them. Their anticipation of the new school year reflected their anticipation of a great life and prospects for the future.

The few special needs students were looked after and protected by a strong core of bright, responsible, caring peers. As a group, they would prove to be one of the best classes I had taught. This is a good thing, since, as it happened, they were my very last homeroom class. Nestled in the trees of central northern Ontario, it was a lovely location to provide these kids with structure, a stimulating curriculum, and firm, but fair, leadership. With pine trees surrounding us, we were embraced by nature. Unfortunately, my self-esteem and my confidence left me as I was unable to make many of the 8,000 decisions a classroom teacher must make in a day. My unfamiliarity with the community, the school, and the philosophy of the principal left me floundering in a sea of fear and self-doubt. Juggling the Grade 8 burden of the curriculum with this field trip likely sent me over the edge.

Any criticism left me unnerved. I continued to wrestle with my demons as I questioned my ability to do my job. I drove home with the CD blasting great tunes. With the wind messing my hair, I sailed past sparkling lakes and trees dancing in the wind. Turkey vultures as tall as the hood of my car vulgarly eyed me as I passed. A sense of peace passed over me. However, I arrived home to more bad news from the LTC home via Brian. Today Dad had wandered down the hall, still in his wheelchair, and had pulled the fire alarm. I was mortified! At least I knew they could not kick him out of this long-term care home. I'd heard that other residents had pulled the fire alarm. It must be some sort of subliminal call for help.

I worried about having to restrain Dad. He was terribly confused and groaning a lot. We did not know if he was in pain, or, if so, what we could do about it. The staff gave him some Tylenol to ease his pain. It might simply have been his arthritic knees that were causing him agony, but again, we did not know. He could not communicate this to us. Brian sent me off to work and then went in to see Dad daily. Brian fed him at the 8:00 a.m. breakfast sitting. Sometimes Brian would leave the house before I did to get Dad up in time for breakfast. There wouldn't have been enough staff to get everyone ready on time if there were some sort of emergency. It was a merciless schedule and it took its toll on my dear husband, my rock and my pillow. He was eager to relieve my burden and did what he could to help.

Pain is not a normal part of aging, but it is fairly common in long-term care homes and ought to be addressed. Chronic pain is pain that persists for three to six months after it is expected to cease, after healing from a medical condition. Persistent pain is pain that lasts longer than a month. Dad had always had persistent pain, due to the arthritis in his knees, and this had never been adequately addressed. He and his doctor had tried many things (e.g., vitamins, Tylenol), but he never found relief. He bought the magnetic wraps that were supposed to help, but gave those up. In the summer we put some topical ointments on his knees. After the radiation treatments on his forehead he put some of this, accidentally, on his forehead when he wasn't thinking straight. It must have been painful, and we felt awfully guilty about this incident. In the past, Dad had indicated he was in pain, but he was beyond that now. This was what made him so irritable in his final years.

There are accepted non-specific signs of pain: frowning, grimacing, grinding of teeth, fidgeting, bracing, rubbing, striking out, increasing or recurring agitation, poor eating or sleeping habits, sighing, moaning, groaning, decreased activity levels, resisting a particular movement, change in gait or behaviour, or loss of function. Dad had all of these and, in hindsight, was clearly under-medicated.

School and teaching continued to give me stress. My hands constantly trembled. I had gained weight. I was fighting with either anger, fear, self-doubt, or insecurity at various times of the day. My boss had been vigilant in disciplining me for mistakes and errors in judgment, and corrected my anticipated bad behaviour with terse letters left in my mailbox calling me to her office. It was my understanding, having been through the principals' course, that it was up to the school leader to help teachers become the best they could be. I wondered if I would be adequate as an educator even if I had help. I had little self-esteem left. I had been experiencing headaches and insomnia for months. I felt helpless and had no control over my own curriculum. The hand tremors began in May or June. I could not remember exactly when they started. Things were such a battle, what with fighting for care for my dad. I needed to stay home for a few days.

Advocating for Dad; anorexia — September 12, 2006

It is important to be an advocate and to ask questions on behalf of your loved one. I was unable to function well enough to do so. It haunts me to this day. I was unable to get to speak with the doctor, who I wasn't sure really knew or understood my father and his care. There was no treatment plan I could perceive. For someone in palliative care, there is a pattern of eventual physical and biological deterioration that is predictable. This must be anticipated, prepared for, and managed.

Dear Brian advocated so much for us. He visited the staff and spoke to the charge nurse, dietitian, and other care staff. Brian had been advocating for Dad's food preferences. Tania called us from the LTC home that day. I was glad I was there to take the call. I could be replaced at school, but I was Dad's only daughter and legal advocate nearby. Dad had crawled out of bed and fallen onto his knees. It was their responsibility, according to the Long-Term Care Act, to inform us. I thanked them. They assured us he was fine.

Dad was unable to understand the function of the *call help* button and would not wait for help. He often had to urinate every fifteen minutes or so. Long-term care was not staffed to allow for a senior to have such a frequent toileting routine. But it is demeaning to lose control of one's bodily functions. There is a huge struggle to hurriedly get up out of bed and go to the toilet. It was a horrible situation. I still have no answers to this issue, with Ontario government standards limited to three hours' care per resident per day.

No amount of discussion with the nurses would increase his pain medications to an acceptable level. I kept asking for more pain relief, but I truly did not know what was indicated, still had not spoken to the physician, and was getting tired of fighting.

Since his agitation was so extreme, they had put him on a drug to calm him. I think they said it was Respiridol, but it was intended to take away his pain. He chewed the tablets. I did not know what the drug was made of, nor what it was for. I had not been told what drugs he was on, nor given any indication of his pharmacological treatments. On the web it said this drug is *contraindicated for those with dementia*. There were risks involved, but it calmed him and I ignored this issue. My brain was full and I had to choose my battles.

We were not informed of its intended or regular use. As alternate decision-maker, I would have liked to sit down for a talk with the attending physician, but that was not to be. I later filed a complaint, which I hope made a difference to other residents.

Dad played constantly with his hearing aids; his ears bothered him. He would try to adjust his aids. Today he refused his bath. His right foot was still painfully swollen. His eyes were itchy and he was on antibiotics for another urinary tract infection. It was a miserable life. His walker, missing yesterday, had been returned. The PSW told me that Dad had been up at night. He "tore up his room," they told me. I did not ask for too much information. He was wandering down the hall. The charge nurse told me that they gave him some Ativan to calm him down. I thought *I* could have used one. I wondered what all these drugs did to him.

After checking with the dietitian, we figured Dad had eaten only about one-quarter to one-half of two meals in two weeks. They kept careful records and weighed the patients regularly. He was refusing most meals. Anorexia nervosa is a disease that primarily affects young women. DSM-IV-TR (APA) defines it as "*a refusal to maintain body weight at or above a minimally normal weight for age and height.*" It is a psychological disorder that has biological effects as the individual tries to manage or control his or her environment by controlling the amount of food he or she eats. This was Dad's situation. I have seen it in many seniors due to many issues. It is a combination of lack of appetite and a means by which one can feel as if they are in psychological control. There was nothing to do about it. He would not have benefited from counselling, as he could not hear or cognitively process a therapeutic treatment or process.

Work stress . . . depression
— Sunday, September 17, 2006

Bullying in the workplace is an issue facing an increasing number of workers (Bredeson, 2003). It is a major cause of physical, emotional, and psychological issues for employees and exacerbates an already demanding emotional burden on the part of a caregiver like myself. In a familiar pattern of emotional abuse, I received an e-mail from my principal pointing out more mistakes that I had made at school;

things forgotten, things she needed me to change or fix. I knew I was not working at my best and I realized that I could not face this work situation. It was intolerable. My father had to come first.

When we have stress it is like filling a glass with liquid. Each time a stressful incident occurs, a little more is added until it fills us up and we soon overflow. This is what depression does to us. We develop inertia and cannot tackle anything that needs doing. Despite needing to complete numerous tasks, we cannot fight the inertia. Fear of failure secures our feet to the ground. I felt threatened as I perceived that my boss was questioning my methods, my beliefs, my timetable, my work with the special needs students, and my commitment to her school, her students, and her community. I was physically, socially, and emotionally exhausted and felt defeated. I realized that I could no longer face her anymore with my increasing self-doubts reinforced by her critical eye. In my readings, I had found that those who were depressed faced increasingly low levels of self-esteem. People like me, who were juggling home and work, despite having previously achieved success, sustain high levels of self-doubt.

I read an article, published in our local paper, that related loss and bereavement issues to a loss of self-esteem. It was an article published by The Caregiver's Support Network, which was partnered with our local Hospice Group. If only I had known that they existed! They abound in Canada, but I was unaware of this and unable to seek help. I thought I had to do it all on my own.

I tried to be tough. I tried to shoulder a burden that was unsustainable. Daily I questioned myself, as a wife, daughter, and teacher. I was having doubts about my teaching ability and my purpose in life. I knew Dad wouldn't last too much longer, and wondered what I would do with my life then. This article talked about setting realistic goals. I had not been able to do so. They talked about a sense of fear, which indeed I possessed. I wondered if I was good enough to do the job I had been assigned. I could not make decisions daily and juggle thousands of lesson plans; I was unable to decide what to teach — or, more to the point, what *not* to teach. Ontario Ministry curriculum expectations are so great that educators have a hard time meeting them all, while integrating learning, focusing on the big picture, connecting learning to students' personal and community life, and all the while differentiating curricula for special needs students. Our two-week fixation on the camping trip left little time to establish routines, set up classroom expectations, and dig into the multi-layered literacy, numeracy, history, and geography units buried in our textbooks. We were interrupted more than daily for bulletins, important assemblies, PA announcements, and changes in plan. It was unnerving.

For me, just getting dressed in the morning involved decisions I was unable to make without forcing myself to keep moving. The article went on to say that low self-esteem could manifest itself by complicating the grieving process. I was grieving my mother, and the father whom I used to know, at the same time. This kind of stress could result in substance abuse, risk-taking, thoughts about risk-taking, suicidal ideations, negative mind chatter, fear of new situations, and distancing oneself from family and friends. I checked positive for all of these symptoms.

I spoke with an absence management representative at the board office. I told her all that had gone on in my life. She suggested I go back to the Employee Assistance Program (EAP), despite my failure to find an adequate counsellor last June. (I spoke once to a counsellor on the phone, and she suggested, after forty minutes, that I really didn't need to talk to her again.) My contact promised she would speak directly to her contact with the EAP Management group. I was glad I had reached out. She advocated for me and ensured that I spoke to someone who would guarantee that I had an experienced counsellor who would guide me through this chapter in my life. What a blessed relief.

I began to see this counsellor weekly. He helped me work my way through the issues that I was juggling. He complimented me on how well I was handling the stress. I had lost all perspective. I laughed a great deal and tried to step back to look at some situations with amusement. This made life endurable. He assured me, after I told him my previous experience with counselling, that I would not be left high and dry this time. I had lost my peer support system and social network by moving away from friends. I felt so much better; now I had someone in my court other than my beleaguered husband and my children, from whom I had unconditional support. As I talked through my issues, I began to realize that my priority had to be me and my dad.

My father required increasing amounts of support from us. While the Ontario government has a plan whereby employees could take six weeks off from work to care for a family member in palliative care, it is leave without pay, and would cost me pension dollars. I had taken time off work before beginning my teaching career, and had little enough pension as it was. The penalties for a shortened career due to child-bearing profoundly impact mothers in their retirement years. In addition, one needs a letter from the doctor stating that the patient has less than six months to live. How could a doctor predict this?

With Dad's ill health and current deterioration rate, I thought that maybe he might have had two weeks left, but it was hard to tell. I had little choice but to take some sick leave now to try to look after my dad and myself. I had to call in sick. I was determined not to let my work determine or limit my ability to care for my father. I would never regret the decision to move to Muskoka.

Until now, I had enjoyed going to work. It took me away from my concerns. It helped me keep life in focus, as opposed to peering into the valley of the shadow of death. I felt that I had much to offer with my background and experiences in dealing with many types of students of varying abilities, disabilities, learning styles, races, colours, and creeds.

My mental health was the most important issue right now. I was truly suffering from a difficult work situation: a new school, new boss, and new culture. My students were delightful; my colleagues had remained supportive and understanding. They lauded me in my efforts. They listened and helped. But despite this support, I could not face work anymore. I felt devalued and unrecognized. I had had enough. I felt very strongly that God had something else in mind for me.

I decided to give up my career and my teaching practice. I held fast to my faith, determined to retire as soon as was possible in December when I turned fifty. As I drove past each school, with a schoolyard filled with laughing children, and school buses motoring on down the road, the regret at ending my career left me feeling like a failure. The shadows loomed in the dusk as I faced my demons.

Brian continued to go in and feed Dad breakfast, while I tried to heal myself and "look after me." This was the advice many, many people had given me based on their own experiences. I had always agreed with the flight attendant's advice: to demand that mothers put the oxygen mask on themselves first, and then their children. I was drained of energy. I found it difficult to begin any tasks, let alone finish them.

We were slowly getting the house in order; it began to resemble a home. I found solace in cooking and going back to being the home-maker I once was when my children were in their early childhood years. I began nesting. I told my counsellor that I wanted to hibernate for the winter. I wanted to cocoon, eat better, drink less, exercise more, and get myself back in shape.

After each afternoon visit with my father, I came home either numb or in shock. We would often go out to dinner, as preparing a meal was beyond us. At times I had an immense sense of gratitude for living in this beautiful place and surrounded by nature (tourists having gone home for the winter). At other times I did not know how to manage my new reality: that of homemaker/caregiver. I ate a lot to keep my hands busy, and drank just enough to be able to sleep. One glass of wine would lead to another until I could not feel the pain anymore. Something would give if I did not stop and take it easy.

Old dreams die hard. I had given up the notion of being a principal here in Muskoka. I realized that once retired, I could not go back to delivering workshops, either. They want current practitioners to deliver workshops. I could not do so. Finally, we had found a good doctor. He worked in a practice with a drop-in clinic and, while I had put off looking after myself, he seemed to be able to help me. He asked me several questions and came to the conclusion that I was clinically depressed. Basically, my neurotransmitters were not firing properly, and it was the fight or flight response to my stress that had sent me off into a tailspin.

I could not go on this way, worrying about school, my father, and our new home. My physician prescribed anti-depressants. I was not sure what they would do to me— many drugs have side effects—but I knew there was something wrong and agreed to take the drugs. The first lot gave me headaches. I could not abide the headaches. I knew one had to start them slowly with a half dose, but I also knew there was something wrong with me that I could not fix with sleeping pills, exercise, or relaxation tapes. The prescription cost $117. Thank goodness for my drug plan!

My doctor gave me a medical note to stay off work for a month. I felt incredibly sad, but quite relieved. I could not live with the workplace stress and the angst I felt at having to face my principal feeling like a failure. I could retire in December at the age of fifty with an early retirement penalty and a huge reduction in my income. I believed that my mental health and my ailing dad were worth more than just money. I filed the papers. As the old ad said, "I am worth it." I had 130 sick days that I had brought with me from Ottawa, and did not have a history of being ill. It was time to use those days. This past year had sent me over the edge. I was travelling at top speed down a slippery slope, headed towards disaster. My teaching career was over. It was a hard life passage to face.

My brother returns — Thursday, September 21, 2006

Robin took some time off work to visit us, at our insistence. We were so glad to see him. As a caregiver and a daughter, I made most of the decisions, all with the support and advice of my husband, checking in with my brother as much as was practical. But Robin works in a mine in the Northern Ontario bush, for two weeks at a time. There was only one cell phone and he was hard to reach. It was easier for me, as I could go about my work independently, without interference from other family members. In some families there is conflict about who is in charge and what should be done each step of the way. It was a relief to have Robin here to see how things were really going now. He did not understand, and I could not convey by phone, the decisions we faced and the issues that confronted us daily. He, too, must be in denial. It was difficult, so far away, to face reality.

Robin is such an affable, very positive, outgoing man. This situation was weighing heavily on his mind, too. He is an ideas man and had great plans to make all our lives better. The time Mom was discharged after cancer surgery number five, he was going to renovate the bathroom and put a full bath in on the first floor. Time was short, however, and that could not be done. He planned on buying us a hot tub, but that never materialized. If you were there with him, you knew Robin had your back. Otherwise, he deals with the crisis there at the time. Underground, in the bowels of the earth, with him in charge of the dynamite, you knew he would be there for you. If you had to move, he would be the muscle to make it so. He has a dear set of friends who look out for and love him. We were glad to see him here to help.

Robin and Brian went in to feed our father. Brian guided Rob into the big brick institution, with brickwork that reminds me of braid and Band-Aids. He showed Robin the sign-in process. Brian kept his badge with him: a special one with "BRIAN" on it in big letters. Many times Brian would be feeding Dad and Dad would forget Brian's name and call him whatever numbers of letters were on his badge: G145, for example. I made myself a permanent badge with "JEN" on it. It made a difference and allowed other residents to call us by name.

Brian showed Robin the routine of feeding: how to get set up in the family feeding room. He got the cutlery from Dad's usual table, set up the serviette, put out the fork and spoon, and snapped a bib on Dad. Dad had a big breakfast. He was hungry. I was sure he was happy to see Robin. All the ladies adored Robin, too. They still asked about him for months afterwards. He is of Scots descent and has dark, curly hair and an attractive figure, solidly built with the sturdy body type of a miner used to moving heavy machinery. His mother came over from Scotland to have him. He was adopted when he was two weeks old. Mom and Dad were so happy to have a boy and a girl; we always felt chosen.

Dad's hands shook so much, perhaps he was still getting used to the level of drugs he was being given. He could not lift food from his fork into his mouth. He could not understand how to use a knife anymore. His brain could no longer navigate the function of simple things. He would spear a large piece of egg and try to shove it in whole. Toast went into his mouth in one whole piece, too. Dad, happy to see his son, was ravenous. He smiled at Robin; his sense of humour was not lost, and he told Brian, "Pour it on!" practically winking in glee at his shared joke with Robin. His hunger strike was in remission today. He was happy and eating well. Robin and Brian phoned me and let me know that they would do some errands and hang around until lunchtime. Meals took the better part of an hour. I was glad to be at home puttering around the kitchen.

New wheelchair — September 22, 2006

Lo and behold, Dad had a new wheelchair. He had been trying to undo the seat's safety belt, which requires a pen to pop the lock for safety. He put his feet on the floor and his behind on the edge of the chair. He fought the restraint valiantly. He wanted me to get him to the edge of the bed so that he could use the rail to stand up. It was a typical hospital bed. He pleaded with me to help him use the hand-rail to get up to go to the bathroom.

"Jenn, please," he said with such fervour. I knew I could not lift him. Instead, I pushed the call buzzer to get a staff member in to help. I thought it futile. He had not been able to use the toilet since he could no longer stand. It must be terribly difficult to be wearing an adult diaper. He was at the point where they needed to use a mechanical lift to move him all the time.

He had spilled food all over his new wheelchair. I went to his bathroom, found a clean set of cloths and towels and wet a cloth, after the ladies were finished, and wiped the chair clean as best I could. His glasses were lost, as were both hearing aids. His bed had been lowered to the floor. This minimized the distance he would fall, should he insist on getting out of bed. There were mats on the floor on either side, as well, to cushion his fall.

Dad was barking again, that half groan, half yell like some tennis players do on the court. When I finally wheeled him into the hall, Igor, another resident, told him to shut up, and I wondered whether to say anything. I rolled Dad down the hall past the ladies who were lined up in chairs and wheelchairs for dinner.

Communication: the whiteboard — September 24, 2006

When Dad was in the Manor, we often wrote things down for him, since he could not hear us. It became humorous, as he would reread notes previously dealt with and would forget that we had moved on with the conversation. I should have taken the scraps of paper and filed them in the circular file. We had to scribble over the old notes so as not to confuse him during our written conversations. It was a complex task to communicate with him.

Brian's brilliant idea was to buy and put a small whiteboard and marker in Dad's room. This way Brian could write down what it was he wanted to communicate to Dad, and Dad could respond orally. I had heard that other families used this method. It really works well, since one simply erases the message to write the next one. Unfortunately, Dad was not quite clear on some concepts. After a time he lost enough of his cognitive abilities that it became useless and then he lost the marker. Back to the drawing board and square one!

Physiotherapy, inhibitions, and dietitians
— September 26, 2006

The things my father said truly embarrassed me. I knew that his inhibitions had been dampened by the growth of the brain tumour. I knew that the indignities he had suffered had had a profound emotional effect upon him. It came out in defiance and appalling antisocial behaviour. He spoke of care staff with the cheekiness that only the aged could display and get away with, except for on TV! He would regularly shout, referring to various staff members: "Here comes the fat one." Or, "Here comes the old one." Strangers wandered in and out of his room, wiping his mess at either end of his frail body, changing his clothes and sheets, and wheeling him down to meals he would rather refuse. Other residents wandered in, lost and alone in this hospital-like world. Their dementia was an unseen issue in their daily lives. Despite previous communication issues, Dad spoke in full sentences to Brian today; clearly refusing toast and waffles. (Wasn't it Dad who had warned me to eat my vegetables, as there were children starving in Africa?)

The physiotherapist, Katherine, had a conversation with Brian, who had taken much of the advocacy burden from me. Brian looks more like Dad than I do (I am adopted!), with beard and bald head. They kept thinking Brian was Dad's son, not son-in-law, and would ask him to make decisions.

The young, attractive Katherine wanted to give Dad some physiotherapy to help him to more easily transfer from the wheelchair to the bed. While Dad flirted outrageously with one and all, and would have loved the attention from this attractive brunette, this was not a good idea. Brian explained to this lovely young woman that we needed to refuse this help, since making Dad stronger in this activity would only jeopardize his safety and complicate his issues. Dad was in palliative care, we had to reassure them, and this was a different situation than most of the other residents. Dad would not get stronger. He was making bad decisions regarding his safety. He would get weaker and required two people to lift him now. There was no sense in helping keep up his strength to defy the care staff. Dad would never be able to manage to walk again. We had to balance out physiotherapy that helped, provided range of motion, and ameliorated pain, versus physiotherapy that added to his aggravated state and agitation. Dad could not stand people bossing him around, even the most jocular of personal support workers (PSW). Each day would bring a whole new raft of PSWs he did not recognize and who manipulated his body: transferring him in and out of bed and dragging him off to meals he did not want.

Brian had a bizarre conversation with the dietitian. We knew that Dad used to like to have an egg a day. Brian fed him breakfast on a daily basis, and this was what he wanted. The dietitian was concerned with his cholesterol. Again, Brian patiently explained that Dad had been given a final prognosis, the brain tumour was inoperable and untreatable, and we wanted him to be happy eating whatever he wanted to eat. Like a teenager with anorexia, he had been asserting his will around the issue of food. It was the last stand for Dad. This reminded Brian of his stepfather, who was in a long-term care home with Alzheimer's syndrome many years ago. They wanted to put him on a diet, as they were worried about his food intake. Our goal was to try to keep my father happy as best we could. He wouldn't live long enough for cholesterol to be an issue!

Selective hearing — September 28, 2006

When Brian arrived for Dad's breakfast, Dad was trying to get out of bed. Brian told him to wait for a PSW, and that settled him down. Two PSWs arrived and did a two-person lift and put Dad in his chair. While he waited, Brian tidied Dad's room. He knew how much Dad liked things neat, having helped him tidy up his room at the Manor. Dad was ranting about the mess in his very small, simple institutional setting. I guess I married my mother: she and Brian joked about the penchant they had for liking things just so. I am a clutter freak and Brian a neatnik.

With meagre curtains, flatly painted walls, and an ensuite two-piece bathroom with handrails, it was nothing like home. Dad had two dressers and one wardrobe; his TV sat atop one dresser. We placed three paintings and photographs around the room. I had bought a live plant blooming with African violets, the planter surrounded by a big, cheery yellow bow, for the bright window. Dad loved his plants and flowers, and I had given away all of his two dozen African violets to the church for their annual bazaar.

On this morning, Brian managed to get Dad to eat a bowl of porridge and drink two glasses of orange juice. There were no eggs, and Dad was really pissed off with this. Also, he complained to Brian that he was feeding him too fast. As well, Brian changed spoons, and that set Dad off. This took me back to looking after my children as toddlers. As my friend, Kristin, said: "Pediatrics and geriatrics . . . not much difference except for body mass." Things had to be just so. Neither the young nor the old and infirm can tolerate any change in routine. Rigidity and predictable expectations make some people more comfortable. It makes everyone feel better to know what to expect.

It broke my heart that Dad had to be there in that institution; but we could not cope with his intense needs at home. I had talked to so many women who cared for ailing family members. The most difficult time seems to be if both spouses are alive — they can cope after a fashion and stay in denial about their abilities to manage in their own homes. It puts a huge burden on their adult children and neighbours, however, as the phone calls for help increase in quantity and severity.

Dad's hearing aid was broken. It was lost, and had been found, but it was really broken. Brian took the one remaining hearing aid away to the hearing aid store. The young lady, Terri, had been very good about cleaning dad's hearing aids. She had attended Mom's funeral and popped in at the visitation last May. The cleaning cost nearly $300. She told Brian that Dad's hearing was seventy-five percent gone in his left ear and twenty-five percent gone in his right ear when he had had a hearing test two years ago. This explained a lot of our troubles.

Tornado and storm — September 29, 2006

The anti-depressants had slowly begun to make a difference for me. It would take months, my doctor told me, but I knew that things would get easier. At this point I could not go in to face Dad on a daily basis, to witness his emotional pain and anger turned outwards. I visited every third day or so. Brian protected me, for the most part. We spent a fortune on eating out this month. It was a ritual of sorts. When we visited Dad, we would be depressed and go out for dinner, too tired to face our own ADL. My waistline was increasing. It was not something I could work on right now, though.

There had been another big storm this month; we lost our power for a couple of days. Our neighbours had been six days without hydro. We were more fortunate. Their power went off when two trees fell, one on their power lines and TV cable. We had to phone the fire department, since the cables were smoking. Our neighbours had to have trees cut up, hydro repair folks in, and a new pole put on their house. Our wires were buried from the post to the house. It was quite distressing, especially for someone like myself who had experienced ten days without power during Ice Storm '98 in Ottawa. I anticipated a bout of post-traumatic stress disorder as all of the same fears resurrected themselves. I knew that if I had any more stress I could not cope. I was grateful that we had everything under control here. A tornado? No power? So what? It was the least of our worries. We used the barbecue and tried to relax.

Temporarily his mood improves — September 30, 2006

By now, Dad was raging most of the time. Nothing seemed quite right. Brian marched down the hall, past the dining room, to get Dad ready. As Brian went past, he noticed that Dad was already at the table. The walls of the dining room were clear glass and Dad waved as Brian zoomed by to begin his routine. He dropped his coat off and returned to the dining room. With about nine or ten tables in the room, care staff would go around and get residents set up at their particular places. Residents unable to feed themselves were grouped at a semicircular table; others sat at tables of four. It was a Saturday and Brian was there bright and early for the 8:00 a.m. feeding. Dad was cheerful, sensible, and happy. One just never knew who he would be each day. He was given his bib, his pills, coffee, and two extra cups of orange juice, and seemed quite happy alone with Brian at a table. He told Brian that the oatmeal was okay, but not great. He was communicating clearly and asked Brian if it was cold out, reflecting an understanding of the season.

Di, another resident, waved to Brian from another table. Di was happy to see him. Brian is such a dear man. He is good with people and a charming host. He had helped me host my staff Christmas party on our third date. He is a gift! In the meantime, Dad was concerned about Brian today and asked him where was *his* food? Dad said he could not start yet; he was waiting for a blonde. He was happy once he spotted the blonde PSW. He spoke to a brunette PSW, as he always did, saying, "What could I do for you, sweetie?" They chatted. Dad told her she best move on, as he did not want to "ruin her." She told him it was way too late for that! It was good to know they were having fun and joking. PSWs treat all the residents as human beings, more like residents than patients.

By nine a.m., Dad was back in his room. He saw his stuffed bear; it was his as a child. Filled with straw, it must be loaded with germs and dust mites, but sometimes I would put it in his lap. He looked at it and said, "There's my dog. It must be five." Try seventy-five! He looked at the photograph of himself and Mom, taken at the formal church photography sitting, and announced, "There's Mom and Dad! I'm going to sing for them." He proceeded to sing several verses of one of his favourite hymns, "Hear Me, Lord." He forgot the next line and had to stop. Then he began calling out, "Joan!" as if she were in the next room. (She'd know the words!) They totally depended upon one another. She wasn't ever far away in life, surely she was there in spirit. "She must be sleeping," he mused.

By now Dad had to go to the bathroom. He became quite disturbed and quite vocal. Brian told me Dad sounded like Marley's ghost out of *A Christmas Carol*. A staff member came and she said she had to get another staff member to help with the lift. It was hard to use the mechanical lift in the small bathroom, as Dad was a tall man. They got him onto the toilet, but it took three of them. For so long Dad had had to urinate every fifteen minutes or so, now he would become agitated when he could not get to the toilet as frequently. It was another sign that he had lost his independence. They could not be moving him onto the toilet this often. The LTC home just did not have the staff for this. They left Dad there with Brian, Dad on the toilet and pants halfway down around his ankles. Brian stood supervising, but could not lift him nor move him. Brian calmed him down, patting his arm soothingly. I could not imagine another person looking after my father so tenderly.

The PSWs returned and lifted Dad up from the toilet chair in his private washroom, into the main part of his room to dress him. Dad got his foot stuck in the footrest of the wheelchair and he became agitated. As they got him dressed he cautioned, "Go slow, please!" Everything was painful, I think. Once he was back and into his bed, tucked in, Brian warned that he had to go now. Dad clearly stated, "Don't go. I haven't got the fireplace straight." Brian sat for a bit longer, leaving once Dad fell asleep.

More signs of pain: fretting, worrying, and gnashing of teeth — October 14, 2006

I was in to give him dinner again. Today, Dad was spooning his water into his mouth. I chirped, "It's water, not soup!" His hands were shaking uncontrollably. Maybe that was why he was spooning it in. I tried to keep a sense of humour about me.

"OOOH," he kept saying. I put my warm hands around his cold ones. "Oh!" He stopped moaning immediately—then started off away from the table. He undid one hand brake and pushed his hands against the table, but the wheelchair did not move. One brake was still on.

"You're moving the table, Dad. Where do you need to go?" The heavy wooden table made of old pine logs and boards started to shift, just like my shifting perception of my foundation. His arms were strong.

"Ooooh!" Clearly agitated. I did not know why.

"What is it?"

"OOOOOH!"

"What were you doing? Where were you going?" I decided to get him back. "Come on back. I need you at the table." I accidentally hit his big, swollen foot with the table, wincing inside. "Put your foot down." I could not get his knees under the table with his foot on the foot support. "Okay. Put the brake on so you don't go anywhere." I knew I talked aloud, basically to myself, but it helped. He pushed on the wheels on one side, not both, and went around in a circle.

Off I went to the kitchen, needing a bit of a change for a moment. I was out of the room and he was moaning away to himself.

"OOOh," he said rubbing his hands together to get them warm. "Oooh. Ooooh. Ooooh."

Back I came. I announced, "I have milk. I have shepherd's pie with green beans and mashed potato. Let go, Papa; let's get you close. Let go! Would you stop it? You twit!" He was trying to push himself away from the table. This normally agreeable man was being a pain in the butt! I could not help but laugh. He was gripping the table incredibly tightly. I often taped my conversations to add to my story. I was amazed how one could laugh in the face of adversity. I look back and realize how much I did do for him.

A staff member came into the room as I wrestled with him, trying to get him close to the table in his wheelchair. Dad talked to her and declared, "I couldn't call you that. She gets to talk to you like that but I couldn't!" He had not called me anything. Trying to settle him was impossible.

"Now, Dad. Stop. Do you want shepherd's pie?"

"What do we got to hear it? The zero fuel?"

"Zero fuel?" I question. We both giggle, knowing it does not make sense. Another diamond reflection of the father I used to know.

"Are you going to do this yourself or were you going to make me do it?" I ask hopefully. "Nice peas and carrots." I wondered if there would be any co-operation.

"That's kind of a . . ." he trails off again.

"Is it okay? Was it warm? Okay, there you go. I'm going to have the coffee Brian bought me. There. How's that?"

"You file it on the warm?"

"No." Lord knows what he means . . .

"OOOOOH." More moaning.

"Here comes some more food. Stop worrying the table!" I scolded him like a child.

"I'm frozen." He was always cold. "Don't talk to the floor," he orders. "No, you do that and you would talk to the floor." He was pushing away with all his might. I didn't know if he wasn't hungry or just being obstinate.

"You're okay. There you go." Another bite into him.

"Um hum."

"Dad, don't push the table. Don't, please. You're going to knock yourself over."

"No more."

"No? You don't like it? Do you want beans? Green beans? Or mashed potato?"

"Ooooh. Did you find it?"

"Yeah, I found it. Some green beans? Good for eyesight or something."

"Oooooh." What was wrong? Was he in pain?

"Take it easy, Dad." Still pushing himself away. "How about some mashed potato? That's a good boy. Chewy, huh? I forgot to check dessert."

"I did not even try it." (Of course not. I hadn't brought it in!) "Ooooh."

"There, some mashed potato."

"Oooh." And still he worried the table.

"You're okay, Dad. Here, still got some in there? Yeah, you do." I did not want to stuff it in and choke him to death. The headlines would haunt me. I got a little more mashed potato into him. He was still trying to get away. "I don't know where you think you're going." He started worrying the chair. "That's not the brake, that's the chair pad. You're okay, Dad. It's dinnertime." He was quite agitated.

"Wants some car caught or something?" Sometimes the ebb and flow of conversation comforts me. It doesn't have to make sense. I could hear Stephen Harper on the news on the TV next door. He was going on about the "best markets" and how our country "presents the largest movement in energy reduction . . . Emerging energy superpower . . ." My reality included very different things. I felt blessed being able to do something for my dad.

"There's your milk." With an itchy nose, he scratched it furiously. Some days he was hard-pressed to make his finger reach his nose, like a drunk taking a sobriety test. He just could not connect the intended motion with the right brain cells. It was like a broken telephone, this lack of communication between motor functions and brain.

"Oops," he declared, as his hand shook. I rescued his milk, about to spill it like a little boy. He had eaten three green beans in the long run. Dessert consisted of mousse and fruit pieces. Dad took the spoon and started scraping up the dish of mousse and worried it for a good five minutes. In hindsight, I should have cut to the chase and gotten some dessert. All of his moaning—further hindsight—indicated pain. Of this I was now sure. I should have advocated harder for pain control. The problem was that the doctor was unavailable to us. It was the charge nurse who phoned him and, on his weekly visits to the floor, checked on patients. With all the different conditions faced by the residents, he could not be familiar with every disease. I don't know if he had ever treated anyone with a brain tumour. I knew Dad was at risk for headaches, but had no means by which he could indicate this. I finished the meal, took him to his room, cleaned him up, and drove home in the dusk.

Case conference for Dad — October 15, 2006

Ontario law states that there must be an annual case conference for each resident in long-term care. Today was the day. Aside from the intake meeting, we had kept careful tabs on my father. There was little we did not know. We found that popping in at different times of the day had kept us apprised of different issues and situations. We had met various staff members who worked on the different shifts. Aside from coming in every day to feed Dad dinner, we popped in if we were in town for an appointment or an errand. I had come to know the reception staff. They were very kind. We shared stories of parental issues. One woman had dealt with these very issues with which we now dealt. Her mother would refuse food in her presence and eat later when her daughter left. Her mother was agitated when she was there visiting—perhaps blaming the daughter for the frailties of old age and the insult of leaving familiar surroundings. Displaced anger.

Today there was an accreditation meeting for the LTC home. Our planned case conference conflicted with this event. Dad's doctor, who was responsible for the entire floor of patients, saw us in the hall outside the nursing station and apologized that he could not make the meeting. We went upstairs to see Dad before the meeting. He said to us, "What were you doing here this early?" It was 10:20 a.m., just before our 10:30 meeting. He must have some remaining glimmer of understanding of time and that we usually visited at dinnertime. He could not really understand what I was saying—that we had a meeting. He was talking gibberish.

The case conference was in our familiar Muskoka Room. I had taken Dad down the hall to where our meeting would occur. (As a teacher, I always included students in our parent-teacher meetings. I thought it an important thing to do.) It was a small conference with the charge nurse, another staff member, a PSW from another floor unfamiliar with Dad's case, and us.

They told me Dad had been aggressive with a PSW. He was agitated and had grabbed her arm. In another example of Dad's trying to maintain control, he was consistently refusing his bath. It must have been scary and upsetting, all these changes: losing his personal space, his home, his wife, his dog, and his independence. For those who are immobile or unable to bathe themselves, baths are given in big rooms with strangers using a mechanical lift to get them up into a large tub. In a fit of violence, not uncommon in long-term care situations, he grabbed the arm of one of the attendants in his agitation. They decided to give up the bath notion. We could not convince him to have a bath for two weeks. This was not the dad who had had a bubble bath every day at home.

As we talked, Dad wheeled his chair around the large, heavy pine table. He got caught up on the table leg. He was talking out loud. "What do we deliver to?" And later, "Where could I go to a radio activity team?" I sat and wrote these things down as we talked. It gave me a focus and a purpose. I found it surreal, these interactions. I had bought a spiral-bound book to record all the information.

My questions went unasked: what pain medications was he on? What if the pain got worse? I did not have the sensibility at the time to ask them. The PSW suggested that we get Dad involved in some activities. I wish! He could not hear. He refused to interact when he was embarrassed. I had taken him in his wheelchair once to visit the parakeet downstairs in the recreation room. It did not go well.

They suggested we get him music therapy. Dad loved music so very much. If he could only hear, that might have been a good bet. On a more practical note, I asked if they could arrange to have the resident hairdresser cut his beard weekly. It grew so quickly. His hair, on the other hand, what was left of it, was straggly from the radiation treatments in the spring. It was very fine and wispy. They told me about the massage therapist, as well. I knew she existed. I had previously contacted her and asked that she try to visit once a week. It would help his circulation and improve his well-being. They provided regular foot care, as it is difficult for many seniors to take care of toenails.

Medical information proved the most difficult challenge of all: trying to talk with the busy doctor, especially at the most crucial times. He was only in the residence once a week. Eventually, I learned that the only person we could talk to was our charge nurse. She knew more of his behaviour, could check his files, and could speak to the doctor on our behalf. We had full power of attorney, both medical and personal, as was the case with about ninety percent of the residents in this wing. I began to suspect that Dad was in pain, but could not be sure. I had to figure out what to do with this information. They could give him Tylenol 3, but it did little to assuage the pain. I should have fought harder, but had no energy to do so.

Another difficult meal — Thursday, October 19, 2006

I wandered down the familiar hallway, peering into the courtyard; the trees were now bare and it was cold. The sunny inner courtyard was used for a barbecue in the summer, they had people in to entertain, and it was a delightful oasis in an austere setting. The plants had begun shedding their summer finery. Upstairs I went to find Dad and settle him into his feeding routine.

Dad was quiet and subdued. As I fed him, two of our dear neighbours showed up. I just kept on feeding my father as I greeted them. I found that sticking to routines comforted me as much as Dad. They stood and watched. He drooled his coffee. I wiped his beard. He could not lift the food to his mouth. Today he ate a little bit of meat, but very little of the vegetables.

Dad saw them walk in but did not pay them much attention. These were the neighbours who had helped care so much for both of my parents. One had done all their banking; the other had cleaned the kitty litter and had brought soup every day for my dying mother. Maybe my father remembered the times the one would put flowers into his precious gardens without permission. Or the time the other one tried to convince Dad to give me signing authority on his bank account. Dad had a long memory for past hurts, a side to him I never knew. He and Mom were mad at the church and refused to attend at one point. I never knew why and did not ask. Dad and Mom never spoke to his one sister over an inheritance issue from my late grandmother's estate. Such hurts are so silly amongst family. We are all drops of water in the sea of humanity.

It was a shock to both of these hard-working women to see Dad in this condition. One had not been to see him since May, I think. The other had been to see him in August, at the Manor, but not since, as far as I knew. There was a big change in him. There was little left of the kind, God-fearing man who would do anything for his neighbours.

Our visitors conversed with me as I fed him. I kept up the chatter, as I always did. It was like feeding a toddler. You talked about what you were doing. You asked questions and made some conversation; you asked aloud if he wanted more. Dad's friends were in shock. They had not been to see him in months, and his deterioration was exponential. They asked me if he knew them, but it was hard to tell. As with Dad's good friends, Dick and Beth, who visited in the summer, it could be that he preferred to save face by not recognizing that these people knew him when he was fit and able. One of the ladies began crying. After some more of his dessert, he happened to glance over at the pair. He nodded to them in surprise, as if he had not already known they were there. Their sorrow was palpable. He was unable to make conversation and did not do so. They left, saying they had to go. It was a short but telling visit. I was relieved to be alone.

Playing dress-up — October 20, 2006

I made my way upstairs to visit, punching in the security codes as I went. Dad was on a medium-security floor. The upstairs was high security for those who were at risk to escape while gripped by the claws of dementia and Alzheimer's.

Dad appeared to be in pain. He was dribbling coffee as I fed him. I noticed that his rosacea was pretty bad. His face was red and irritated. I would have to phone the charge nurse later; the staff were run off their feet at mealtimes. His fingernails and his hair were growing long. I imagined that he was not co-operating for the hairdresser or caregiving staff. This was becoming standard behaviour for him.

He was upset and angry at life today. When he saw me he said, "You're here. That's good. I need all the help I can get." My heart broke for him. "It's awful. I feel awful. I couldn't do anything," he went on to say. As much as I wanted to help, I could do little. He was stubborn about his food. In the meantime, Brian had done errands and brought us all coffee. Dad drank my store-bought coffee instead of his, and ate only his pudding. As we left, he said sadly, "Are you leaving so soon? Goodbye, baby." I knew he still loved me. It was comforting, and the sparkle of the shining diamonds kept me going that day. He knew I was doing all I could. Brian stayed with Dad for a bit. I left him so I could have a visit with Michelle. Michelle had her own battles to fight. She was having trouble finding a hairdresser she liked. Her pain was increasing.

Michelle is our friend and was in a room across from Dad's. Suffering from spinal stenosis and arthritis and unable to stand up, she required staff to lift her and put her into a chair that kept her fairly horizontal. A retired nurse, formerly of Vancouver, she had moved here to be nearer her sister. She monitored Dad for me. I would visit with her when I was tired and stressed from seeing Dad. She had a great sense of humour, despite her situation, and we were kindred spirits. It was difficult for her, having been a nurse and now stuck in long-term care. She knew too much. She was in constant pain and was given morphine three times a day or more. She was able to access legal marijuana for pain in B.C., but we are a little more backward in Ontario!

I had dressed up for this visit. Michelle told me that I looked very nice. How nice to hear kind words. I loved the reaction from all of the ladies as they sat in their wheelchairs in the hall, waiting for their meals. They oohed and aahed over my bright colours and my snazzy earrings. I always tried to dress up somewhat. I told Michelle the story of my mother's friend, our Aunt Darya, who passed away a long time ago due to cancer. Mom's good friend Darya had come to visit her in hospital after one of her two miscarriages. I remember the story vividly. Aunt Darya had dressed up in a bright red hat and a splendid red coat. I could still feel the warm glow of that outfit as Mom told me the story. Mom explained how good it made her feel to see someone looking so good and dressing up as if she were somebody important.

Choking and swallowing — Sunday, October 22, 2006

Good news and bad news. Dad greeted me with a kiss today. Then three times he tipped over in his chair. I think his equilibrium was being affected by the tumour. He juggled right-of-way in the doorway with another resident, Tom, as he tried to leave the sitting room. They were crashing about with wheel chairs, running into one another. He became angry. "I can never do anything well, dammit." How do I recall for him the home repairs he had done, the work he did over the years, supporting his family, and the care and love and attention he lavished on us all?

He choked on his milk and he could not swallow properly. He recited "762," the first three digits of his home phone number, again. I left to get his third cup of milk and when I returned, he was surprised that I was there. He said "Oh. Look who's here!" As if I hadn't just fed him two cups of milk. He insisted on spearing his own meat that day. He managed to get three pieces into himself. He had much trouble doing it. "Shit. Nothing's worth a shit," as he missed the small piece I had cut for him. He drank a total of four glasses of milk that day. He was quite thirsty, but I feared he would choke to death, and the headlines would say, "Daughter stands by while father chokes to death on milk."

Dinner repartee — October 24, 2006

Again, I took a tape recorder in for my visit. I was intellectually fascinated with the changes in my dad and the ways that his expressive language had changed. Having had training in expressive and receptive language issues, and done some research on the brain and early childhood brain development and learning, I was interested to see how a brain deteriorated. I needed to rewind each day and examine what happened, partly, I think, to see if I could see patterns, and partly to try to predict what to expect each day as he declined in health.

"Aaaaaaaagh, Aaaaaaagh." His moans last five seconds or more each.

"Dad, you have to keep your seat belt on. You have to stay put."

"Aaaagh."

"Dad, you have to stay put." Dad spent a lot of time trying to worry the seat belt off of his wheelchair. He was prone to falling over and out of it. He was so strong that they had to tie a knot in the end of the belt so he could not pull the belt right off. Some days he worried it down to his knees.

"Why am I locking that?"

"Well, you have to lock it so you don't go anywhere." He seemed to hear my conversation — sometimes.

"Oh, my Lord!" I said.

"Aaaagh," continued Dad.

"I guess it's off his chair," Brian said, referring to a handle that Dad must have broken off his chair.

"I can't understand anything," complained Dad. Brian and I were conversing and trying to figure out what Dad had done to his chair. Dad's moans kept on as he worried the seat belt. I felt bad that he could not hear us unless he was looking at us, but sometimes that worked to my benefit. It was helpful to talk to someone about my concerns. Brian was an effective sounding board. He often relieved me when I tried to cope with the situation.

"AAAaaggh. Haaaaaaggh. Seven, six, two, five — five five . . ."

"Five-five! Seven, six, two, five, five, five, five, that's right, Dad." It was his old phone number. He knew he wanted to be at home. Staff did not know what he was talking about, but we did! It was a familiar chant for him. I should have told the staff about it. They must have wondered what he was talking about. Dementia was a familiar story around here, but this was a logical plea for things known.

"Aaagggh. Aaaaggh," as he pushed up on the belt, trying to remove it.

"Take it easy, Dad. You're okay. Relax. You're okay. Relax." Nothing I could say would help him. He was agitated and wanted out of his chair. I could not abide the moaning any more. It was time for us to go home for our dinner.

Dinnertime delights — October 25, 2006

I continued taping Dad's conversations. I had been faithful in writing down Brian's daily reports, too. Having a degree in Early Childhood Education and being profoundly interested in speech and language development, I found Dad's communication issues to be both similar and dissimilar from normal speech acquisition patterns. Children begin by using one word to communicate, and usually nouns. "Juice!" was a frequently heard demand in our house. Eventually, two-word sentences appear in their vocabulary and "Mommy, up!" was short form for "Pick me up!" The indication that Dad's tumour was developing in the area of language processing occurred when he could not retrieve nouns, as I noted previously. Eventually, we could piece out subjects through the content. It was a frustrating and sad affair.

Much of the time, as many sources told me, one realized that arguing did not work, and agreeing was the easiest and best route. It was a puzzle. I could not figure out what was going on in his brain cells. Some days he was capable of social interaction; other days he was "whacked right out of it," as Brian would say.

Just to keep me on my toes, Dad ate 100 percent of his dinner on this day: his pork chop, baby potatoes, and Brussels sprouts. He started using his fingers to capture the Brussels sprouts, as they escaped his fork. Sometimes I would get another fork and spear food for him, quickly taking away the other fork. I had to move each Brussels sprout closer to him so that he could reach it. Blueberries were for dessert. He scraped up every last one with a spoon.

He was drooling and spilling his food. I noticed that one eye was rolled up slightly, at a different angle from the other. The pupil was dilated and it wasn't in the centre of his iris. I wondered if this was creating a problem for him. It took me an hour and a quarter to feed him. I was late for choir practice, but felt the need to help him, since he had suddenly decided he was going to eat. As the nurse left, after coming in to give him his pills, he said, "You take care!" as if he were always so affable; a wee gleam of the father I remember.

I had joined a local choir to give me something to do. It was a joy to sing in a choir. It gave me a false sense of belonging somewhere, when I had no friends or family nearby. I had sung in choirs since I was young, with my parents in church choirs for many years, and I felt good about this. I had sung with the choir director in my teens in our Toronto church—one familiar face in a sea of strangers. He used to sit beside my dad in church choir in the seventies. When I told my father this good news, he was simply angry that he could not sing anymore.

Characters in long-term care
—Tuesday, October 26, 2006

Dad was in the TV room upon my arrival. As I sat there visiting, Donny wheeled himself across the room, around the corner, and into the games room. I had never spoken to this man. He had never spoken to me. A slight man, he impishly rolled over to the radio and turned it on. He turned it up full-blast, and then wheeled his way out the door, quite innocently. I had to go in and turn it down. The little devil! Some sort of act of rebellion for a man reduced to the indignities of life in a long-term care home and confined to a wheelchair.

I had ceased asking my dad how he was each day. I knew better than that. Every day I would ask if he had "behaved" or if he was being a "good boy." The same was true for Michelle, bedridden and unable to walk due to her illnesses and frustrated by her immobility and dependence upon others. It was our standing joke because, of course, she had not!

Lois, another resident, was sitting in front of the TV. An older woman, sitting in a wheelchair, she was missing some of her teeth and had wild grey hair. She was watching *Star Trek*. Data, that genial robotic character, was on the screen. "Hello," she cheerfully said to him a couple of steps away from the TV screen. "Aren't you beautiful?" He was, rather, when you looked at the tortured bodies and aged limbs of the people that inhabited this care facility. Every time I saw Lois, she would tell me she loved me and that I was beautiful. Lois was one lady who was always glad to see me. Bizarre as it was, it warmed me. I liked to go and see her and hug her.

Dad, meanwhile, appeared to strain himself in his chair, raising himself up on his arms to the full extent his feeble muscles could manage. He was incredibly discontented in his chair. He moved his milk around on the table constantly. His speech was slurred and he was talking bafflegab. I pushed him up to the table in preparation for dinner, "Don't push me too far." He always surprised me when, out of the blue, he could articulate such things. His hands were steady holding his teacup.

"AAAAgh. Aaaagh. Tell the took full. I don't know what they are. All hell, we'll—"

Trying to put some sense into the conversation, I asked, "Where did your knife go?"

"Aaaah, well—"

"Lost your knife. There it is." This was painful. His groaning and moaning, and his attempts to get out of the chair.

"Every get the bloody back jaws."

"The bloody what?"

"He would have washed my—"

All I did was try to pretend that I was comfortable with this new normal. I was used to feeding toddlers and working with children with special needs. I knew that one had to model appropriate behaviour and model the language one expects. I was tired of being good and polite. The old dad would have been shocked.

I looked at Dad's dry skin. "What's the matter?" Dad took off the brake. I put him back into the table. "You need to be right there for dinner. Where is your watch?" I asked. His watch never appeared again! He was always incredibly concerned with time. He could have put it down anywhere. It was a big, heavy, gold-looking watch.

"Oh. Shit." His commentary on the whole experience was right.

"Yeah, it is shit!" I agreed. Oops. Off he went from the table again. "You need to stay here, Dad. This is where we eat our dinner."

"I don't know what the hell to do."

"There's nothing to do, just wait for dinner. Wait patiently for dinner." Off he tried to go again. "Where you going?"

"I don't know."

"I don't know, either." Once in a while I liked to pretend to be an agreeable sort.

"AAAgh."

"Where you going? You have to stay here for dinner." He glared at me. "Don't look at me like that. It's not *my* fault." Lord knew if he heard me!

"Aaagh." He didn't look thrilled with this whole process.

"Well, it will be a good dessert. You like your dessert."

"Aaagh. Oh shit."

"Ah, shit. Yeah. That's how I feel!" I replied with a show of cheerful agreeableness I did not possess. He ate, perhaps, five percent of his meal.

Grooming 101: the beard-trimming event — October 28, 2006

Brian popped in this morning to visit Dad. We both thought he needed a beard trim. Dad didn't like anyone touching him anymore. Brian had a wicked cordless electric beard trimmer with an attachment that gathered up the clippings. He took it in to work on Dad, but the batteries died. I needed to give it a go. I was not used to this trimmer, but I did have a hair trimmer I had used on my children's hair. How hard could this be?

I popped in early to do our evening dinner ritual and routine, trimmer in hand. Dad spoke as if there were marbles in his mouth. I was looking at his beard. "I think we need to trim it! "

"I don't know. Pieces, suspended on the—"

"Yeah. Brian did his beard this morning. "

"I had three oh packages of it." He sounded drugged, which was okay. I still suspected that he was in pain, hence his vocalizations. I was not sure.

I could hear Marjorie across the hall, yelling "Help!" as she did continually, in her state of dementia. "Help me! Help me!" Sometimes she would sing the words.

Dad was lying in his bed. Dad seemed calm as I cleaned him up and prepared to trim his beard.

"Do you have any bacon?"

"Yup," I say, knowing he means scissors. His inability to retrieve nouns did not faze me anymore. I did not correct him. "I'll get a towel."

"You want to know. Not what you left. A get back to get up."

I sat him up, cranking the head of the bed. He gave a big yawn. "I did not have any relax."

"Oh, no?"

I started trimming. It was quite long, with his mustache growing into his mouth. I was tickling him, and he moved away. "It's okay. Sorry, I'm tickling. I'm doing my best, but not giving up my day job, though." (Oops. Actually, I had.)

I kept working at the beard project and I was relatively successful. It was a bit crooked, but better than it had been. He tended to get so much food into his beard and mustache that it helped if we kept it short. He had always been so meticulous with his appearance. He and Mom had made regular visits to the hairdresser. Dad always got dressed every day in a shirt and pants.

As I worked at his beard, the PSWs came in and asked if I wanted them to get him up. I told them that he would be ready shortly. Off we went to dinner again.

Singing and sambuca — October 30, 2006

The change in weather was a blessing. The animals were preparing for winter; the cooling temperatures were welcome, as we knew they were bringing a new season. As I drove by one person's mailbox, I spotted four huge turkey vultures standing in the driveway as if waiting for the school bus. They were as high as the hood of the car and quite a shock to me, city girl as I was. I always tried to wrestle as much peace and harmony out of the natural world as I could before we drove in to see my dad. I had Brian with me for moral support.

Dad was singing constantly today. He was quite affable. He slept from two until four p.m., talking nonsense when he awoke. His hands were shaking; today he ate all of his roast beef and his cake. He had no eye-hand coordination and kept falling out of his chair. I tried to lift him up, the way I had seen the PSWs do with one arm under his armpit. He was a heavy man, despite his extreme weight loss. I did my best, this now being my day job.

As I sat with him, a nurse came in. "Oh!" he said, as always perking up when someone attractive walked in. "There's my girlfriend."

"Ray!" she scolded with a warning tone in her voice. "I don't know what my husband would think of that!" We giggled. He had been reluctant to take pills some days. They had to let the residents know that the pills were important. She showed him the pills. "I brought you a drink, too!"

"Rye and ginger!" I chirp in hopefully.

"Oh, there we are. There you go." She gave him his pill. We continued to joke.

"With a shot of sambuca," she suggested helpfully.

"Yeah, we'll have to remember that for next Saturday. Sambuca all around!" said my non-drinking husband.

Brian had a secret non-drinking habit. That was what my mother called it. It was her joke. For our wedding present, several people had given us wine and some gave us wine with wineglasses. One gift was a lovely set of hand-painted glasses that we cherish to this day. At our wedding luncheon/reception, Mom, ever the classy hostess, warned us that, just to be polite, we needed to pretend that Brian did drink so as not to hurt anyone's feelings. That was fine by me, as I got to keep the wine all to myself! The funny thing was that this started at our wedding luncheon and reception that Mom hosted the day after our small wedding by the lake. Since we were not allowed to tell anyone, we had to pretend for years. Mom was in charge, you see. (There was Mom's way and the wrong way!)

My cousin was put in charge of the wine at the reception, and he offered to fill glasses at our table. I knew that he did not realize that Brian did not drink. My cousin came around and refilled Brian's glass while Brian was talking to some one else. I grabbed Brian's glass from him, previously filled with grape juice, and said he best not drink it! It was a funny moment that we all laughed over for years. Mom and Brian had many good jokes together.

A chocolate bar was a hit — October 31, 2006

Again, I was in to visit my father. Dad was in the hallway near the dining room. I took my coat and handbag into the Muskoka Room and put them on the chair. He followed me into the room, where I always fed him. These were the rules — so as not to disturb other residents. He was very angry. He would not hold my hand. He was banging on the table. Dinner came in and it was a chicken pot pie. He said, "Not mine." I thought that he and Mom liked those. (I loathe them!) He refused to eat one bite of it. He was swearing. Dessert, as usual, was a different story. He took the spoon and went at it. He was eating coconut pudding and fed me a bite. Another brilliant "diamond" of a moment. When he dropped some or spilled, he swore. The moment passed quickly.

He started pouring his leftover milk into his pudding. Once upon a time, he would scarf down two cups of milk. Today was a different story. He was wiping his hands on the wet cloth that I would always bring for cleanup. He was prone to spills with his hand tremors.

I had bought him a Sweet Marie chocolate bar. Mom and Dad loved those! I think they're good, what with the nuts and caramel. He needed energy, since he wasn't eating much. When he saw it he said he thought that it might be nice, raising his eyebrows in pleasure. I broke up the chocolate bar into pieces, after he had seen the thing whole and knew what it was. (If you have fed toddlers you know what I mean.) He began to put spoonfuls of pudding on a morsel of chocolate bar. Sure enough, he ate the whole thing. By 5:50 p.m. I had him back in his room. I washed his face and left him to be put into bed later. Worn out again.

My children visit — November 4, 2006

Caitlin and Jean–Luc came from Ottawa to visit. It was heartwarming to have them here again. They both work outside their home, and I knew they were working hard on renovations inside their home. They had incredible friends and a terrific social life, with the kids helping each other in their respective houses. Poor Caitlin. She had been incredibly supportive, but this was hard on her. At least she knew what to expect this time.

It was decided that she and I would go and visit Dad; the men would take care of dinner. We set him up in the familiar ritual in the Muskoka Room. She sat with Dad while I popped out to the kitchen cafeteria to get his food. She was very good with him. When I came back in, Dad said to her, "There's your mother!" He knew us both, and that was a relief. I went across the hall later to visit Michelle while Caitlin held down the fort. Dad chose that time to confide in her. He leaned over to her and said confidentially, "She's keeping me here." Ah. The guilt! I was, indeed. We had no choice.

He was drooling, drank two glasses of milk through the straw, thanks to Caitlin's help, and a large coffee from Timmy's. He choked, drinking from the mug, and we had to go back to the straw for the coffee. He was reciting his phone number again . . . 762–5555 . . . 762, over and over.

We were glad to go back home to where the men had dinner under control. This was such a drain on one's energy. Caitlin and J–L stayed for the weekend. What a welcome relief to have understanding children, friends, and visitors: people who did not wonder aloud why we didn't bring Dad home, or try to tell us how to manage our lives. I felt refreshed with someone here to share our grief and our pain, as much as our joy to be living in this beautiful place. They helped with chores and brought a fresh energy and spirit into the house. Jean–Luc rebuilt a shelf that was not wide enough. He is a brick.

His invisible friend — November 8, 2006

Back to routines, and Dad was in his room. "There isn't even a bit of anything," he complained to me. "Hey, Ban!" he said, eyeing the floor. I wondered if he was hallucinating and picturing his precious dog, Bandy, at his side. (This was a symptom I had read about.) I missed Bandy, regretting I could not care for her. She was a bright, if spoiled, dog. I knew Dad missed her a lot. He was always so happy with his animals about. I mourned his old life and shared the grief of it all with him. I remembered the Dad who walked his dog daily and looked after his gardens. Dad and I had things to do, however. Off we went to dinner.

The man with the red ball cap and his arm in a sling, and a stuffed brown animal on his wheelchair tray, went by us. He was hunched over, seemingly tired of sitting up, tired of life. He wheeled around the hall, using one foot to propel his chair. Dad chirped, "I don't give a shit!" I was not sure if he was talking about his life, his dinner, or me, but I hoped he was referring to his lack of appetite and food issues. Never mind. I was learning not to take these things personally. Even if I was not doing the right things, I knew I was making the best decisions I could with the information I had at the time.

One-two, skip a few — Sunday, November 12, 2006

I skipped my Saturday visit. I did not feel up to it. I needed a break. When I arrived on Sunday, *Newsworld* was showing on Dad's small television in his room. I just sat and watched. It showed a suicide bomber. The bomber had set off a device that killed men walking on the way to seek work. A second bomber blew up people who were helping those who were stricken. Meantime, Dad still slept. The calm in the room belied that bomb growing in his brain. Two workers came along to change Dad's diaper, clean him up, and get him ready for dinner. I did not even leave the room now. I was used to the whole business. The smell was wicked, but it was all part of life and death.

Bill, another resident, was quite out of it and seemed preoccupied. I didn't know why he wasn't in the dining room with the rest of the residents. The dull routine of their days was punctuated by their three meals. Bill was standing in the middle of the hall with his pajamas and his adult diaper around his ankles, drooling and disoriented. His family jewels were sparkling in the light for all to see. It was rather a shock. Two PSW staff spotted him. They gently asked him what was wrong and took care of him. They thought he'd tried to change his diaper on his own in his room and was unsuccessful. They were so loving and kind. Nothing shocked me anymore, even a strange, naked man with the evidence of his gender for all to see. Off I went for home for some wine and some dinner and my "normal" husband.

Nutritional issues and drooling — November 18, 2008

Today, I walked right past Dad. I went in to deliver to my friend Michelle the candies and McIntosh apples she had requested. We always asked her what she needed. As I went by Dad's room, I noticed he had his pants down at his knees. Thankfully, his diaper was still on, and he was, again, wrestling with his seat belt. He was singing hymn-phrases still. I dropped off the goodies for Michelle and went back to Dad. I wheeled him into his private room to pull up his pants. He was fiddling and worrying the seat belt. It was so painful to watch him. He looked into his sock drawer, singing, "I don't know what to do." As if trying to speak and, failing that, he could still sing. He sang again, "I don't know what this was for." It was so hard to know what was going on in his mind.

He sat and worried the seat belt some more. I reached into his sock drawer and pulled out one of the hard candies he and Mom liked so much. He clearly confirmed, "Oh, that'll be nice!" But he could not unwrap it, nor could he get the candy to his mouth. I gently held his hand and tried to support his hand to let him get the sense that he was feeding himself the candy. Dignity was a marketable commodity these days.

He was drooling his lunch; little pieces of food were falling out of his mouth. His beard had traces of his afternoon juice. Since I had choir practice that night, I checked my watch, fearful of being late. As I did so, he again spoke in a full sentence, looking at me intently, "Are you okay?" It was surprising and it came out very quickly after my actions. I think it indicated that he still understood the implications of someone looking at a watch. My parents were most careful about being on time all of their lives. They never once were late for choir in forty years.

For a time he was peaceful. After he finished his candy, he looked over at the name tag that a kind staffer had fastened to his bed. They had labelled his articles left around the room. Some staff member labelled his wardrobe, wheelchair, and soap dish, too. He read the name aloud, "R. Jilks," then pointed to himself. Then he indicated that he wanted me to help him get into the bed. I could not do so, as it took two strong people to lift him. I had back issues of my own.

There were times when he knew he wanted a pen to release the mechanism in the seat belt. He was so upset that the belt was keeping him in. We had to be firm about this, though; since his balance was gone, he would fall over — even while in the chair.

Advocating and agitating — December 5, 2006

I had visited Dad the previous day and spoken to the charge nurse, who told me that he had been quite agitated for several days in a row. She decided, with the concurrence of the doctor, to give standing orders for him to have his sedative daily. Once pain was quite severe, it was difficult to overtake it. It was better to be proactive and prevent pain rather than to ameliorate it. There are doctors without experience in this kind of persistent pain. With large caseloads, they are unable to understand the problems of a patient the way family members can. There were intervention strategies that could be applied. None of the comfort measures we had tried so far had seemed successful, nor were they implemented on a consistent basis.

I had to learn to trust my instincts. It was too distressing for him to be so upset. He kept singing those hymns without words, piecing together all of the words and phrases he could recall. He was incapable of logical thought, as far as I could tell. He was eating little. He gently shook his head after eating a small amount. I did not know if he was not hungry or if his subconscious was telling him to reduce intake to reduce pain. He was slowly wasting away before my eyes.

Many people told me that they had experienced similar behaviours from their elderly parents. Once an adult child made a decision that a parent needed to go into a home, the child was blamed. There was anger and confusion. One must be strong enough to make the right decisions at the right time. Many families have issues around such decisions, as well as the type of palliative care. I wonder how much I had prolonged Dad's life while almost forcing him to eat. I am glad that my brother and I agreed on care issues. I tried to keep him informed as much as I could.

Treats — December 6, 2006

Brian went for his physiotherapy appointment. The poor man was now having persistent pain, which we attributed to the time Dad was desperate to be lifted into his bed and Brian moved him. This caregiving was physically and emotionally demanding. The back strain was obvious when leaning over to feed Dad. (Brian's slipped disk still gives him trouble two years later.)

Brian popped in to see Dad after his appointment. Dad was singing or shouting, we weren't sure which. I was not sure if he could keep track of time. Dad saw Brian and asked him where he had been. I guess he missed him. Brian told him that he had a bad leg and was even using his cane. Brian shared a chocolate bar with him, breaking it into manageable pieces. Dad said "Thank you" every time he gave him a piece. He was quite happy to share the chocolate bar.

Bandy revisited — December 9, 2006

Dad seemed to want to have the dog visit him. He could not articulate it very much. He pointed to the photos, spoke of happy things and gazed at Bandy's picture saying things like, "It would be nice to have that happen." I give him a candy and a chocolate kiss. His sweatshirt had food on it and I changed it for him. When I arrived home later, I phoned the family that took Bandy for us, but did not receive a response. I could not imagine anyone wanting to visit here. It was difficult some days to see the joy. We were Dad's only visitors, for the most part. They did have pet visitations, with trained workers who would bring their dogs in to visit with residents, but Dad was too grouchy and in too much pain to go. There was a busy activity schedule, but Dad could not be part of it.

The LTC home was all dressed up for Christmas and Hanukkah. There were decorations everywhere. An artificial Christmas tree was wedged in beside the comfy sofa in the front hall. Gifts sat underneath. Poinsettias were here and there. On an end table someone had placed a little piano-playing snowman. If you pushed the button, he pretended to play, "Oh the weather outside was frightful." I would go over and push the button and then continue to sing loudly as I walked down the hall to go to see Dad. (I always sing when I am stressed. It is good therapy.) The decorations continued down the hallway: lots of angels, candles, and lights.

On the second floor, Dad was stuck in the activity room, wedged beside a chair, and could not back up out of the space. I reminded myself to ask about having his wheelchair pad pumped up. His skinny butt bones were hitting the hard metal base, with the pad so deflated. The nurse said she would look into it but must have forgotten. It requires a pump. The wheelchair has padding, which I would sometimes clean, since he would stow food in it like the squirrel saving for winter. Later they told me that the pump was kept by the physiotherapist, who only comes in three half-mornings a week. Great. Another phone call to make to ensure that this happened.

Christmas decorations — December 18, 2006

To brighten up Dad's room, I put up Christmas lights, as well as the Santa light that plugs in and glows a bright red and white. It dates back to my childhood. It was garish and old-fashioned, but seemed to be just what I needed to do. After my chore, I went to find him. He was in the TV room, somewhat upset. He was looking down and saw me after I touched his hand. He said, "You aren't who I was looking for." Too bad, so sad, Dad. You're stuck with me! He looked at my name tag and wanted to know who I was and he tried to read it. The PSW had said he was swearing today. Not a good day.

Our mealtime ritual went on again. Finally, I went into the kitchen to get dessert for him. He was yelling for me when I came back into the room, trying to get out of the wheelchair, despite the seat belt. His face was very red; he was agitated and very determined. Outside the room, I had heard him calling and talking. He said, "I'm going to die." A couple of times he simply stated this aloud. Then, as I entered, he said it again. After another trip into the kitchen, he was yelling again for someone. As I re-entered, he chirped, "There's my bee-bee [baby]!" My old Dad was back; another diamond.

He suddenly reverted back to his normal bad behaviour. Dad would not eat the broccoli. He addressed the potatoes with a "Puh!"

but I snuck a few in. He kept trying to spear the chicken leg bone, rather than the meat that I had cut off for him. I ended up taking the bone away to the garbage. He looked at the small piece of cake I had brought. He said, "You shouldn't eat that until after the chicken," clear as a bell. No dessert without eating your dinner. He knows the rules! He managed to drink most of his juice, but could not get the last drops. He could not figure out how to tip his head back and drain the cup.

Christmas, birthday, and December travel plans

Christmas was coming. I didn't feel much like celebrating. Depressed and very tired, I planned on picking Jesse up in Toronto and driving with him to Ottawa to see family and friends. I later found out that while I was agonizing over leaving, hemming and hawing over staying home, rather than leaving Brian alone over Christmas, Brian and Caitlin were frantically trying to figure out how to ensure I made it to Ottawa. I kept waffling, afraid to leave Dad and not feeling particularly sociable. But Caitlin had planned a surprise birthday party for me with some of my friends. Who knew?

My biggest problem remained in making decisions. I could not face packing. I put it off until the morning that I was to leave. I stood in front of the closet with a blank mind. I simply could not make a basic decision: to choose which pants, skirts, blouses . . . and changed my mind several times. Later, I found out that this was part of my depression symptomology. My medication was working and I was feeling better in some ways, despite my hot flushes, but I found it hard being with people.

I packed too many clothes, hesitant to decide what to put in and what to leave. We were only to be away for a few days. Brian could not go since his back pain was still very bad and he could not stand a five-hour car trip back to Ottawa. His physiotherapy continued and he did his exercises faithfully. He had reduced his pain medications, but it was still flaring up. He had had to give up his precious walks and many other pleasurable activities.

Caitlin had begun planning the party last August. What a sweetheart she is! We had a terrific party, I saw some dear friends, and I did not worry about Dad, what with Brian in charge of things at home.

I phoned every night and was given an update. I had forgotten how good friends make one feel loved and part of this world. Sometimes you just have to act as if you are normal. (Terry says that is the best advice I have ever given him!)

I closed off the year feeling a bit better about myself. I knew I was loved. I had a wonderful family. I vowed to take better care of myself to help my healing. We were conscientious about eating nutritional food, knowing that this helps in times of stress. I knew to take in the daily requirements of the four food groups, having taught the requirements to classrooms full of reluctant students (and not: junk food, fast food, fried food, and chocolate). But I helped assuage the emotional pressures with my comfort food (popcorn) and eating out, which always means too-large portions. I had been working out faithfully three times a week, but I was not and never will be a slim middle-aged woman! This really helped a lot. I wanted to work out more faithfully.

2007: Dad's Passing

Obsessive-compulsive, belligerent, angry — January 2, 2007

It was a new year. With the new year I hoped to better understand my situation and my commitment to helping my father; and ease his way through this maze of palliative care. I was only doing what I could, without pressure. I was also hoping to be able to deal with life better. My calorie reduction plan was in force. I had used food as a comfort — popcorn was what Dad used to make as we watched *Wonderful World of Disney* every Sunday night. It took me years to figure out why I wanted to have popcorn so much when stressed.

I could still remember the sound and the smells in our Toronto home as we huddled around our old-fashioned metal popper waiting for the first two kernels to pop. Dad would put in the oil and only two kernels. Then, once we heard those wonderful two pops, off came the lid and we would put in the rest of the popcorn. The smell of oil cooking still takes me back. Once it was popped, my brother and I would go into the living room and watch *Wonderful World of Disney*. It was such an easy time of my life. Life was wonderful. My parents were loving, God-fearing, caring people who were well respected in their community. There were no worries. My father was infallible and made the best popcorn in the world.

Visitors and strangers — January 3, 2007

Strangers had a hard time figuring out what was going on with Dad. To look at him, one might have thought he was simply frail. I knew better. Today Dad was asleep. I looked at the indentation above his ear on his temple. My research showed that it was in Broca's area, a part of the brain that governs language. I don't know if it was the place where the tumour was growing, or what caused it, but it seemed to fit. On his forehead there was a large horseshoe-shaped scar that remained from his original surgery. The staples long gone, the scars and the horror of it all remained when I looked at it. I thought the crevasse had grown. But when I looked back at the photos taken previously, I realized it had not really grown at all. It was his temple that had become increasingly concave as he continued to lose weight (thirty-five pounds since September). My perceptions were very peculiar. I often looked back at old photos. It was becoming difficult to remember the strong, responsible, loving father that he had been. I was consumed with the present and determined to honour the past.

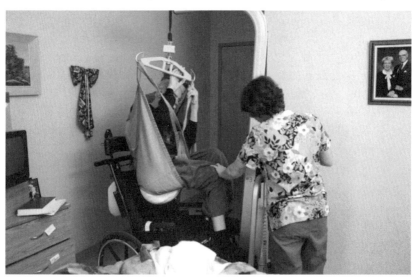

How difficult it was for me to see my father incontinent, immobile, drooling, and unable to manage his activities of daily living at any level.

Hymn sing — January 4, 2007

One of my parents' favourite shows was **Hymn Sing**, on CBC from Calgary. They performed the old faithful hymns and anthems that my parents loved, memorized, and sang frequently and for so many years. When I arrived, Dad was alone in his room with the door closed. My friend across the hall had asked the care workers to put him in his room with the door closed because he was disturbing them so much. His voice remained strong; he hadn't been able to sing in August, as his voice was rather scratchy. It was a good voice — if only he could remember the words!

As we were sitting there singing, I flipped through the hymn book and sang loudly the ones I knew. It was most comforting. It was a lovely hour together. I would gaze up at the photo of Mom and Dad, taken about ten years ago before cancer hit them both. I kept praying to Mom to help me do the right thing. I prayed for strength. This was so hard for me—one of Maslow's Peak Experiences that I would learn from, if it did not kill me in the short run!

I typed out the music to his favourite two hymns, using a large font, since Dad had lost his glasses. (We had continued to look high and low for them, but they had disappeared.) Dad could figure out the first line or two of "Lead Me, Lord," but he could not move on to the third line. I had high hopes. I thought the problem was not that he forgot the words, but that he could not keep his focus. His yelling continued; a clear indication of pain. I kept at it. I went into some form of a meditation as I sang. I hoped I was helping him. I imagine not, since he couldn't hear me well, nor could he sing himself, which must have frustrated him. Eventually, he managed the third line of the hymn; I just kept at it. I have pleasant memories of that session. Music was so important to him. However, when I sang for him in September and talked about the choir director I sang with, an old friend of ours, he became quite agitated, as he couldn't sing the way he used to. It was more distressing than a comfort.

In listening to CBC, I heard a show that spoke of death rituals. Specifically, they spoke of an Ojibwa ritual in which the dying person sings to his maker of his readiness for death. This seemed fitting to me. The rituals were comforting. I hoped I was assisting Dad in his journey.

Last night I went through some of the family slides from the early years—the seventies and eighties. Dad hated to show them. The slide projector was fiddly and difficult to use. The slides tended to fall out of the tray and must have frustrated him. Mom protected Dad, and we had not viewed them in recent memory. I have so many questions about some of them. I paid to have them put into a digital format. They are comforting photos and a celebration of the good life we used to have. I toyed with the idea of showing the photos to him,[6] but thought he probably couldn't face the beautiful slides showing

---

6   Good therapy; I made a YouTube video of our slides: **http://ca.youtube. com/watch?v=aVqnmplKDe4**.

us all working on the land here at the cottage. The slides show the family clearing up brush, giving us more land on which to garden. There were family slides of trips and big extended family dinners. The "good old days"!

Personal grooming — January 6, 2007

On January 6, I arrived in good time for a change. I seemed to procrastinate when leaving the house. There was always something else to do. It might have been a subconscious avoidance, having been a schoolteacher whose every moment was scheduled in the day. Today, my plan was to shave his beard and trim his hair again. He was looking like a wild man. That, combined with his singing and chanting, made him appear rather odd to strangers, which was only right, I mused. He was quite sedated; he'd obviously had some Lorazepam. Praise be — my advocating worked. I sat him up, to better get at his head and beard. He was quite dopey. I put a towel around his neck and began the process.

A personal support worker popped in; Dad had stopped singing, and she was worried about him, especially with the door closed. She told me that she'd tried to do his beard, but he had become agitated. He trusted me and I figured this was my chance. I knew that veterinarians liked to see their grooming patients when they were unsedated, for good reasons, but I carried on, hoping to get him tidied. I managed to give him a good shave and a trim with our clippers. I used to do Brian's hair, before he went back to shaving himself bald. It was not so bad. It felt good doing something for Dad. It wasn't a good job, but I cleaned him up and he looked more civilized. I resolved to bring in scissors next day, to get the stray hairs I'd missed.

Dad also had mini-massages scheduled. Given in the seated position, a hand and arm massage soothes these seniors. The process gives residents relief with mobility and circulation issues and provides some nurturing, physical contact. A regular part of grooming included having foot care. These seniors cannot take care of their feet. Their toenails get long and can become ingrown and infected. It was not something I felt comfortable doing and asked the local foot care nurse to take care of this and bill us.

Activities of daily living — January 8, 2007

When I arrived on this day, Dad was in his room, sitting in his wheel-chair beside the TV, which was on. Dad was nodding on and off. He tried to find something to talk about but could not. He said to me, "I want to go lie on the couch!" nodding towards the bed. Staff were just beginning to realize that he had a right to choose to eat or not, and if he missed a meal, it was not such a big deal. He was very, very tired. I sat with him, unsure of what to do. I could hit the call button and ask them to put him to bed. I waited a bit as I thought about it. The PSWs were conscientious about following their general routines: they had to get everyone in the wing of the institution up from bed and into wheelchairs if they were immobile. They had to take care of toileting routines and regular personal care practices. They concen-trated so hard on doing everything the same way for everyone that they could not treat individuals individually. There was not enough time to figure out if a resident wanted to stay put, or if there was a reason to respect a resident's wishes to stay in bed. Bedsores were a huge issue with these seniors, and there was a certain amount of pre-vention that was a necessary part of their job. Individual care was an issue for all concerned.

Dad appealed again to be put to bed, and I hit the call button. When the worker came, I explained that he desperately wanted to go to bed. We needed to respect his wishes. She told me he'd had a good breakfast, but lately was eating only one good meal a day. I was trying to figure this out. She disappeared and came back with someone to assist, and they lifted him up using the "arm under armpit" technique. It was amazing to see. It was a task that required two. They were effi-cient and strong. This was clearly something I could not manage at home. I felt as if I had people on my side as I tried to cope.

I measured the dent in his head. It was 1/2 cm long and 1/2 cm deep—about the size of my baby fingernail. It must be the tumour. His forehead was a red colour, with red spider webs of arteries where the tumour surgery scars remain. It was hard to believe that the tumour was growing underneath, stealing the blood from the brain cells. Eventually the tumour cells would starve the brain cells. In the meantime, they were just on a diet, which resulted in his increasing lack of inhibitions (swearing and inappropriate comments).

I wound up his hospital bed to a sitting position. He slept. I had brought his lunch from the kitchen, but he did not want it. It was a salad and an interesting pizza with a deep crust. Since I had missed lunch, I ate it. I was embarrassed when I took his dishes back to the kitchen and the staff member commented on all he had eaten. I corrected her, feeling rather silly. She smiled! It was good to focus on simple tasks, one task at a time.

I sat for a while and read beside his bed. I wanted to observe his behaviour. I wasn't in a rush and felt good just being close with no pressure and no yelling. He seemed to wake after about fifteen minutes of drifting away to Never-Never Land. He looked at his window and at my new decorations. The sun shone on his face. *Look towards the light, Dad*, I fervently prayed. I had removed the Christmas decorations and left the angel on the suction cup. On the suction cups from the Christmas lights, I had put the string of heart-shaped lights. They were a gift one Valentine's Day from my husband. They required two batteries and did not work anymore, but they twinkled when the sun shone through. I put up a store-bought sign with a Cupid and the word LOVE on it. It was cheery and showed that someone cared. Dad seemed to like it, but who knew for sure? The rooms are so institutional and drab.

Dad woke a couple more times—about fifteen minutes apart. His noun retrieval was terrible, and I was hard-pressed to figure out what it was he was trying to say. He seemed to wonder if he could do something for me, but it was peaceful to read and sit quietly. I think he was worried that I was bored. Another diamond—a beautiful moment shining in the sun. I was reading a book called *Pink Ribbon, Inc.,* which explores how much big business was milking the donor-fatigued public for big bucks in the name of cancer research. Do we need research or do we need help in dealing with the disease? Everyone in business is getting into the business of raising money. They seem to spend more on fundraising than the donations bring in.

A little later on, a PSW popped her head in to make sure Dad was breathing. I will call her May. We chatted a bit. She told me that Dad had been flirting with her this morning! The old devil was up to his usual tricks. Two staff got him cleaned up, changing his adult diaper, washing his buttocks, and getting clean clothes on him. He was asking for kisses from them. It seemed his hearing would come and go, although I think he was using his lip-reading skills. In a loud voice he would ask them, "What are you doing to me?" They would reassure them that they just needed to get him into his wheelchair and up for breakfast. He wanted a drink then, but they told him he had to go to breakfast. He moved toward May to shake her hand, and then she gave him a hug. It was heartwarming. He ate up all his breakfast.

May's parents were similarly ill. Her dad was dealing with Parkinson's and her mom was failing and showing signs of dementia and the impact of a couple of strokes. They were ready for a long-term care home. It was such a fight to get these seniors out of their homes when it was time. They did not realize the burden on family and friends. May was thirty-five years old. She had divorced a spouse and was living on her own. She would go over to their home after work and get their garbage ready. I told her she would burn out if she did not take care of herself. Her parents got help in five days a week. It was hard to find care staff here in the north to help these seniors. So many new grads prefer the city and the opportunity to meet other young people.

May told me that she had been having headaches and her arms were shaking with tremors. She had a diagnosis from the doctors and had told her father and brother that she had a small brain tumour that would require radiation and chemotherapy. Fortunately, the prognosis for such interventions was more positive for young people than for seniors.

May had set up a meeting later that day to talk to her father and brother. They had to decide whether to tell her mother how ill she truly had become. They were afraid that her mother would experience stress and have another stroke if she were given the bad news. I felt for her, knowing how much I missed confiding in my mother. She thanked me for listening, and I reminded her, again, to look after herself. She came over to officially introduce herself and shake my hand. I asked her for a hug instead. There was a bond in sharing your difficulties as an adult with caregiving responsibilities. Caregiver support groups abound, but I was too depressed to attend them! Here May was helping to care for my father, doing things for him I could not do. I came home very tired.

Many of the staff did not understand Dad's issues. Personal support workers have only a fourteen-module training course in some colleges. LTC homes are staffed at just over three hours per day per resident. This includes other support staff and simply does not reflect the actual needs of severe cases. Dad's tumour was progressive, and they could not see the big picture: keep him comfortable and as happy and as pain free as possible. They had been trained to intervene, to keep residents mobile, and I had patiently explained to numerous staff members about Dad's prognosis. They did not have time to read all of the files of the many residents. Often staff were bumped from floor to floor (there are three floors) and did not know routines or expectations. Continuity was sadly lacking. Staff were assigned where they were most needed. I would pop in later that night to try and make contact with the night staff, having created a pretty good relationship with the day staff. Dad's loud talking, yelling, and singing was disturbing to all of us. I wanted to see what went on in the evening.

As I left, I spotted the new RPN who was doling out meds. I spoke to her and asked if she could tell me how much Lorazepam Dad was getting. She checked the book and found that he regularly had one with meals. I trusted our charge nurse and that she knew this was the right thing for him to be taking. I explained that Dad's "singing" appeared to be a sign that he was in pain. He could not communicate otherwise, and despite several attempts to determine if he was in pain, we couldn't be entirely sure. She said she'd put a note on his file for us advising "at the family's wishes" to give more Lorazepam at night if he shows the least bit of disturbance. I was quite relieved.

Dad was thin and cold. I always placed his wool blanket on his lap when I arrived. He kept moving his wheelchair in and out from under the table. I did not lock his brakes, as I think it good he was moving and thinking about where he was sitting—until he banged the chair wheel into my leg. Then I decided to lock the brakes. He still had some manners. He said, "Sorry, sweetie," which broke my heart. A diamond, something I haven't had in quite a while. He was still there, in between the medications and the tumour, which was eating away at his brain cells. How much longer would he last? I guessed when he was ready, he would go.

His food came, and it was the macaroni and cheese I chose for him. He refused to eat it, with a nearly imperceptible shake of the head. I still could not figure out if he was being stubborn, had no appetite, or if he had developed anorexia, as he tried to control his fate. I would not argue with him. He inhaled his dessert. (Was it canned fruit, again? I forget as I write.)

We rolled on down the hallways to his room, where I rinsed a cloth in hot water. He enjoyed this act, no matter how sick he appeared. He almost purred when the hot water washed the leftovers from his beard and rinsed the dust of the day from his bald head. I wheeled him around the corner and beside his bed. He looked up at the professional photo he and Mom had posed for at their church. They were lovely, formal portraits created for the church's member directory. He pointed to the photo and said, matter-of-factly, "Mom and Dad." I nodded in agreement. I didn't know if he was confirming a life well led or reminding himself of who he was. Was he disassociating himself from his old life?

Valentine decorations — January 16, 2007

Today I went in and put up some more Valentine's Day decorations in Dad's room. I guess I miss setting up a classroom for each new time of year. Dad was somewhat dozy, sitting in the hall, prepared for dinner by the staff. He was nodding off as I worked—I could see him in the doorway. I don't think he was aware of my presence. When I finished, I went across the hall to visit Michelle. Michelle and I chatted a bit, talking about one thing and another. Eventually, after a few minutes, I could hear him talking in the hall, "Where's my daughter?" He continually surprised me, as he could not always call up the words as his brain required them. He had not truly registered my presence or acknowledged that he knew I was there. But he was very aware.

Dinner ritual started again, Dad started eating a bit. It was lamb, and he liked his meat. He often burped as he drank his milk. He was falling over on his left side, heavily leaning on his chair. I wondered if this was the tumour affecting his balance. He was not using his right hand at all. The tumour was in the left part of his brain, which controls the right side of the body. He ate the whole chocolate bar I brought for him. I resisted the urge to test it. Food had been such a comfort to me lately!

We finished up and I rolled him back down to his room and to his washroom to clean his face. We sat in his room and he looked over at the small photo in which he and Mom are at a wine and cheese party. Both in teal-coloured sweaters, glasses of wine in hand, smiles on their faces, celebrating at a friend's Christmas party. He reached over to the photo and I handed it to him. He spoke of "grandma"—he sometimes confused nouns, but I knew he meant my mother. I told him that Mom was waiting. "Where?" he responded with a look of query on his face. I just had to smile. He was drooling and vague again. I had to leave.

Food issues — January 20, 2007

Dad was sitting gaunt and miserable in his chair. The Valentine decorations were shining in the sun, the light passing through the red candy-like lights in his window and reflecting on his cold floor. I did not think I would last until lunch. I had brought juice boxes for Michelle and decided to see if Dad wanted some juice. He did. The abscess or indentation at the side of his head looked deeper, but I could not tell for sure.

The PSW told me that he was not eating breakfast. The last time I visited, they told me he ate a good breakfast, but usually had only one good meal a day. The nurse wanted them to mash up his food, as staff thought he was unable to chew it. He was just not hungry. He refused to take pills from the RN. She asked if I would give it a try. He refused again. The pills were often ground up and put into a spoonful of applesauce or pudding to make it more palatable, much like for a small child! He had been chewing his pills for that past month. They were quite creative in figuring out how to encourage him to take these meds. Bless them every one!

I told the nurse that I thought Dad needed to see that he was eating real food. Today it was ham, and I did not think he wanted it minced. Only old, sick people had that done for them! I was right. Dad refused to eat any of his mashed meal. Dessert was another story. "He's a great dessert eater!" one staffer told me. I knew that! I often only wanted sweets, no veggies, when ill.

Today I gave Dad a Ghirardelli chocolate when I arrived. Brian and I visited San Francisco, where these chocolates were made, back when we could more freely travel and take weekends away. It was a terrific visit to a lovely tourist area. The chocolate factory had a large sign, unmistakable to those visitors who were keen on such tours. We took a boat tour of the harbour, strolled around the boardwalk visiting expensive but entertaining shops. What a way to go—immersed in chocolate!

Joys of nature—January 25, 2007

As I continued to cope with my emotional distress and depression issues, I tried to appreciate the beauty around me. On this beautiful day, the sun shone, and, despite minus eighteen-degree temperatures, the landscape was very healing. I was out playing in the powdery snow yesterday, collecting and cutting kindling. It had the texture of icing sugar. I barely felt the cold. The icicles were sparkling in the sunshine. There were wisps of cotton candy clouds drifting slowly across the horizon. Seemingly reluctant to pass through this gorgeous scene, they paused when I stopped to take it all in. Occasionally the wind sent cotton balls of snow from the branches to the ground. The scene was full of dark brown tree trunks, green pine trees, and many red-tipped buds waiting for spring.

The squirrels (grey and black), chickadees, and blue jays shared the birdseed. Well, that was the theory. I spotted a blue jay dive-bombing a hungry squirrel that had parked herself on top of the seed, stuffing her whiskered face on the spot. Two- and four-legged critters had been shovelling a path across the deck railing as they scoured for our dropped birdseed. We hadn't seen the nonchalant raccoon in a long time; she must be in hibernation. Confrontations scare us more than her. Cheeky big devil.

Goldfinches, in their olive-green, muted winter coats, had ravaged the millet seed. They must be eating a cup a day, dropping hulls below, bombing those lower on the pecking order that were checking the deck for spillage. It was a joy to go out to refill their feeders as I listened to them chirp encouragingly in the branches overhead. Maybe they were telling me to hurry and move off to allow them to get back to their grub. Their wee footprints were a reminder of their presence. I liked to get up in the morning, feed the cats, and then check the deck for footprints to see who had visited in the early hours.

The cats sat inside and watched, happy that I'd put on a new show for their pleasure. The fisher's footprints appeared in the snow and ice down by the lake. His favourite meal, the ducklings, had grown and flown since he used to troll the shore for easy prey. I took the time to appreciate nature and to seek its healing powers.

Same old, same old — January 26, 2007

It was nearly lunchtime when I visited today. When I arrived, Dad was sitting, apparently asleep, having a chair massage. Susan was doing his arms and legs as he sat in the TV room. The TV was blaring, as usual, with Lois (who loves me) parked in front of it. Dad, Susan told me, was making noises and singing when she arrived, but dozed off as soon as she started his massage. I tried to explain our theory that when he sang, he was in pain. She was surprised and opened her eyes wide in disbelief. Who else, however, would know my Dad as well as I? I had a hard time convincing many professionals of what I knew and felt in my soul.

Dad's knees were terribly big and swollen, as was his foot. The remaining areas of his legs, and his arms and face, were thin and gaunt. His knees were in stark contrast to the rest of his body and had been painful for years. His ribs were visible, and his tailbones protruded with little padding. He had chunks of food in his mouth, sometimes drooling bits as he sat dozing away. It was not a pretty sight.

I went off to visit Michelle. She was doing all right. She told me that Dad was noisy last night. I still did not know how to monitor this. She wouldn't phone me if there were a problem. There was a standing order for more meds if Dad was agitated. She complained that they let him sleep in the day, but I was not sure he did. She could only tell he was sleeping if she couldn't hear him. I often came across him in another room. The staff was good at getting him up and moving him to other places. They got him up thrice daily. He protested, but that I left up to their expertise. Sometimes one had to let go.

Back I went to the TV room. I said good-bye to Dad. Lunch was ready, and Susan had finished her treatment. We both left, meeting in the foyer as we signed out. I had more chores to do, milk to pick up, mail to deal with and send off. I had gone through the family photos at home and had chosen the old photographs from my mother's folders of aunts and uncles that I should send to my cousins. I had not heard from any of them in a long time. I knew they were interested in these old black and white photos of the generations that had passed.

My cousins were in their seventies and looking for mementos of the past. Having just hit the big five-oh, I understood this passage in life.

I spent days going through the family slides, culling the ones I wanted to save. I knew how difficult it would be to go through the photos. I had finished, however, and weeded through all of them. It was time to let go of the past, honouring it in my own way, and moving on. I had begun to throw out things such as my high school report cards. I shuddered when I thought of the work my children would have to do if this task were not completed now, while I could put myself in their shoes. There was no reason to hang onto much of this stuff. The locker with Mom's and Dad's old possessions was being cleaned out. This task took me a long time. I still shudder even now as I drive by the storage facility: remembering my trying to lift boxes that my husband could not lift due to his back injury. It wasn't as if I needed to sell their house. I had time to decide what to keep and what to pass on.

I spoke to a young teacher who was interested in some of my teaching resources. Soon the decision would have to be made whether I hold a garage sale now or later to share these materials. None of it was new—education just recycles some of the same ideas—but the books would soon be stale as the authors fade into obscurity. Although, like bell-bottom pants, some ideas will come back after a time, I did not have the space to store all this!

Dreams and hymns — January 30, 2006

It was peculiar, the dreams I had been having. This morning I thought I was at home in our family house in Toronto. I must have had a subconscious wish to go back to those times when the living was easy. We lived in a small, semi-detached house in the inner city. It represented security and safety and a time when all was well. I loved that old house, with the ivy growing up the back wall of the neon light factory behind us. We went back to visit it a couple of times, but never went inside. When I was a child, there were long, deep lawns, with three-storey, 150-year-old houses across the street. The large, old house directly across the street had been remodelled into six apartments. We played softball on those lawns. The kids would have pick-up games on the lawn in the same way kids play hockey in the streets. There were tall trees and large homes with huge front porches. The cement pillars were magnificent.

As I sorted through the family slides, I found lots of photos of the street. There were a few showing the big tractors and backhoe that demolished these houses in the eighties. In their place, perhaps twenty years ago, they put up massive townhouses, with a parking garage underground. These large, glass edifices that redecorated our view were intended for folks anxious to remain living close to the downtown in the busy city.

In my dream I was up in my old bedroom. Somehow I made it down to the kitchen. I was preparing breakfast for my mother, father, and another young person. I was trying to make toast, but the toaster wasn't right. It was a long, flat toaster, for which bread must be sliced horizontally across the plane of the bread. Dad buttered a piece of toast. I was upset, since he had used so much butter it fell off the plate. Mom's toast, which I had to wait to cook, did not cook enough. There was nothing worse than raw toast! I was sure there was something meaningful in this dream. Mom had been eight months in the other world by this time.

The old family slides show my dad building a shed in our backyard, carefully cultivating his gardens, cats sitting in and about his roses and geraniums. The front yard in Toronto was tiny, as was the case in many of these older Toronto homes. It might have been ten feet by ten feet. We planted a large, crimson king maple tree there. After we left, the new owners had given up on the lawn and had created a massive garden. I was quite pleased with the result.

Walker Avenue, the street on which we lived, had been named for my aunt's grandfather, who had owned the farmland on which these houses were built. This aunt had married my mother's brother. Her brother lived next door. We called him Uncle Dee. He was a clock repairman. He had clocks and timepieces and wonderful tools and pieces of equipment. I could remember hearing them at night when they would walk up the stairs to go to bed. It never scared me. Eventually, after Uncle Dee died, my cousin took over that place. He totally gutted and renovated it, replacing the old wiring and plumbing: the lead pipes were incredibly out of date in this home that had to be a hundred years old.

I was in a new phase of my life. Dreams die hard. I trucked into Orillia. I was auditioning for a solo part in choir. After I auditioned, the artistic director told me he wanted a "boy soprano" sound. That would be a hard one to fake! Here I was, middle-aged and in menopause. I was quite distressed with another perceived failure. I felt as if I were having little success these days.

I went to the LTC home to visit with my father, as I felt it might do me some good to help another human being. I truly did not feel up to it. Nevertheless, in I went. As I arrived, I heard an alert: "Code Red on the second floor!" I kept on going up to the second floor, where my dad resided, dreading what might be happening—did he pull the alarm again? Was there an emergency? Would I have to walk past someone who was very ill? The kind care staff knew I was fretting and a couple of them assured me that it was just a drill. Bittersweet relief.

Dad was awake and singing. He had one of his hymnbooks on his side table. I dug his glasses out of his drawer, the really old pair, and put them on him. They kept slipping off and he kept having to slide them back up. I hoped he could see enough to read the words to his hymns. Unfortunately, he could not follow the lines across. He was mixing up the final word of the third line with the final word of the first line. I sat with him, trying to sing for him. I really couldn't tell how well he could hear. My suspicion was that he heard very little. He tried to take the two hymnbooks away from me. I had memorized his favourite hymn and tried singing it with him. He kept going back to the same verse. It was emotionally difficult after all the Thursday night choir practices we had attended together. I remembered singing so often with my parents. It started in Grade 9 when I joined the church choir. They were good times.

Exercise and stress relief—February 1, 2007
I worked out today. It felt so healthy to get the body moving and those endorphins firing throughout my body. When Mom passed away, a worker involved in her care had suggested I get help in dealing with my bereavement issues. I thought I just had to cope on my own. I knew that I had experienced many depressive symptoms over the past eight months, and exercise would be a good antidote. To that end, I was working out every other day. My goal was to walk the two kilometres to pick up the mail every day. I had great goals! I would do so, I promised myself, when I did not have the responsibility of my father pressing so hard on me. My weight management program

was working and the weight was very slowly coming off as I limited my intake and gave myself more time away from Dad. I had stopped seeing my therapist, since after my retirement my employer would no longer be paying for my therapy.

Consistent care — Friday, February 2, 2007

I often wondered how I could get messages across to all the caregivers that served my dad and met his needs. Continuity of care was important. They had little understanding of my goals, even though I left notes on his bed, his wardrobe, and the walls. He was always cold, and often they did not put an undershirt on him under his sweatshirt. They would drag him out of bed for meals he did not want to eat.

I went in to visit Dad just before lunchtime today. Wearing the cap Caitlin had crocheted for him, he looked jaunty in a peculiar sort of way. His eyes were wild and he knew he didn't know certain things. He was in the TV room, stuck, with his wheelchair wheel lodged against a chair. I suppose there was irony in this! He said, "Hi. How ya doin'?" I noticed that his beard was a mess and I began to wheel him back to his room to get a face cloth. He probably had drooled his snack in the afternoon. He forgot to chew and seemed to fall asleep during the process. As I moved him into the hall, he noticed the regular group of residents waiting to go into the dining room and said, "Look at them all!"

I parked him in the doorway of his room and moved around him to put my coat on his chair. He seemed so frail and he was terribly cold. Many who are quite ill are cold, as their bodies begin to shut down and metabolic rates become slower. I picked up his woollen blanket, which by now had gone through the long-term care home super-duper washers and dryers. I should never have left this fine Scots tartan woollen blanket there. It was looking a bit the worse for wear. I did not know how to keep it from eager housekeeping staff who would throw fine articles into their industrial machines. I placed the blanket on his lap. I thought I might take a photo to show Caitlin how cute he looked in her handiwork, but first I lifted the blanket to straighten it and tuck it in at the sides. He grabbed the blanket from me and said, "Hey, were you going to steal it?" The shock of hearing my father say such things overwhelmed me. In the institution, he needed to protect himself a lot.

I tried to do things for him and hoped that he knew that this was me, his daughter. I wet a face cloth and washed his face with hot water. He always enjoyed this and nearly purred, again, with contentment. I dried his hands and put cream on his dry hands and bald, dry forehead. His skin was beginning to break down as his body was shutting down. He had dry, scaly patches, and many liver spots.

I perched on the bed, remade with clean sheets that were simply awaiting his presence. The sheet protector sat smack dab in the middle, like a baby's change table pad, as he had been incontinent for months and could make a mess. Despite the adult diaper, feces were apt to fall out. I was never prepared for that. He began to wheel away from me on the other side of the bed and moved towards the window.

"Where ya goin', Dad?"

"I don't know . . . Nowhere."

Then his song began anew, "Help me. Help me" sung several times over in a beautiful rendition of an opera, almost recognizable but not truly so. We miss the lady who used to sing this song. Marjorie, I think, was her name. I must ask what had happened to her. There was a board with a candle and a place where they put up notices in memoriam of residents who had passed away. I always looked at it and half expected to see Dad's name there. Why I would come back and visit after his death, I did not know. I kept mentally preparing myself. There were stages to grief. I had accepted some of them. The reality was different. To this day, when I do something or have to face another trial or tribulation, I catch myself thinking I should phone Mom and talk to her.

"What do you need, Dad?"

"Everything." Out of the mouths of babes.

It still took me aback when he suddenly could carry on a superficial conversation. I think he read lips and sometimes could comprehend. Perhaps it was just the social patterns that were ingrained in the hard wiring of his brain. I started to grab my purse and got ready to take him to lunch. He recognized my actions and said "Where we going?"

"It's lunchtime soon!" I went over to him and yelled in his ear and asked if he wanted me to help him with lunch. He shrugged his shoulders. I figured that this wasn't a "no," and I wanted to feel useful. "I don't know how we get to a bedroom," he told me. I think he meant the dining area. He was quite confused about some things.

I ran back and forth fetching Dad's soup, coffee, and milk. He wanted no part of the coffee or the milk, despite the fact that I had two different people trying to find the straws from the new order that had been put somewhere and disappeared. This was the result of having insufficient staff to stock shelves and cupboards. One cheerful soul said she'd ordered them, they had come in, but did not quite know where they were. It was good to have a project to complete! The hunt began. After two more people looked, we found them, and I popped one in dad's milk glass. He did not want his milk and I popped the straw into his coffee. He did not want that, either. "Ah, me," as my mom used to say.

I knew dad had a lot of pain, but I was unable to get him onto stronger meds; not until the final week.

Before lunch arrived, and the real fun began, Dad's geriatrician arrived on his rounds. He was the doctor attached to the institution and the second floor. He visited one day per week. The doctor had no idea who my father was, or had been, especially as he existed now.

The charge nurse accompanied him and gave explanations about each resident as they moved through the wing. They tried to talk to Dad, who did not understand who they were. I told them that he couldn't hear them speak, although he wasn't bad at lip reading. The doctor made no attempt to speak to me or to ask if I had any questions. I was frozen, caught up in my regular feeding routine. There was no bedside and no bedside manner. So much for integrated health care. I was so distraught I could not fight for some time with this doctor. I should have been asked if I had any questions. If I had been healthier, I would have spoken up. I wanted to talk about pain and medications and the treatment when Dad's time came.

The pain begins in earnest — February 6, 2007

This was the first time that I clearly understood that my father had pain. I knew his knees had been bad, but this exceeded anything that had gone before. Headaches were typical of brain tumours. He was in his wheelchair; I sat down on his bed and drew his wheelchair over to be closer to me. His hands were freezing cold and his sweatshirt hood was up. He looked like a wannabe street kid; very thin and his eyes hollow. I covered him with his wool blanket. I put up a few more Valentine decorations. The sun shone red through the red heart-shaped lights. He had moved his wheelchair along the foot of the bed, but it was stuck at this point. I was putting up more cardboard hearts, a large, stuffed fuzzy red rose, and rearranging the window. I had bought a soft, heart-shaped, red pillow at the grocery store, of all places. I put it in his lap. He did not seem to understand what it was. I hung it on a hook that I had mounted over the door. It had held his Christmas wreath. The pillow was a bright red spot in his room. It cheered me and I had been told that it cheered others. It showed that someone cared.

He proceeded to leave the room while I was perched on his bed trying to visit with him. I had lowered the bed, since it was raised up high to more easily get him in and out of the chair lift. I kept asking him where he was going. I wasn't sure if he thought that he had to go down to dinner, since I was there and I always fed him dinner. He kept going back out the door. A respite worker was walking by. He said, "Hi. How are you?" She spoke to him for a few seconds. I laughingly told her I was trying to visit and he had left me alone in the room! I left him there while I finished up his window. When I brought him back in the room—I appreciated the privacy—he was becoming more agitated. He seemed sedated, but in pain. I held his hand under the blanket. He kept pushing up with his right arm—as if trying to escape some pain. I asked him many times and in many ways if he was in pain.

"Are you in pain?" Pausing for a response. "Does it hurt?"

I clearly enunciated each consonant and he kept asking me, "Pardon?" turning his bad ear towards me. I wondered at this!

"Do you want a pill for pain?"

"A pie for pay?"

If I hadn't been so upset and worrying about what to do, it would have been funny. There was no way I could help him understand. Eventually, however, it became abundantly clear. He kept saying, "Ow! Ow!" paired with a sucking in of breath through clenched teeth. This time I went to found the nurse. There were several levels of nursing care. There were nurses who gave out the medications. There were registered practical nurses (RPNs) and registered nurses (RNs). There was a charge nurse who was above the RPN and was "in charge." These were the people we phoned if we needed to get something done. They were wonderful people, but quite busy and seldom at their desks. Muskoka has a hard time keeping trained staff here. The young people want to go to the cities where life is bigger and more opportunities abound. There are not enough nurses to go around.

I found the floor nurse and spoke to her. She obligingly came down to Dad's room. One of the ones with a wonderful bedside manner, she must have spent fifteen minutes with us. She went through feeling his abdomen to see if he had any reaction, and therefore pain, in that region. He did not wince at all, and so she kept at it. I pointed out the huge concave places in his temple, lovingly smoothing it with the back of my hand, and he winced. She kept asking him if he had "pain, hurt, or an owie," but he couldn't hear the words. We ran out of synonyms. She felt his head: the top, the sides, and the back. We thought he might be having headaches, since there was no indication of pain elsewhere.

At the very least, he needed something. It was an hour before the next meds were to be handed out. At this point he was getting

Lorazepam (Ativan) to reduce the agitation, as well as the pills to prevent seizures (Dilantin). The Lorazepam calmed him down enough, but it wasn't a pain medication, as I had previously thought. She went down and got his regular meds and crushed them and mixed them with applesauce. These days it was hit or miss whether he chose to take them. I was worried. She smiled at him and tried to coerce him into taking them. Eventually, as I stood behind him with bated breath, he took them. I thought that sometimes he refused to take them if he knew I was watching. It was hard to say.

It was time to change his meds. She told me that we would have to get doctor's orders to increase the medication. She asked if I had talked to the doctor at all. I told her I had seen the doctor doing rounds the previous Friday but we hadn't spoken. She asked if we had had a case conference, and I said we had, but the doctor had not been there, since it was the day of the accreditation meeting. I asked how I would be able to talk to the doctor to ask for a pain prescription. This was not the last time I had trouble getting to talk to the doctor.

All the way home, driving through the snow-covered forests, I worried about what to do. When I made it home, obviously agitated, I looked up the doctor's office number and phoned. The office was closed, to reopen later that evening for a walk-in clinic. I knew that the charge nurse was the person I should speak to and I phoned the front desk. The receptionist said she could put me through. She said there was no problem in phoning the doctor. She would phone me back with a report later. Sure enough, after a few minutes she phoned back. The doctor's office was closed but she had left a message at his home to call her. The charge nurse said she would let me know later what happened. Eventually she phoned me back again and reported that the doctor had given an order for Percoset, which would help Dad with pain. Percoset, which I looked up in my pill book, was acetaminophen with codeine—prescribed for mild to moderate pain. I hoped it worked. I thought he was beyond this type of pain. I decided I would go in early the next day to see if it was working.

What to expect?— February 7, 2007

Dad was not putting sentences together very well—he could draw up many nonsensical words. He was napping every few minutes. He had some of his lunch still in his mouth. He was gesturing towards the bed and I knew he wanted to sleep. We pushed the call button and Cynthia came to our aid. She told us she would get Sharon to come and put Dad into bed. Sharon had a lovely sense of nonsense! Dad always smiled when he saw her. She is an attractive woman, perhaps in her thirties or forties, with dark hair and a winning smile. She always made a point of bending over, or kneeling down, and getting at his eye level. She told him she was going to get him into bed. I loved it when they treated him like a person and someone who might be sentient, even though all indicators pointed to the other end of the spectrum.

They brought in the big mechanical lift. This was a piece of equipment about five feet high that was plugged in to charge its batteries when not being used. On wheels, it could be rolled and moved around the room easily. Sharon made Dad lean forward. They put the jacket around his shoulders and up under his legs. She told me that he really did not like it. She apologized to him, even though he couldn't hear her, for having to use the lift. It was a touching gesture and I think it helped. It certainly helped me. I remember one time that he enjoyed it and was laughing and smiling at me as he was being lifted. Once he was in bed, he was asleep in thirty seconds. We tucked him in. I kissed him goodbye and left.

I adored Sharon's bedside manner. She was always respectful, kind, and caring at a level that went beyond her training. Her spirit embodied that of the PSW: she treated Dad with such dignity and respect at all times. Despite his inability to hear her, she always explained what she was doing. Jill Bolte Taylor, in her book *My Stroke of Insight*, demonstrated the respect, or lack thereof, that some staff members or visitors display to those who are perceived to be ill. Dr. Bolte Taylor suffered a life-threatening blood clot in her brain and wrote of her experiences. Since she had moments of clarity, with little brain function on the left side of her brain, she was able to understand emotions and feelings without having the language to articulate them at the time. She reminds caregivers and staff members that the best way to help those who are ill is to let them sleep. Beyond that, a caregiver's respectful attitude is perceived on a deeper psychosocial level even by those with brain injuries and apparent dementia. She found that those who came in to visit her, if they possessed a positive attitude, and brought energy and a strong spirit into her room, gave her added energy. So many burned-out workers in LTC are hard-pressed to keep their energy up. So many of our RNs and RPNs are stressed-out beyond their abilities to cope. This has a profound effect on those in care.

Another issue that bothers me is that most staff members called my father by his Christian name. People of his generation, potentially four times the age of their caregivers, are being spoken to quite casually, as one would to a peer or acquaintance. I found this most disheartening. A generational thing, I would prefer more formality.

This new level of Dad's illness created in me a visceral reaction that still haunts me. I kept fighting the reaction. It affected my whole being: body, spirit, and soul. It was very upsetting, and I kept thinking that I would be getting better soon. I would learn to manage my grief for my late mother, as well as grieving the loss of my father as I knew him. Each stage had an effect upon me. I took my emotions out and examined them like the clothes I was planning on wearing to our Valentine Ball on the weekend. I kept weighing my choices: I had two long dresses, more cocktail dresses than ball gowns, a new tulip skirt with a blouse I had bought. I spent some time trying them on, looking at myself this way and that. It was the same with my grief. I went back over events and put them up on a hanger to look at them from all angles. Eventually, I would pick the clothes that fit best. I would come to terms with all I had been through.

I dreaded the next levels from here in Dad's care. I could not find out any information on what to expect. From a Web site I found out what I could expect in the last forty-eight hours. Eventually, it said, cancer patients succumb to a brain hemorrhage as the cancer cells fight for oxygen and destroy the brain cells. I figured that there would be pain, as there was for my mother during the last years of her life. I remembered going in every morning and after school, checking to see if she was still breathing. When I went in to see Dad, he was very still.

Canadian Cancer Society peer support — February 10, 2007

On a Saturday morning, I had a long conversation with Marg, one of the Canadian Cancer Society volunteers in Peer Support. I arranged to talk to her weekly as I dealt with this stage of my father's battle with the tumour. What a wonderful person she is! Our stories were incredibly similar; which was what the Canadian Cancer Society (CCS) tried to do. They match caregivers to a peer volunteer whose family members had succumbed to cancer in the same circumstances. Marg was an experienced volunteer. She had seen her mother through a brain tumour, and a father through Parkinson's disease. She was a wife and teacher with children my boys' ages (early twenties).

As I told her my story, she said some things that meant a great deal to me. She told me that she had searched for information on living through such experiences and did not find anything on dying with a brain tumour. It compelled me to keep up my writing practice. She asked if I was writing about my feelings, and I assured her that I was doing this. Like my fancy dress choice for the Valentine Ball, the examination of my reactions really helped me to digest what was going on in my body, mind, and spirit. Clarifying my story and putting it into words really helped me put together the chapters of this time of my life. She told me that I sounded like an amazing person. It was gratifying to hear, as I understood that I had been through a great deal. There was a saying that "The things that don't quite kill you make you stronger." I did not feel strong right then, but hoped I would eventually. I hoped, too, that I would be able to help someone else in these circumstances.

Marg's role as my peer support person was to be someone to whom I could unload and find some understanding. It was not a reciprocal arrangement, in that I did not provide her with the support that a friend would expect in return. She was there for me. The purpose of her association with me was to support me by listening. She phoned me weekly, monthly, or however often I needed her to call me, and provided a listening ear. She had a phone calling card from CCS and I did not need to worry about her paying for this.

We spoke of many things: how family continuity means a great deal to the patient. How both of our respective parents' brain tumours blocked their understanding of the function of things, such as the TV remote, but by using non-verbal means, a caregiver could come to understand their issues. We both had had to take antidepressants to get through this period of time. The serotonins and endorphins simply weren't getting produced the way they used to. The brain, in its fight or flight mode, was unable to effectively produce the right reactions. In time, this would diminish, but to get through the here and now, my doctor's prescription was priceless.

Symptoms increase — February 11, 2007

I went in to see Dad before choir practice in Orillia. A PSW had just changed Dad's sheets. I had seen her from the parking lot as I looked up at Dad's window. His Valentine decorations were a bright spot in an otherwise bland institutional building. Snow had piled up and there was quite a chill in the minus fifteen-degree brisk winter air. Once I made it up to his room, I found him in his chair, with his head lolling over to one side. I mentally kicked myself, since I had washed his Obus form cover and had forgotten it at home. This is a soft U-shaped pillow that helps support the neck when the care recipient no longer can keep his or her head erect. It would have helped him greatly. He would not lean back and put his head on the headrest. Occasionally his head would shake with tremors. It pained me to look at him.

He was trying to form words but could not speak clearly. He spoke as if he had marbles in his mouth. I thought I heard, "Yie down," meaning he wanted to lie down. He spoke this phrase several times, too ill to gesture any more. He just could not relax. I heard him say, "Aaggghh." I knew that there were two staff members on breaks after the meal they had just served at five. I could hear staff calling for help with "lifts," putting residents into bed. I decided to sit and wait until they came, as I knew they would eventually. I did not want to make demands on an already beleaguered staff.

The PSW came into the room. She mentioned that she had just changed his bed, as it was quite messy and smelly with bowel movements. I thanked her for doing so and showing such concern. We spoke of his ear problem. There were crusted bits in it. I told her he had big wax problems and she thought that he had an ear infection. Likely the least of his worries, I told her that I thought he was in more pain than the medications could help.

When they began to change his adult diaper there was a big problem. Nursing staff had given him a laxative, since he had been constipated. No wonder — he hadn't eaten anything in ages. The

ladies began to lift him; he groaned as they did so. He could be having any number of symptoms, but I was sure he was in pain. He
had been seemingly nauseous for months. I could see the bones in
his back sticking out. He was as gaunt as a holocaust survivor. He
had pressure sores from his bones digging through his thin buttock
skin into where he sat on the cushioned wheelchair. They wiped and
washed and changed him several times, as he was still evacuating his
bowels. They kept their sense of humour and smiled. He grunted and
moaned. I knew the man was in pain. I wondered why the Do Not
Resuscitate order did not include such invasions as laxatives.

After this difficult scene I got into the car and drove to choir. I
was still shaking after the thirty-five-minute drive. It felt good to have
something else to do. Focusing on singing and reading the music
brought me out of my fog. I could not get the smell of Dad's feces out
of my nose. I wondered if I smelled this bad or if I was just remembering the scent and worrying.

Moira sat beside me at choir and she listened while I vented.
I explained that we were having trouble advocating for Dad. She is
married to a pharmacist. She said to keep advocating. We knew Dad
best and knew what we wanted done for him. Once a senior is in
LTC or under the care of CCAC, the family loses all control. Policies
prevail in their need to meet standards of care that may or may not
apply to individual cases. I spoke to her husband, the pharmacist,
at the break—he had experience in such matters—and he strongly
suggested that Dad could go on morphine at this point. On the way
home, I popped in to see if Dad was asleep. It was ten o'clock, very
cold and dark. The place was deathly quiet. He was sleeping, and I
was relieved. Off I went home, determined. I sat down with Brian. He
listened to my story and agreed and suggested I either call the doctor
or call the charge nurse. I did both the next day.

Phone tag, dietitians, and pain
—Wednesday, February 14, 2007

The day started with a bang. Literally. The new roof was being built
on our cottage, and about half of the shingles were completely off of
the roof of the main house. We had construction crews all over. I had
to be careful to shower at the right time, since the bathroom window

did not have curtains, and I did not want anyone falling off the roof in shock. We haven't lost a contractor yet!

I went in to have my visit with Dad and had a talk with the dietitian. She gave me some valuable information. He wasn't eating much, usually one meal a day, and about one-quarter to half of that meal actually got into him. It was a slow and painful process. One PSW would feed about four seniors at a time. It looked like a bizarre scene in a day care from hell. In September, he had weighed 165 pounds. At five feet, ten inches, he now weighed 135 pounds, she told me. It was in the reports. Over the past few months, he had eaten about one meal a day. He ate well when I visited, she told me — which had not been often over the past month, as I could not face visiting every day. I did not feel bad about this, since there were many patients who did not get as many visits as we had been able to make with Dad. I knew it made a difference seeing someone one knows and loves, despite living in an institution. I wondered whether our feeding him had prolonged his pain and suffering.

Dad was still keen on chocolate! That's about all I could get into him on many of my visits. I had not fed him for several days. I then called the charge nurse. She checked his file and told me that Dad had refused meds on the 12th, and then yesterday had spit out one-fourth of the pills she had ground up into the applesauce for him. I wonder how much of the meds were actually getting into his system? If he was refusing to take his pain pills, then we must get something into him. And, how many of the pills were still necessary?

My friend had told me that they could administer morphine in a liquid form. That might be the route to take. Due to governmental rules and funding, they must follow protocol and be very careful. The legislation was very heavy-handed on requirements for patients in order to protect vulnerable seniors. Nursing staff asked me to talk to the doctor. I tried. He was not in his office today, being Wednesday. He would be at the Regional Office the next day and wouldn't be back to his clinic until Friday.

This couldn't wait that long. I felt powerless. This was intolerable. Health care is the right of every Canadian. What an abuse of a situation! I had been listening to the CBC show *White Coat, Black Art*. Who was making the doctor accountable? No one. The nursing staff, my only link and the best people to judge our needs, were not nurse practitioners who could prescribe meds. I was between a rock and a hard place.

I received some advice from a staff member. She suggested I talk to the Director of Care and request a multidisciplinary conference team meeting. I wondered how much time that would take.

Many seniors, I had noticed, refused meals or really weren't hungry. (Except for desserts, which were usually incredibly good!) PSWs had to be vigilant to ensure that these seniors, already frail or feeling upset, would get up out of bed and eat. It was their duty. I still had a hard time convincing people that Dad was in palliative care, and forcing him to get up and go to meals was as abusive as keeping food from him.

I had three concerns: 1) physical supports to his fragile frame, e.g., pillows under his knees, raising the head of the bed, which helps those with headaches and/or brain tumours; 2) pain management; and 3) nutritional needs. I felt that getting him out of bed and taking him down to meals when he wasn't eating them was a waste of time and his energy. I wanted to get him back into bed as soon as possible after a meal. They did not have enough people to do this immediately, yet personal care was so important.

The concern was that he could develop bedsores; he did have pressure sores. I saw them when they were cleaning him up and changing him. He had red blotches, like liver spots, all over his arms and legs. The danger of letting him stay in bed was pneumonia. I asked if they could just get him up once a day. I left a note on his light asking that staff just keep him comfortable. Some people did not know he had been declared palliative. It was not the kind of thing they would post on a resident's door.

The Director of Care (DOC) phoned me back and said she would arrange a meeting for us. Apparently, the care staff knew Dad was going to have a bad day when he woke up and asked for his (late) wife. The DOC wanted to know my schedule, which by now was pretty flexible, my having given up working. She asked what I needed to talk about and I explained it to her: I told her I had spoken to the dietitian and I understood that I needed to let staff know that he isn't to be forced to get up and eat. Staff did not understand that I wanted him left alone in peace. She also offered tray service, meaning a staff member would feed him in his room. I wondered silently where they would find personnel for that. They were hard-pressed to get people back into bed for those who need assistance for bedtime. Nevertheless, she couldn't guarantee that the *doctor* would be there.

I was overwhelmed by Dad's situation. He was clearly in pain, and mouth breathing with great difficulty. On my way out the door that night, I had a message from the nurse that we would be able to talk with the doctor tomorrow. That never happened.

Brian had made a late reservation for a Valentine's dinner for us. We went off and had a delicious meal at the restaurant. It was wonderful to be looked after with sumptuous oysters, salad, and main courses. I worried the whole time, although satisfied that I had done all I could.

Aside from the brain tumour that was growing and sucking nourishment from brain cells, Dad had severe arthritis in his knees and edema in his feet. The pain from these two physical issues alone had always been terrible. His pain was increasing and there was no reason not to expect it to continue to get worse. I spent a great deal of my time pleading with staff to give him more medication. He was clearly under-medicated. This was a familiar story among friends who care for ailing seniors. There was great reluctance to give more painkillers. I really did not understand this. The RPNs only had time to give each person their regular doses as they did their rounds. Since we were fully paying for all of his drugs, I was constantly bothered by this issue. It remains an unresolved issue for me and haunts me to this day.

Preparing the way — Thursday, February 15, 2007

The phone rang at one a.m. The PSW had gone in to visit Dad, which they did hourly, and he seemed to be very badly off. They would touch his arm and speak his name. I am not sure why they would do this. Surely it would be better to leave him in peace, sleeping? He was unresponsive at this time. They thought I should know. They were not sure if I should go in or not. They were not sure how quickly he might leave us. They agreed to call me back at 3:30 a.m. and keep me updated. They did not call back, and I fell asleep at around three. I woke at seven a.m., hurriedly got dressed, had some coffee, and packed up a blanket, a thermos, and some other things.

I had gone into the LTC at around eight-thirty a.m.; I saw the nurse in the hall and asked if she could tell me about the rest of his night. She hadn't had time to read his file but promised to get back to me. I went into his room. He was lying on his back with an oxygen tube in his nose. Apparently, even when mouth breathing, enough oxygen got into his lungs through his nose as he sucked in the air. Dad was mouth breathing, with some rattling in his chest. There was paraphernalia on the table beside him; large Q-tips, a container of Vaseline; another of something like mouthwash. I had no idea what it was for. His eyes were one-quarter open, and he was unresponsive.

I had brought in a big comforter, which was washed and returned later, along with several pillows and pillowcases. They proved invaluable later on. The PSW asked if I wanted him to go to breakfast or if I wanted them to bring in a tray. I knew he couldn't eat. I had tried giving him some water on Tuesday and he could not suck from the straw. At this point he hadn't had anything to eat or drink in twenty-four hours. He couldn't eat or he would choke. From time to time he would hiccup. I thought he might have had a slight convulsion. He kept on blinking, but did not say anything. I dug under the covers and found a hand to hold. Surprisingly it was warm. His feet, remarkably, were not so swollen anymore. This was peculiar, as this condition had begun in the summer and had not gone away despite diuretics and his special socks.

There was a call in to the doctor, who did not work on Wednesdays but would be in his office later. Were we not entitled to health care and visits by a doctor? How enervating this was! The RNs had no control without the authority of a doctor who did not even bother coming in to see my father. Finally, at ten a.m., we got an order for Dad to have injections of morphine, 2–5 mg every two hours, as needed. It was such a relief. They gave him 2 mg and he seemed more comfortable. Some workers thought he was not in pain, but I knew better. I knew him so well by now. He was in a hospital gown. I asked about the toilet seat, which had been changed for a higher one. He hadn't been on the toilet for months. I asked if they could put a regular one on now, as I knew it would be a long few days and it would be easier if I could use his private bathroom toilet rather than going down the hall. The custodial staff needed a nurse's order to remove the booster seat. The only public washroom that I knew of was on the main floor. This would make it very handy for me, as long as no one walked in on me! In fact, I nearly collided with a staff member when I came out of the door a couple of times.

Audrey, from the front desk, came up to the room and told me that the Director of Care would be in to see me before long. This was good news. The PSW said to hit the call button if anything changed, or if I needed anything. They looked after me. They had put a radio in the room and they were playing some old songs. It was comforting. They shifted him at 10:30, but did not otherwise disturb him. I decided to go and get something to eat. Brian had poured me a coffee in his travel mug and I knew I was getting light-headed. I was scolded affectionately for not staying out and having a relaxed breakfast, but I wanted to get back to Dad. I had my second cup of coffee and breakfast sandwich in Dad's room.

I phoned Brian. He said he would come in around noon. Then the Director of Care (DOC) came in. She found us two chairs, and we settled in for a chat. She explained many details to me: outlining what I could expect in the next few days. She gave me some information I had not heard on mouth care, signs of death (see the final section of this book) and what they would be able to do for us. She said he could have his morphine injections until the end. It was a judgment call when he needed another injection, but I was the one in the best position to make that decision. It was far better to err on the side of comfort, rather than not enough. He had been aphasic (uncommunicative) for days. She explained about the oxygen. If they don't have oxygen patients could panic because they cannot breathe. It was a comfort measure. She explained that the body could go three minutes without air, three days without water, and three weeks without food. Dad was two days without water at this point. Food was a distant memory.

The DOC explained the symptoms of approaching death, all of which Dad had demonstrated in the past few days. His breathing softened and came and went over time. We could expect apnea (periodic cessation of breathing), Cheyne-Stokes respiration, cyanosis, and other symptoms (see Part Two for more details).

A Web site entitled, "As Death Approaches" says: "The fear of the unknown was always greater than the fear of the known," and that was true. It was comforting to know what to expect, not that all of this had to occur. She reminded me to look after myself, to take regular breaks. She said to talk to him and let him know I was there.

She felt for his heartbeat, which was weakening. She showed me how to do mouth care and told me that the mouth care he had received so far was excellent. (I was still not giving up my day job!) Staff came in and helped check his position. Dad was moaning and he was twitching. He could have been having more seizures. His forehead, where the tumour was growing, was a brighter red than elsewhere.

Brian arrived to spell me off and I went home for a break. He phoned on his cell phone every few hours, while I supervised the roofers and chatted with them. At five p.m. the clouds began rolling in, and we were having snow squalls. I told Brian to come home. I had put a phone call in to my brother to tell him what was going on. He was out in his camp at the mine and hard to reach.

I made it back to the hospital for five-thirty p.m. after picking up a Sub sandwich, a couple of juices, and potato chips—to hell with the weight management. At 5:50, the doctor arrived—he had decided to pop in and see if I needed anything. Not now, thanks! The RN came in at 6:50 and every hour from then until she left. She checked Dad and asked if I thought he needed more morphine. In hindsight, I wish I had given him some. I did not see evidence that he was in pain, but felt that he had no way of letting me know. He was comatose. He was still blinking; his forehead and hands were red. He was breathing five times every ten seconds. I don't know why I measured it. It was good to have something to do, other than the mouth care.

I rearranged the big easy chair twice, eventually pulling it out and putting the comforter and three pillows on top. It was comfortable. The oxygen tank pulsed all night, a form of white noise that cancelled out all the noises in the hall: people chatting, pages for various staff members, residents wandering the halls. I had brought my computer with family photos on it and was sorting the photos, travelling down memory lane and remembering all of the wonderful things Dad was and had been for me and for many others: father, husband, chorister, churchgoer, and volunteer. At eight p.m., he was breathing six breaths every ten seconds. By ten p.m. I had inhaled my food, had one of my juice boxes, and watched four *CSI*'s[7] in a row! It was bizarre and most surreal sitting there checking him every so often. It was comforting to watch TV and remove myself from the situation from time to time. It was a breather of sorts.

---

7   An American TV show about crime scene investigations—CSI's.

I went closer to Dad for the umpteenth time, looking for signs. The RN had checked his feet for cyanosis, but I found it in his hands. I looked at one eye and a tear was starting to fall from it. For some peculiar reason I hesitated — do I ask for more meds? He was otherwise quiet and did not appear in pain. When Dad's other eye began to tear I pushed the buzzer and asked for morphine. It was 10:45 p.m. I looked at Dad's ribs sticking out; his organs were so small; there appeared to be nothing left of him.

At 11:00 p.m. I did mouth care for him, just as Diana had done. I made a mess and got Vaseline on his beard, but did not worry about it. I knew he would forgive me. I held his hand and watched more TV.

Dad's passing — Friday, February 16, 2007

At 12:15 a.m., two PSWs came in and repositioned him, shifting his weight to his other shoulder. Dean, one of the PSWs, was a kind caregiver. He offered me tea, coffee, or juice, and I asked for some tea. Not a tall man, with broad shoulders and a kind manner, he brought a firm foundation of competence, and I trusted myself with him in these last few hours of Dad's stay in this institution. Dean brought me a tray with tea, milk, and sugar. I held Dad's hand, rubbed his bony shoulder, rearranged his blankets and looked at his mottled hands again. I counted his breaths at 12:50 and he was breathing seven times every ten seconds.

By 1:00 a.m., he was up to eight breaths. At 1:15, I heard Cheyne-Stokes breathing. His breathing stopped for about ten seconds or so — it was hard to tell, as time stopped for me. It wasn't upsetting at all. I sat beside him holding *my* breath. When he started breathing again, I was upset. I did not know how much longer I could take this! He needed to finally be out of pain. Mom, his parents, his cats and dogs; all were waiting on the other side. Our faith was strong and true, and Dad's cycle of life nearly complete. I had three cups of hot tea and made several visits to the bathroom, darn glad I had had the toilet seat changed back. I think I nearly took out the PSW in the doorway again, the bathroom door being behind the entry door, when he came to check on us for the umpteenth time.

Dean told me that he had quite enjoyed caring for my Dad over the past while. He told me he had ensured that Dad had pain pills, as needed, on those nights that Dad was clearly agitated and loudly vocal. He, too, recognized Dad's pain. Some days they could hear him singing down the hall and around the corner, in the nurse's office. They made sure that they gave him the pills before they moved him to give him care. I was grateful. Every move seemed painful in the last days of his life.

Dean spoke of how they had had to watch him carefully. Dad liked to get out of bed in the night. Holly, his first charge nurse, found him a bed with raised sides. Even then, Dad would position himself at the end of the bed, bony legs and feet hanging over the side. They had to laugh. He was a challenge, but Dean thought that he must have been a good man in his prime. Dad was always polite and thanked them for things they would bring him.

I took a break; the room was dry, and I needed to stretch. I walked out into the hall. Here was Donny, a resident, using his feet to wheel himself back and forth across the end of the hall. It looked like a Monty Python skit; back and forth in the darkened, surreal hallway, disappearing in a doorway. I asked Dean if Donny was always up at night. He said no, but that it was likely he had slept all day. Back into the room I went, to try and get some sleep. I was on edge and weary.

At 1:24, Dad had an apnea episode and stopped breathing for two seconds. I thought back to a time in the Manor, when I was running back and forth between work and home and Gravenhurst, that Dad had said I looked tired. Then he patted the bed and said I could sleep there! Now, here I was, keeping him company at last. Finally he had his way.

I had another flashback. When I was a child, I was afraid of the dark hall I had to travel to get to the bathroom. I remember that there was a red glow in the base of the light, a wall lamp, a reflector of some sort. It scared me. I would go and stand and wait beside his bed until he woke up. He would ask, "What is it, Jen?"

"I have to go to the bathroom."

"Well, off you go, then." I think I just needed to know that someone was there for me. I was glad to do the same for him.

I settled back into bed around three a.m., feeling that it would be a bit longer. I drifted off to sleep. I jerked awake at 4:20. I turned my head slowly. All was quiet. Too quiet. I could see that Dad's colour had changed profoundly. Nervously, I approached him and felt his face. It was cold. He had stopped breathing, with his eyes one-quarter open, as they had remained for hours. Suddenly, the door swung open and Dean came back in. He said he had just checked in on Dad and found that he had passed over. He did not know whether or not to wake me right away. He went and told the nurse. I was glad to get some sleep; there was nothing I could do.

The nurse came and checked on Dad. His core was still warm. It hadn't been long ago that he had passed over. I felt as if a burden had been lifted from my shoulders. No more guilt; no more worrying over whether I had done enough or done the right thing. I asked what would happen next. They said they would call the doctor at seven a.m.; there was no rush to pronounce him dead. It had been expected. Staff had rounds to finish, residents to check.

I decided to pack up Dad's room then and there. I couldn't face going back there later that day. I am sure there was someone who needed the room. They told me I had a couple of days to clean out his things, but I felt quite awake and I did not want Brian to lift anything and set back his physiotherapy treatments. I carefully removed the Valentine decorations from the door and the window. I went into the bathroom and threw out his toiletries and other personal items. I checked his drawers, folded up my comforter, placed the family photos in the pillowcases. The PSW came in and washed Dad's body while I took his things down to the car.

It was a lonely process going up and down to the second floor. I loaded up the car, under the starlight, and drove home. It was quiet and peaceful. I had not phoned home—I knew Brian needed his sleep. The place was quite dark. The snow crunched under my boots. The only thing I unloaded was Dad's plant, not wanting to let it die in the minus fifteen-degree cold. I did not bother bringing anything else in from the car. These things could wait until dawn arrived. It was six a.m., and I saw Brian standing at the top of the stairs. I asked him if he would make me a coffee. The cat was halfway towards the stairs, not knowing if she was going to be fed, or if I would go to bed. Brian went to get his robe, and I followed him upstairs. I said, "He's gone." He knew.

By seven o'clock, I had phoned my daughter, knowing she had to get ready for work, and told her the news. I woke her husband first and we chatted. I explained that Robin and I would not be doing a funeral until spring—this had already been decided. Jean–Luc said that Caitlin wanted to come now, but, with my brother arriving Saturday, we would cope. Jesse was to visit on Wednesday, and that would be great.

I had found that the time immediately after a death in the family was the easiest. With a long list of things to do, and comforting words of those one meets, there was a sense of purpose. When everyone goes home and the void begins to form where the loved one used to be—that was the most difficult. A funeral demands much time and energy. I would focus on that.

I made phone calls. I made an appointment with the funeral home for the afternoon; I gathered papers: birth certificate, certificate of marriage, legal documents, and so on. By nine a.m., the roofers were back. The cat was quite perturbed. Brian said she was quite worried about those BIG squirrels on the roof. She would sit there and look up at the ceiling with great concern. The banging of the roofers went on all day. It began to irritate me after some time. I mentally kicked myself. Here were these men working in sub-zero weather giving us a new roof. Eventually it was time to go into town for the errands.

Brian and I went into town for our appointment with the undertakers. By then Dad's body had been brought from the LTC to the funeral home. Brian went to the home and gathered up Dad's clothes for me while I met with Cathy, who was the funeral director. We planned out what we needed to do, determined which legal documents I needed to find, and I gave her a copy of the obituary notice I had prewritten with input from my brother. We wrote up a contract for services.

There was a set form, with lines for the various components of a funeral arrangement: consultation, fees, funeral home reception and supervision, procuring and completion of documents, embalming, shrouding, use of facilities, memorial stationery, visitors' register book, transportation, transfer to the crematorium, coroner's certificate, death registration fees, casket, and urn. I, as executrix, had to sign the contract. We priced various urns.

Then Brian and I went to see Dad's body and said our goodbyes. My brother chose to remember him as he was. He would be cremated immediately. That gave us time to plan the memorial service later in the spring. In hindsight, I shouldn't have gotten the register or the thank-you notes from the funeral home. The register was barely used. The thank-you cards were exorbitantly expensive and we had tons left over from Mom's funeral. I did not call all of Dad's friends — I assumed people would know from the announcement in the post office and the newspaper. This was a mistake, but I could not deal with speaking to any more people. I should have delegated the task. I always tried to do everything myself and should have reached out for some help. I was desperate to get everything over with and finish what I had tried to accomplish: assure Dad a death without pain and a burial with dignity.

More funeral preparations; legal requirements — Monday, February 19, 2007

Robin arrived later on. With big hugs, my brother and I began with coffee, chats, and fond memories. I had had insomnia and went downstairs to have a change of venue. I had awakened at 5:30 a.m. I prepared a fire and nestled into the couch with a blanket over me. Later we hustled to get ready, lulled into a slow start to the day. Robin and I went back to the funeral home.

Robin, the funeral director, and I went downstairs to see the other urn we had had our eye on since Mom's passing. We had noticed it at the time and thought it might be suitable for Dad. It was either that or the one with the painted slate cover with two loons on a lake, a spring scene. Mom's was a nice wooden box, with top made of slate and a hand-painted scene of winter. We looked at the one that had two hockey players carved into the side of the wooden urn. I thought that we could hang the two slate paintings in the cottage, after we interred them in the summer. We began to tromp back upstairs. I was in the lead, Robin and then Cathy behind me. We left the main room and turned the corner to go into the hall. I remember that I had my handkerchief in my pocket. I reached for it. As I walked, lifting the hankie to my face, something fell out of my pocket. As I walked I accidentally kicked it.

By the time we spotted it further down the hall, Cathy was beside it. She picked it up. She couldn't figure out what it was. It looked like something you would plug a hole with. It was a Rollo. It was peculiar, since I hadn't brought any with me. Brian had brought some to Dad last week. I had started eating them the night before Dad died as I sat in his room. They were in the basket we kept on Dad's dresser, with his hymn books and Bible and his straw bear. The outfit I was wearing was a long jacket that I had not worn in months, and certainly not to the LTC home. We were a bit spooked. I couldn't figure out how it had gotten there. I felt it a nod from Dad—that we were headed in the right direction and he was pleased.

We went to see the lawyer for an hour and a half. We went over the list of things we needed to do. We needed to sign papers as administrators, the legal term being "application for state trustee with will." Mom's estate still hadn't been tied up, but it should be fairly easy, since she had a will and it all went to Dad. We needed to list all of Dad's debts and assets, send the bill from the funeral home to the bank, transfer ownership of the van, change the van insurance and house insurance, file taxes for Mom and Dad for 2006, then for Dad for 2007. Once all that was done, the will would be settled and we could disperse assets and call it a day.

Well, it would take months; in fact, more than a year! We would need endless copies of the death certificate; many places would only make the required changes with an original copy of the certificate. I gave up on cancelling Mom's Sears card. I just could not be bothered. The funeral home arranged for the death certificates, as well as the certificate of cremation required for burial.

The mail continues — February 26, 2007

After a week-long visit, my brother left to go back home to British Columbia. I resumed preparations: a death notice was put in the Ottawa and Toronto papers on the weekend. I deliberately waited to post them until the weekend, when it was likely more people would read them. In the meantime, Brian and I trotted around town, doing errands, and we bought new fixtures for the cottage bathroom. I was uneasy and anxious while out. My hands became shaky. I was feeling unsettled. It was amazing how much of a physical impact the stress had on me. We went to the post office to pick up the mail, which was the hardest part of this process. The mailbox held several more sympathy cards. The death certificates had arrived, along with the bill from the funeral home. I had to figure out how to have the bill paid. The bank had frozen Dad's account as a matter of policy. I would see, as executrix, if I could have them pay the bills for me—another difficult chore I must tackle. I found that this part of the job of executor was the hardest. Mail continued to arrive for Mom and Dad. Letters would arrive and I would have to call these agencies back and let them know that Mom and Dad had passed over. It was part of the grieving process, as well as graciously accepting condolences from friends and strangers.

The house needed more cleaning. I managed to find the energy to vacuum. I was lethargic and uneasy. The bathrooms needed a good clean, what with daily use. I would have to wash my brother's linens, too. He left to go home, and while it was good to have him around, I felt uncomfortable having to play host. I certainly had not been able to grieve. There was such an emotional and physical reaction to being with Dad as he died. I flashed back, from time to time, to those last difficult moments with Dad. My psyche would put my hands up in front of my face for protection. I felt my stomach churn. I flashed back to the times when I fed him and looked after him. There were many times when he was angry and upset, and agitated and frustrated. Flashbacks are a big part of the grieving process. I tried to deal with them and carry on.

Paperwork and estate woes—March 2, 2007

I had not yet taken Dad's clothes to the Salvation Army store. That was a difficult task. I continued to collect my parents' mail and dealt with that on a daily basis. *Reader's Digest* thought Mom might win a billion dollars. That was the most heartbreaking mail—week after week they inundated me with large envelopes, her name boldly inscribed on them. I could not figure out how to make them stop until I finally found an address for a PR person. I wrote and demanded he make them stop. They must have killed a tree with all the paperwork they sent.

The lawyer called. I needed to identify the value of my father's assets. We had to figure out how much the house, the car, and Dad's assets amounted to at the time of his death. Most upsetting was that to do the simple paperwork of naming me executor, rather than my cousins who were named in the will, the government would suck back taxes at the rate of fifteen dollars per thousand dollars of assets. For the issuance of mere paperwork; I was appalled. Another tax grab on money previously taxed, since Mom and Dad did not have pensions — they had socked money away in investments. These were after-tax dollars as it was. What a waste of time (mine, the lawyer's, and his assistant's) and money!

Dreaming of love — April 10, 2007

This week of her grandfather's funeral, Caitlin had a dream. She dreamed that her grandma and grandpa had visited with her. As she hugged them in her dream, she could feel the texture of their skin. Caitlin has always been sensitive to the other world. My mom responded with the comforting words, "We'll see you there"; i.e., the funeral parlour. It was a comforting and a beautiful dream. Mom and Caitlin always had a strong bond. Mom would often "see" things. She foresaw my uncle's death, seeing an ambulance in his driveway just before he died. These incidents, while scary to some, were comforting to all of us.

Arranging the visitation room at the funeral home — April 12, 2007

Caitlin arrived with Jean–Luc for yet another funeral. Again, at the funeral home, she helped me set up the photos and memorabilia and arrange the potted spring bulbs, daffodils, and Easter lilies I'd bought. Our respective husbands went to the cottage to think through dinner. We had work to do here in town.

We brought little artifacts that told what Dad meant to all of us: the sign with the dog's name from the dog pen, his hard-earned degrees from summer school, photos and plaques from big events, and the community groups with which he worked. We debated over bringing Mom's ashes and I thought we should. She was going to be there, we knew. Caitlin's dream had told her! We set up the room and it looked lovely.[8]

We went out to dinner before the visitation. It was good to visit and bond as a family. Back we went to the funeral home with

---

8   For the photos see: **www.jilks.com/Ray**.

tummies full of good food; God bless those in the service industry, which comprises about thirty percent of the workers in our region. We were recharged and re-energized for another difficult emotional few hours.

At the visitation that night, good friends of Dad's, his look-alike friend, Dick, and Dick's wife, Beth, came to chat with us. They had visited Dad in the Manor from time to time. They told me that he kept asking them, "When is Jennifer going to come?" It was good to know that he needed me, remembered me, and wanted me there. I felt that I made a difference, despite the issues with which I had to deal emotionally. I had been told that the most important thing you can do for loved ones is simply to visit with them. The gift of your time and attention, while difficult, is profoundly important.

Retirement—September 2007

It was in July that I began to do my M.A. in Counselling Psychology. I spotted an ad in the paper for an on-line course, run from Fredericton, N.B., and thought that the information I could find on depression and bereavement would help me better understand myself. I had found it difficult finding support, our living so far from town. I did research on many topics and learned a great deal about the biological, psychological, and sociological issues related to depression, middle age, bereavement, and caregiving, all information I could use. Years ago, I had wanted to retire up here and write a book about education. Who knew that my diaries and records would be more useful to people like myself who had to shoulder the burden of caring for ailing seniors?

Summer approached and then passed by, as the seasons tend to do. The shoulder season in Muskoka is my favourite. We sat by the lake. No boaters. No screaming kids on tubes. Lazy cat languished by the shore. The ducks happily patrolled the waters seeking food for travel. They paused on our rock, rested, stretched, preened, and went back to work munching on greens, bobbing quietly, and with more of a sense of security than when they were tiny, since the fishers seemed to have lost interest. One remained on guard as the others reached for the bottom of the lake and the succulent weeds. These large ducks, formerly the downy ducklings I had eagerly photographed, were much wiser now and could escape the quick death that had taken their long-lost siblings.

There was a peace and beauty in the song of our wind chimes. The wind made the leaves dance in a chorus celebrating the new season. Many leaves had changed colour and had fallen in the dry spell that was August. Water washed up on the shoreline, adding a layer of rhythm to the dance. The lake had receded so much that the beach was greater than ever. The changing seasons always bring us a sense of security in knowing that the planet continues to move through its orbit. The light levels had changed. I looked out and saw that my garden no longer got the high noon sun as it did. I hoped my vegetables would ripen in time. The spaghetti squash was doing its best to complete the age-old process of seed, germination, plant, flower, and fruit.

I looked forward to the changing of the leaves and the new beginning. Life unfolded as it should. This was the first time in twenty-five years that I did not have to start preparing for the school year and begin to build a classroom community. It was bittersweet. There was an excitement to the first days of school; everyone on their best behaviour until the honeymoon was over. All of these new challenges help us to grow. I looked forward to what the new season might bring.

Healing and the grieving process — October 19, 2007

The work I had done at my father's LTC home had been noticed, and I was asked to participate in the Aging at Home Project. Each Local Health Integration Network (LHIN) was charged with finding appropriate regional responses to the issues of old age and the dearth of health care. Weekly I travelled to Orillia to work with some phenomenal men and women representing various stakeholders who served seniors: LTC; Alzheimer's groups; private, profit, and non-profit groups; medical professionals: a geriatrician, geriatric nurses, CCAC nurses; and so on. It was an interesting process and I learned a great deal about the health care system while participating in this project.

In regards to my psychosocial health, I knew that time healed all. It was getting easier to move around this place and deal with the little things in a day that had raised my ire a month or two ago. Small things in the past year would overwhelm me and cause me to cry. I forced myself to stop, regroup, and let it all go. New projects kept me busy. I could see, now, from my involvement with projects related to seniors and aging, how I had learned from all I had been through. I could see that now. It has been eight months since I lost my father; more than a year—nearly a year and a half—to grieve for my mother. Where does the time go? I still found myself wanting to take Mom photos to show her places we had been or to laud the achievements of her grandchildren. As I look forward to being a grandmother, I know that the circle of life completes itself, as it should.

The more I talk to others, the more I realize that things were not as they should have been in the final months. Mom denied all that was happening in an effort to not allow it to be so. I still feel regret that I was not here to help her pass over. She thought, I believe now, that I could not have handled it. Always, one had to remember that our children are our future. We need to model death and dying, as much as living. Our children need room to grow. The old trees fall over in the forest and leave space for the younger trees to grow and seek the light; we age and step aside for our young ones. We could prepare for it and encourage them to be individuals and to be independent. And, when it was time, we could let go and let them become adults and contributing members of society. It is in the giving that we receive.

As I prepared to go to Ottawa to my daughter's baby shower, I hoped I could pass on all I had learned. Another part of me wondered if I needed to. The lessons we learn are ours and are learned in a different age and time. We can do no more than provide roots and wings. The trees grow; they pass their time in the seasons of the sun, then, when we shed our leaves for the final time we know that others will follow. No one stands in the forest where and when and as I do. I would not shelter my children. I could give them shade and support. I had to trust and have faith.

Restless nights — November 15, 2007

4:00 a.m.

another sleepless night
the dark before the dawn
worries, fears, and sorrows haunting the shadows
they sit lurking in the corner
bedside lamp banishes the ghosts
dawn arrives
sun's soothing fingers massage the corners of my aching room
ghosts flee as the grace of daily obligation calls
cat burrows deeper into blankets

—J. Jilks

I woke from troubled sleep, a familiar problem for me. After I struggled with relaxation techniques, listened to soothing music, and read, I had troubled dreams of my parents, despite being well on the road to recovery in the grieving process. This morning I dreamed I was on my way to attend my Dad's funeral. In the wee hours, at four a.m., when I could not sleep, I had been thinking of the funeral plans we had made. In my dream, my hair was a mess and I remembered trying to use a blow dryer to give it some body. The hair dryer I picked up belonged to someone else and it did not work. I had no choice but to leave my messy hair, as the funeral was going to begin and I did not want to miss it. I drove through the entrance to the parking meters for the funeral home and did not put my five cents in when I should have. I had to hand it to the parking lot attendant. The peculiar thing about this dream was that in our wee town we do not have parking meters. I do remember thinking, before I slept, how so few people had attended Dad's funeral. In hindsight, I realize I had not phoned everyone as I had when my mom died. I still have guilt feelings about that. People were phoning me irregularly to find out about Dad's condition. But at this funeral, in my dream, there were many, many people.

We anxiously awaited the birth of our grandchild. She arrived in December of 2007. The cycle of life is simple and true. We look with hope to the future and the great possibilities that it holds for

our children and our children's children. There is dignity and responsibility in being the matriarch. I have seen and done much: lived,
loved, raised children, and had a career. I have been blessed in many
ways. The work I do in the field of aging would help others to have
better end-of-life care. I am optimistic that the future is bright, that I
will find a purpose and a new meaning.

December 9, 2007

My trip to Ottawa to see my grandchild confirmed the circle of life. I
have seen much more of my son Jesse, as he lives in nearby Toronto.
He brings his actor friends to the cottage, and we have wonderfully
inspiring visits from the young people in his cast and crew.

The situation of the aged holds a special difficulty for those who
have lost meaning in their lives. Loss of relationships (work, retirement,
or the loss of a parent or spouse), work productivity, financial conditions of retirement and old age, and the ensuing lack of mobility make
demands as we endure the aging process. With a loss of choice of home
and a limit on fun activities, a frustration can result that is palpable. I
try to keep active and motivated to participate in society. I adore the
outdoors and the fresh air of the country. I find that each day brings
more healing and a sense of peace. The next stage for me requires that
I develop some purpose and meaning in my life. By keeping mentally
active, one can offset the potential degeneration of brain cells.

I miss my parents, their unconditional love, living in the bosom
of family, and the deep laughter we all shared. I continue to wander
to the phone to let my mom know what is going on in our lives. I
believe she watches over us, as does Dad. I often feel chills in those
quiet moments of peace and stillness.

Victor Frankl, holocaust survivor and existentialist, wrote in
Man's Search for Meaning, "suffering fills the human soul and con-
scious mind, no matter whether the suffering is great or little." Frankl
quotes Nietzsche: "*He who has a why to live can bear almost any
how.*" During the past few years, I could not see the forest for the
trees. I had lost my purpose in life: my children, my parents, and my
work. My panic and inability to advocate for my parents resulted in
such anger and frustration. When one watches loved ones die with
death's lack of dignity, it is a painful process.

I sought some joy each day, as Mom and Dad diminished in cognitive and physical abilities. Their suffering I endured with helpless grief as I felt powerless to heal myself. I now take great joy in the small things in life. We have nestled into the routines and rituals in our community. Settled in, we participate in volunteer work in various facets of senior health care. We have reconstructed our lives in a meaningful way. Brian delivers Meal on Wheels. I work on several boards of directors. It gives meaning to our lives and a sense of purpose. We are there for the children again, despite virtually ignoring them for the past while.

Keeping mentally and physically active ensures the longevity of the heart, mind, and soul. For a time I lost my mind and my purpose. Immersed in Mom's and Dad's care, I did not know where to turn. In my depression I could not reach out. Mental health is based on reaching out for life, finding a purpose in your place here on earth.

I feel compelled to share my story. It is with great hope that I write of our journey.

Recovery from depression and stress
— January 20, 2008

As I recover from depression and grief, I continue to seek solace in nature. After giving up my career, my Ottawa home and garden, familiar colleagues, my old city life, and losing my parents, I take it slowly. Walking heals me. Today it was glorious out walking in the dusk. I kept an eye out for the wolf that appeared last week when Brian was speaking on the phone to Caitlin, my daughter, while I was out at work. He was gazing out the window while he talked and stopped mid-sentence, awed by the sight as it hustled by. I think it was looking for our turkey vultures that visit our feeders — it was the cycle of life. You could see its footprints in the snow as it trekked across the lake. The colours, the shades and shadows, as well as the creatures that continue to survive in the minus double-digit temperatures always stir me.

This morning, the blue jays were puffed up for warmth. I had filled the feeders last night — I knew it would be a cold night, ten degrees below zero or even lower, and they would be hungry. I counted five jays negotiating for a spot at the feeder. The squirrels, in that endless hide-and-seek game, had wee faces covered in snow as they doggy-dug, trying to first bury and then find sunflower seeds or peanuts. They were a hungry lot today, and I may give them all a second sympathy feed. The rest of us were on diets, but we don't have to live outdoors. I was glad for no yard duty anymore. Supervising inadequately dressed teens, hell-bent on jockeying for yard position, was no fun. I spend more time outdoors now, but it is my choice and I can move around, take photos, and explore nature.

I am so glad to be on the upturn emotionally. I still find it hard being in large groups. The winter was passing, and spring would come, just as it had for the previous fifty years of my life! I endeavour to get out every day to walk or do other outdoor activities. The Vitamin D is necessary for us old folks. I have been off meds for long enough to know that I don't need them right now, but I know that my doctor is there if I need him, and he is happy with my progress. Quitting antidepressants too quickly or suddenly can result in setbacks.

I had worked hard at doing my M.A. coursework: research to help me navigate through the past few years of depression and stress. I feel that I have made many gains. There have been days when I felt sad and tired, and re-experienced some of the warning signs of depression (sadness, anger, fatigue, inability to make a decision, and insomnia), but they are less frequent. When I recognize the warning signs, I make sure I work out more, get outside in the sun, take time for me, do something for myself, and it passes. What a relief.

In the spring, Caitlin and Jean–Luc brought our granddaughter for a visit. She was thriving in the joy and love of a wonderful home. We visit lots with Jesse, who lives the closest, in Toronto. I regularly communicate with Terry, too, and he visits from time to time. All have been grieving the loss of their grandparents. We often speak of the fond memories that we hold dear: trips to the cottage and trips to town; tons of photos and slides are on hand.

Part 2

The Perils of Aging and of Caregiving

— The Research

Major depressive disorder is defined in the *DSM-IV-TR* (the bible of the American Psychiatric Association, 2000) as characterized by a period of at least two weeks where a person has (a) a depressed mood and/or (b) loss of interest or pleasure in regular activities. Beery, et al. (1997) examined the changes and the effects caregiving has on elderly spouses. They are profound: spouses can experience traumatic grief, as well as depression symptoms.

If stress persists, there are chemical changes in the body. I could see this happening in me as I fought for Dad. These changes are not restricted to the body; they impact one's life psychologically and socially. In the research I did for my psychobiology course, I found that there were many signs of depression:

- Lack of interest in formerly pleasurable activities
- A change in eating patterns
- Changes in sleep patterns
- Feelings of worthlessness or guilt
- Energy level decrease
- Problems making decisions
- Thoughts of suicide

I experienced many of these symptoms in various stages. Depression can be brought on by an extreme response to life's normal passages (moving, a new job, childbirth, death of a loved one). I hit a lot of these milestones in one go! Depression could occur during the entire adult stage of life, but it was more frequently diagnosed in early adulthood with new challenges faced by those just navigating the path of adulthood, and less frequently in late adulthood as a healthy adult adjusts to life in society (Sigelman and Rider, 2006).

One of the things I had been told was that one must keep up exercising and releasing the endorphins, which provide emotional release. When you are under stress, your body releases chemicals. It is far better to exercise and release endorphins to help you maintain your health. According to the International Stress Management Association, our bodies release more than thirty different chemicals during extreme chronic stress. Now, as I look back at my journey, I can see how I was affected by the illnesses of my parents.

Avis (2003), in an attempt to determine the answer to the question of depression as it relates to perimenopause and menopause, concluded that these factors did not cause depression. The stage of life in which a woman finds herself: an empty nest (or adult children returning home), ailing parents, and other life passages, can cause a depressive reaction unrelated to the changing hormones (estrogen and progesterone). She felt that most studies examined patients, rather than the general population, and many women do not suffer from depression during menopause. Further examination found that the length of menopause and more than twenty-seven months of symptoms (hot flushes, night sweats, and menstrual problems) resulted in an increased likelihood of depression due to the effects of the symptoms, rather than from the condition itself.

Depression can be related to particular medical interventions, such as cancer treatments (Capuron, et al., 2002), open-heart surgery, and brain injury. The elderly are at risk due to life-changing circumstances, ill health, and as a reaction to changes in environmental circumstances (Alexopoulos, 2005). Disorders Association of Ontario stated that depression accounted for thirty percent of all disability in large companies in Canada. Employers were becoming more aware of not only the cost to the health care system but of the loss of productivity. Employers, including school boards and other large groups, are developing employee management plans to assist the employee in recovery and returning to work. This trend continues as the loss of productivity in employees becomes increasingly significant.

Pharmaceutical responses (pop a pill) by the medical profession do not address the underlying causes of this disorder, especially when it is due to bereavement issues. Freud's dream therapy could be helpful in assisting the patient in understanding her subconscious mind. Doidge (2007) cites work on recurring dreams, which contain memory fragments buried in the brain. Educating clients, providing research-based information and literature, and clarifying expectations regarding the progression of the disorder helps empower them to assuage fears of what is normal and what could be expected. I faithfully tracked my dreams and they gave me clues about my mental condition.

Caregivers are seldom looked after, as the health care system focuses on the ill care recipient and ignores the well-being of the caregiver. Health care focuses on the needs of those who are ill. The rules and regulations of family health teams do not take into account the needs of those providing care, whether spouse or family members. Alternatively, the focus must be on the family as a whole, in which the needs and wishes of all involved are understood to affect the treatment plans and outcome. To allow a frail caregiver to provide care to someone with dementia is a horrible, myopic way to treat a family. The financial outlay and number of hours of care need to take into consideration the family, as spouses on the borderline of becoming frail become ill with the responsibility of caring for others. Those who deliver home care to loved ones can experience cognitive, physical, and behavioural issues that result in emotional fatigue, a sense of feeling trapped, anger, or depression (Anhensel et al., 1995). Many care recipients are too ill to understand the impact of their ill health on their caregivers.

Interpersonal struggles between care recipients and caregivers, as well as disagreements between extended family members regarding care, predict anger and depression (Semple, 1992). Caregiving, whether the caregiver is a spouse, an adult child, or a grandchild, can lead to depression even when the ill care recipient is institutionalized in long-term care (Gaugler, Zarit, & Pearlin, 1999). Conflict is seen in families between spouses and siblings as a primary caregiver places a loved one in LTC.

There are rewards and benefits of caring for loved ones in the home, including feelings of being appreciated, opportunities to grieve and mourn, time to share special moments, and feelings of hope for the future (Burton and Merriwether–deVries, 1995; Emick and

Hayslip, 1999). The cycle of life is to be lauded and embraced. Providing care in a home setting in which familiarity supports the care recipient *and* the caregiver is a positive activity if easily accommodated and warranted.

Workplace stress results in thirty-five million workdays lost each year, according to the Alberta Mental Health Board (AMHB). Mental illness accounts for up to forty percent of short-term disability insurance claims and fifty percent of long-term claims. I knew I was not alone in feeling depressed. I knew that my situation was out of my control. My pressure at work was causing me more stress than I could imagine. It used to be a safe place where I could escape my worries over my father and deal with an incredible class of young people.

A 2006 publication by the AMHB states that many employees in the workplace reporting a "consistent level of stress" were twice as likely to become depressed. They go on to say that stress in the workplace has been narrowed down to these key factors: ". . . lack of control over daily tasks, office politics, lack of communication, inconsistent or unreliable performance reviews, work/life conflicts, lack of company leadership or direction, unclear job expectations, random interruptions, and unreasonable workloads." I knew I was well up on this checklist. I wondered back in September of 2006 if I shouldn't find someone to talk to, but I was worried, due to my former lack of success there, about having to go through the Employee Assistance Program (EAP) again.

The agony of the divorce process gave me much grief back in 1993. I took advantage of counselling through my workplace at that time. It made such a difference. As a caregiver, I should again have had counselling; once you experience a depressive episode, it gets worse each time and requires more effort to recover. The brain reacts in the same manner if you do not change your coping mechanisms and find positive means to adjust your response. Rabbi Kushner said, *"We need to get rid of the life we planned to prepare for the life that is waiting for us."* These are very profound words. He also said to *"liberate yourself from the tyranny of dreams!"*(Kushner, 2006)

My physical health continues to plague me. For more than three years, I have fought hot flushes. I often wake at around four or five a.m., unable despite all measures to get back to sleep. After a couple of hours of listening to my iPod, or doing meditations, sleep comes, and wicked dreams ensue, until 7:30 a.m. — as predictable as clock-work. I had several symptoms of menopause: increased facial hair, acne, inexplicable lumps; but the insomnia I attributed to my depression. My doctor suggested we deal with the depression first.

My research tells me that the depression, the menopause symptoms, and the stress are interrelated. I was referred to a compounding pharmacist, who suggested a saliva test for my various hormone levels. Apparently, while our Ontario Health Plan pays for a blood test, the saliva tests are more accurate, but quite expensive. Women secrete various hormones: estradiol, cortisol, testosterone, progesterone, and DHEA, all affecting us in various ways. The absence or imbalance of hormones leads to many symptoms: insomnia, weight gain, weight loss, fibroid tumors, thyroid complications, acne, irritability, and so on. I would suggest that we do more work in this area: connecting menopause with stress and depression. Hormone creams and supplements should be pursued by a woman's family physician. There is no need to lead the kind of life I have led over the past few years.

Those years of my life have taken their toll on me. Years of hot flushes have been the bane of my existence. A voracious reader, I read many books on parenting, menopause, sexuality, pedagogy, the aging process, cancer, and psychology. I liked to review the literature and glean what I could from various resources and try to do some self-help work. (As in many fields, such as education, health, and psychology, we do a great deal of research in North America, but we ignore much of it.) Currently, life expectancy for an aging Baby Boomer population is 78 years for men and 82.7 years for women (HRSDC, 2008). We need to incorporate these new data for these previously under-researched demographics. This puts new demands on the health care system as we face increased longevity. With seniors living longer and adult children facing the issues surrounding frail parents, much education needs to be undertaken in the areas of health, the management of ADL, and services to seniors.

Once outside agencies are involved, adult children feel better, yet they are not kept informed and have no right to intervene, nor to ensure that the level of care is appropriate for the senior. In our case, my parents were in denial about their ability to manage at home. We all suffered. My mother had dementia due to her medical interventions, yet I could not ensure that caregivers could enter her home to assist me and give me some respite care. She refused all help. This is not an isolated case. Intake workers are helpless to inform family members of the seriousness of the issues in the home: their inability to manage medications, to keep safe and clean, and to eat properly.

I have come to terms with being a retiree. I have learned to seek peace in nature and to accept my new way of life: waking with the light, not the alarm. Guilt-free, I acknowledge twenty-five years of spending the school year working around the bell or a buzzer every forty minutes. Still, when I pass a school, the bell increases my awareness, and as I listen to announcements on the PA systems I get the heebie-jeebies! It is a profoundly different way of life. No bells, carving a life from activities I choose to do, with only personal and little financial reward. We take our days much easier. I find some reward in working on my board of directors. I get some relief from working on the Aging at Home Strategies our regional health group has created in response to the need for more support for the aging in a rapidly aging society.

In *Mistakes Were Made*, social psychologists Tavris and Aronson (2007) write of the cognitive dissonance that occurs as we attempt to make sense of our lives. We recognize that decisions we make profoundly affect our cognitive and thinking processes. Our subconscious mind attempts to reduce this dissonance, or inconsistency between our actions and our beliefs. We try to convince ourselves that our actions were right in order to deal with our regrets. We downplay the negative and accentuate the positive as we make thousands of decisions each month. This kind of justification leads to theories of Mass Destruction, amongst other irresponsible behaviour. I have seen this at work in myself as I chose to leave a great career, house, and neighbourhood, to travel 430 km to a new life caring for my ailing parents. I often wonder what might have happened if I had not been here to help them prepare for death. Feeding my father every day extended his life, and I wonder at the propriety of this action.

We make the best decisions we can at the time, and I now believe that what I have learned, I can share. The importance of family and caring for one another trumps finances, location, and our professional work. On the other hand, as my mother lay dying I could do nothing for her and blamed her for not choosing to allow me to help. In discussions with my brother, I must come to terms with this useless ego action. I have to admit that my mistakes were simply mistakes: at times not doing enough and at others not letting things take their course. It is time to move on and let go.

The statistics of the senior years

We are living longer and contracting a wide range of illnesses. In comparison, in 1901, men and women could expect to live to ages 47 and 50, respectively. Most frequently seniors experience arthritis (44% of 65–74-year olds) and high blood pressure (40% of seniors). In addition, 79% of senior men and 84% of senior women have vision problems. One in ten seniors over the age of 75 need help with activities of daily living at home, compared to one in 100 individuals between the ages of 25 and 54 (Statistics Canada, 2006). Adult children, specifically daughters, deliver most home care assistance, although ailing spouses and neighbours help in many situations. Neighbours can become enablers as they cover for the inability of seniors to manage alone in their own homes. The quality of life in such situations is frightening, I learn as I speak with various private personal support workers and intake coordinators who identify the needs of frail seniors.

Without proper medications taken as directed, seniors suffer more pain than is necessary.

According to Statistics Canada (1997):

- 30% of seniors aged 65–74 years have pain and discomfort
- 37% of seniors aged 75–84 years have pain and discomfort
- 25% of seniors over 85 years will develop Alzheimer's disease
- 50% of seniors with dementia live in LTC facilities
- 39% of Canadians die in LTC facilities

Typically, seventy-five to eighty-five percent of home care is provided by family and friends, with a high proportion of spouses and adult children, who may be seniors themselves with their own health issues. The Canadian Women's Healthcare Network (1998) estimated that one in five women of ages thirty to sixty-four spend at least twenty-eight hours a week caring for someone chronically ill or disabled. Most likely it is a woman who takes most of the responsibility in assuring that a senior is cared for whether at home, in their home, or in out-side care (O'Rourke & Tuokko, 2000). Home-care assistance can be arranged for the care recipients and their caregivers, but it typically averages out at sixty-three hours per month, or 15.75 hours per week. This is not nearly enough support. Many organizations benefit from government funding in order to facilitate home care, but there is little information for the providers. Without a Patient Navigator to coordi-nate services and organizations, a caregiver can get lost in the system.

Oncologists

Especially, there is little information on what to expect of an oncologist. And which questions should we ask? Should we take notes? Should we take a family member or friend? The patient is entitled to a treat-ment plan to establish treatment goals and to understand the ramifica-tions of treatment based on age and comorbidities. In addition, with these goals of care in place, the patient needs to be monitored for medications. We need to ask if particular medications are effective; the dosage; the correct directions, if there are clinically significant drug-drug interactions; what the duration of the therapy will be; and if there are other alternatives (Holmes, et al., 2006).

Oncologists, especially, must be accountable to their patients to identify a treatment plan. Patients, or their caregivers, must ask the hard questions to determine whether the treatment plan will interfere with quality of life. Essentially, with seniors there are statistics that can predict the quality of the treatment, its impact on the patient and care-givers, and the probability of its success. A patient and family must assess the impact on the quality of life during and after treatment and determine the outside resources available if, for example, the patient is incapacitated by radiation treatment or chemotherapy. The impact of radiation can vary widely with patients, but one result of this treat-ment is the destruction of infection-fighting antibodies. My father was taken to emergency the day of my mother's funeral, and no one recog-nized that he had a prostate infection due to the radiation treatment.

Lymphedema

Unfortunately, no one told us about lymphedema, either. My mother had her lymph nodes removed to prevent the cancer from spread-ing (metastasizing) to other parts of her body. There are risks to this procedure. Once the lymph nodes have been removed, or damaged with radiation, twenty to twenty-five percent of patients develop lymphedema within twenty years post-cancer. This risk was not explained to her. Patients need to be warned that there are risks of blood clots, or back-ups of the clear lymph fluid in the skin tissues, which causes painful swelling. **Lymphontario.org** provides more information about this. Catherine Cotton (lymphontario.org) says that in order for such a procedure to be successful, there needs to be accurate assessment, a comprehensive treatment approach, and ongoing education and support for patients and their caregivers. This did not happen in our case. Our GP was unaware of these treatments, and I spent many hours trying to research solutions. Mom was in such needless pain due to this surgical intervention. I felt incredible stress, since I could not figure out how to help her. There is a huge risk of complications with this treatment and we were totally in the dark about its implications, despite research and the best practices clearly being available.

At some point, a treatment plan may need to become a palliative care plan. This is a crucial part of the process and must take into account the patient and his or her family. Unfortunately, my mother went to oncology appointments alone and may have had some dementia due to the invasion of her cancer. She had hearing problems, and I am not sure that she heard or understood what she was told. Information was withheld regarding etiologies, morbidity factors, survival rates, and consequences of medical treatment, especially associated with an elderly patient. Medical personnel did not ensure that a very deaf woman, in the aftermath and shock of a cancer diagnosis, understood the information presented to her and the treatments she faced. My parents were exploited by a system that did not take the extended family into consideration and failed to determine appropriate treatment for failing seniors.

Brain Tumours 101

Only after Dad was quite ill did I come cross a booklet he had been given called *The Brain Tumour Resource Handbook*. It is published by the Brain Tumour Foundation of Canada (BTFC: **www.braintumour.ca**) and it has a great deal of information on the structure of the brain, facts about brain tumours, the difference between benign

Lobes of the Brain

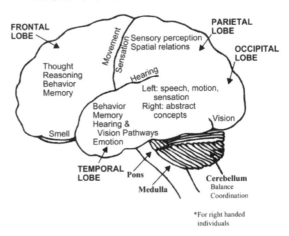

(Courtesy of The Preston Robert Tisch Brain Tumor Center at Duke, Durham, North Carolina.)

and malignant tumours, the difference between primary or secondary (metastatic) brain tumours, the grading system of brain tumours (they run from grades 1 to 4), the types of treatments, what to expect at the hospital, arriving home after treatment, nutrition, community services, and other items. They have a terrific on-line Powerpoint presentation called "Brain Tumours 101" that offers much of this information, with diagrams and photos to explain treatments (CAT Scans, MRI machine).

I will not delve into this information here, except to say that each type of cancerous growth, no matter where it is in the body, is graded by oncologists to determine the type of tumour cells, which then predicts the growth rates, the treatment, and survival rates. This system is based on the World Health Organization Classification of Brain Tumours.

These are questions that one can ask the oncologist: what are my chances of survival with and without treatment? What are the consequences and potential side effects of treatment? If a friend or relative has a different kind of cancer, there are many organizations that provide information on specific medical conditions, and you would be wise to consult these sources. Wikipedia presents some interesting photos and graphics as well.

My father's tumour was in the left frontal lobe, in the prefrontal cortex. It was a low-grade hemispheric astrocytoma and defined as an anaplastic (malignant) oligo-astrocytoma (mixed oligodendroglial and astrocytoma cells). It was surgically removed in early 2003 and returned in 2006, at which time he had radiation treatments that failed to reduce the tumour and give him more time. They told us in 2003 that they could not possibly remove all of the tumour (due to its location) and that it would come back eventually. He had MRI scans regularly to determine this. I knew it had returned, however, as he began to have symptoms in 2006: he could not retrieve nouns. (His tumour was located in the language area of the brain.)

In a study of long-term recurrence and mortality or survival rates of patients with astrocytic and oligodendroglial gliomas, Ohgaki and Kleihues (2005) found that the low-grade (World Health Organization grade I) astrocytoma median survival rate was 5.6 years, and the anaplastic astrocytoma grade II survival rate was 1.6 years, with 0.4 years for glioblastoma. For oligodendrogliomas, the mean survival time was 11.6 years for grade II and 3.5 years for grade III.

Dementia and delirium

Aside from the natural aging process, dementia and delirium in old age have many identifiable characteristics. Dementia is associated with, but not limited to, Alzheimer's disease, vascular dementia, alcoholism, toxic reactions to medications (a huge risk in seniors), infections, metabolic disorders, malnutrition, and brain tumours (Pinel, 2006). Dad could have been suffering from any of these things, but no one was able to help us diagnose it. There is some confusion between delirium, dementia, and depression, and these require clarification, as well as early diagnosis by geriatricians. In *The Hazards of Health Care* (Heckman, 2004), warnings are given for undiagnosed dementia and delirium. The May 2008 issue of *BP Blogger* explains the difference between delirium and dementia.[9] They say that it is the most common complication of hospital admission—between thirty and sixty-four percent in varying medical issues. One can have both delirium and dementia at the same time. Delirium is preventable and treatable; dementia is not.

---

9   See: **www.rgpc.ca**

Dementia is an abnormal progressive deterioration of neural functioning. It involves:

- Memory impairment
- Diminishing intellectual ability; confusion; forgetfulness
- Poor judgment
- Difficulty with abstract thinking, e.g., math, time, thinking skills.
- Personality changes, e.g., stubbornness, agitation, poor or inappropriate social skills
- Sleep disturbances

Delirium can occur in response to stressors such as illness, surgery, drug overdoses, interactions of drugs, and malnutrition (Cole, 2004), and can change daily. Between 32% and 67% of hospital patients are discharged with undiagnosed delirium (Rudolph and Marcantonio, 2003), and some 16% of seniors are readmitted to hospital (Forster, et al., 2004). It affects up to 50% of elderly hospital patients and can result in:

- Disturbance of consciousness
- Disorientation, wandering attention, confusion, hallucinations
- Increased LTC placements, infections, and increased mortality (Rudolph and Marcantonio, 2003)

Alzheimer's disease accounts for 70% of dementia cases and affects 5% of the population age 65 and over (Blazer, 1996 and Regier et al., 1988, as cited in Pinel, 2006). It affects 40% of those over age 90 (Williams, 1995, as cited in Pinel, 2006) and patients die, on average, eight to ten years after the onset of dementia symptoms. The number of Alzheimer's cases is predicted to increase by twenty-five percent by the year 2010 (Cummings and Jeste, 1999). Yet no one had examined Dad for these signs. Not all dementia is Alzheimer's disease, but the work done by the Alzheimer's Society[10] has provided much information on the signs that usually develop two to three years before dementia sets in, such as difficulty in learning and remembering verbal material. The first significant sign is memory loss. It affects simple activities: eating, speaking, recognition of family members, and bladder control. Callahan, et al. (1995) found that 23.5 percent

---

10   See **www.alzheimer.ca** for much research-based and practical information.

of those with moderate to severe dementia were identified as having a dementia syndrome.

Dementia: etiologies, risks, prevention, and amelioration

Dementia is defined as an acquired, persistent impairment in two or more cognitive areas of executive functions, which include the ability to control and regulate behaviours, receptive or expressive language, and memory. Executive functions include planning, organizing, sequencing, and abstract thought. Dementia results in attention, motivation, and depression disorders and other unseen risks to the safety of seniors.

It is caused by other medical and health issues (comorbidities) such as Alzheimer's disease, polypharmacy (more than four prescription drugs), metabolic issues due to hormonal imbalances, endocrine concerns (overactive or underactive lymph glands, infections), infarctions (blood clots, diabetes: tissue dies), or hormonal imbalances. Other biological causes include folic acid and niacin deficiencies, neurosyphilis, HIV, hypothyroidism.

Symptoms and biological consequences of dementia

The person with dementia is frail, defined as premorbid and at risk for biopsychosocial issues; there is an inability to fulfill physical, social, and emotional needs.

Twaddle, et al. (2007) believe that prompt referrals with planned admissions to the best settings ameliorate the need for placements in facilities such as intensive care units and promote early discussions in situations such as palliative care for greater clarification of treatment goals. They found that palliative care study patients were more likely to access medical care through emergency departments. These patients were discharged from American academic/university hospitals at a rate of forty-two percent without follow-up home care services, despite histories of severe illnesses.

This model of crisis intervention is replicated amongst the friends that I know. My father's discharge from the ER with a urinary tract infection after radiation therapy, with no diagnosis, in July, 2006, is a prime example of this situation.

Seniors do not like this term, yet "frail" paints a very complex and complete picture for family members and caregivers. Dementia can be caused by trauma (falls, broken hips) due to frailty, leaving the senior unable to perform ADL. Nutritional issues can then worsen the condition of an already frail senior. (An empty refrigerator is an eighty-percent predictor of problems with dementia.)

Dementia leads to an inability to communicate, and comorbidities such as infections, infarctions, or subcortical issues, such as plaque and damaged brain cells, will remain undiagnosed. For some seniors, aphasia (language disturbance), apraxia (loss of understanding of the uses of things), agnosia (failure to recognize objects), or affective disorders such as depression, Alzheimer's disease, or sleep disorders (insomnia or hypersomnia) can result in those who must receive more support than might be obvious to outside observers or even close neighbours. For some, impairment of the senses (hearing, vision, the olfactory sense, touch, taste) results in a quality of life that creates frustrations for both care recipients and caregivers.

A frail senior who has had surgery will have a higher risk of infections due to the immune system that is compromised, as well as to the frailty of skin and tissue. For those with delirium, drugs are purported to be responsible for eleven to thirty percent of hospitalized patients (Feil, et al., 2007). Nutritional inadequacies, such as a lack of vitamins or minerals, can result in dementia, and can be identified, or even prevented, with liver function tests and calcium, and glucose tests (Wenger, et al., 2007).

For those seniors who live in their own homes, it is my belief that family members must be contacted to provide them with information. My friend Kristin said to me, "Geriatrics or pediatrics: the only difference is body mass." We have the right as well as the responsibility as parents to care for our children. We regulate workers in day care and nursery schools. We must protect our children and advocate for them. Why is this not the same for seniors? Why do we not regulate long-term and private home care? Once an outside agency becomes involved in the care of a senior, privacy laws should not interfere with the rights of adult children to ensure that their parents' needs are being met.

Seniors are often placed in LTC due to dementia. Of those with dementia, fifty-five to seventy-seven percent have Alzheimer's disease.

There is a high correlation with depression (and caregivers as well are at high risk for depression). It can be ameliorated with improved social outcomes by cognitive screening tests and medical, behavioural, and social interventions. It can be prevented or lessened by these measures, but it will not be cured. It must be diagnosed by medical professionals who take a history of the resident within two weeks of entering LTC (Feil, et al., 2007).

Quality indicators for medication use in seniors demonstrate that seniors fill an average of twenty prescriptions per year (Shrank, et al., 2007). Once a senior has a need for hospitalization, he/she may be sent home with an additional prescription and might not think to ask his/her GP if he/she really needs these medications. In addition, those in LTC do not always have the benefit of seeing a doctor. An RPN may simply phone a doctor without any assessment or review of other medications. There are some lucky institutions with nurse practitioners who have the ability to prescribe medications, but health care is so closely guarded by self-serving physicians that many health care providers are finding it hard to access clients. Government legislation controls many providers of services: pharmacists, midwives, and providers of holistic services such as massage and reflexology.

Wenger, et al. (2007), recommends the clock drawing test, Beck's depression test, and medication reviews and adjustments, as well as other measures they call Assessing Care of Vulnerable Elders (ACOVE). The impact on seniors, their families, and friends in an aging population requires that we seek to identify more of the signs, symptoms, and causes of dementia, as well as other infirmities of the aging body.

Medications and polypharmacy

The Ontario Government recommends that seniors be monitored carefully to determine if polypharmacy is an issue causing more harm than good. H.M. Holmes and colleagues (Holmes, et al., 2006 and 2008) have done much research in this area. There are questions we must ask regarding polypharmacy. Many studies exist, but many more exclude seniors in their study population. Some have studied chemotherapy (defined as any prescribed chemicals) to better manage cancer in older patients.

Researchers show that cancer is related to the sequential muta-
tions of key genes that control cell growth. Cumulative damage, such
as exposure to carcinogens due to smoking or workplace risks, has
contributed to the incidence rates. In addition, as seniors age, their
defences are lowered and their immune systems become compromised. In a recent study (Balducci and Carreca, 2002), it was found
that the diagnosis of cancer occurs eighty percent of the time at or
above age fifty-five. Two-thirds of all cancer-related deaths occur in
those over age sixty-five, and they found that patients over the age
of sixty-five were less likely to be treated than those younger. While
advanced age is not a contraindication to cancer treatment, we must
be vigilant in determining the risk versus reward of treatment, based
on studies that tend not to include older patients. The toxicity of
chemotherapy presents great risks for those already frail, and dosages
must be carefully prescribed.

Caregiving in Canada

Caregiving has been related to both physical and mental health issues
and an increase in depression in several studies (Gallagher–Thompson
and Coon, 2007; O'Rourke, Cappeliez, and Neufeld, 2007). Depression rates in caregivers of terminally ill cancer patients range from
18% to 55% (Tang, Li, and Liao, 2007), with other studies reporting
high rates for various morbidities between 20% and 30% (Grov, et
al., 2005; Kim, et al., 2005). To promote the well being of caregivers,
interventions should address improving social supports for caregivers. Lack of social supports, such as counselling and respite care,
have been associated with increased levels of depression among caregivers (Redinbaugh, MacCallum, and Kiecott–Glaser, 1995).

The stress involved in caregiving relationships is exacerbated by
the age and health of the caregiver, the degree of illness or disability
in the care recipient, and the supports and outside resources available
to the caregiver; the effects can be: arthritis, hypertension, insomnia,
pain, stiffness, headaches, and hearing problems (Emick and Hayslip, 1999). There are limits to the ability of a caregiver to look after
both herself and her loved one.

Pagel and Becker (1978) studied the impacts of social supports
and self-esteem on depressive thinking in caregivers, finding that

caregivers with high levels of depressive cognition had high levels of depression only if social supports were low. They found a need for interventions with caregivers to alleviate stress by addressing social supports and controllable life stressors (see also Redinbaugh, Mac-Callum, and Kiecott–Glaser, 1995).

Caregivers tend to have work responsibilities (two-thirds work outside the home, according to the Women's Healthcare Network [1998]). They tend to have problems with being absent from work, which impacts their rates of pay, career advancement, physical and spiritual health, pensions, and long-term financial security.

Caring for ailing or disabled kin is an international situation. Schreiner and Morimoto (2003), in a Japanese study, found that persons with a higher sense of mastery, the degree to which caregivers believe they are not governed by forces outside their control, and their sense of efficacy, agency, and autonomy tend to affect their sense of control, and they have less stress and strain and depressive symptoms in contrast to Western caregivers (Morimoto, Schreiner, and Asano, 2001; Magai and Cohen, 1998).

With outsiders enabling my parents' transition from independent, self-directed individuals to totally dependent patients, my parents began to call upon friends, family, and neighbours to meet their IADL and ADL. The health care system failed us as my parents managed, in denial, to continue to live in a small town where they could not pick up their mail, mow their lawn, shovel snow, shop for groceries, or meet many other needs. When my mother was dying at home, no one gave me suggestions or support in finding respite care, hospice care, or any other resources that would help me help my mother. I ended up "retiring" early, with a huge cut in my anticipated pension, so I could look after these needs. I am not the only daughter or daughter-in-law who has had to change her life for this reason.

I would like to see the statistics that support an argument in favour of this approach. It is a faulty one. My parents did not want help from me; my mother prevented me from attending doctors' appointments, including those with the oncologist and the surgeon. She did not hear well, misunderstood what she was hearing, and avoided allowing me to help her and share the burden of her health care.

Patient navigator

The *Brant Long Term Care Best Practices Work Group* (2007) reference guide says that we have to be advocates for our family members. I tried, but could have used the help of a professional. For me, the solutions would have included a Patient Navigator who could assist a patient at a most trying time. It would include a family health team that would provide health care that integrates all the services and supports available to a family. When one person has cancer, or suffers the vagaries of old age, the entire family suffers. I really must hope that in the future the patient navigator concept will spread across the country. The American Cancer Society has such a program. It has been used for women with breast cancer, but needs to be initiated for all medical disorders.

It is important that we benefit from family health teams that can determine, plan, and coordinate care. Upon the diagnosis of a significant illness, the health system should include a patient navigator as the hub of the wheel. In 2001 in Nova Scotia, Joanne Cumminger spearheaded this concept (*Cancer Care Nova Scotia*, 2008). A patient navigator has many roles that make a difference in quality of life; he or she can:

1. Be a counsellor who can listen
2. Be someone to ensure that support systems are in place, with referrals to agencies such as the Canadian Cancer Society, the Alzheimer's Society, hospice care, respite care, adult day-away programs, palliative care, human and agency resources
3. Be an advocate for case management, assisting with the determination of treatment goals and the generation of questions for the oncologist
4. Help the patient or caregiver to understand forms, terminology, and pathology reports
5. Make sure ethical concerns are being met: is the treatment working? Is the treatment worthwhile and an effective use of time, patient energy, and resources?
6. Demand a geriatric assessment to determine quality of life. The effect of radiation on a seventy-five-year-old is different from the same dosage on a forty-five-year-old.

There may be other comorbidity factors such as infections that contraindicate treatments.

7. Have the appropriate education to navigate through the maze of tests, appointments, and treatments

8. Help with symptom management. Dad's radiation gave him a urinary tract infection, which was undiagnosed by the technicians and the emergency staff. A list of signs and possible side effects could have helped us understand what to look for.

9. Fight for adequate pain relief. There is no reason for someone to be in pain. There seems to be a fear of providing too much pain relief amongst RPNs, but once the pain is out of control, it is much worse and more difficult to rein it in.

10. Help to make arrangements for yourself and/or your loved one before the final days. The patient needs to let family members know what he/she would like to do. Dementia sets in fairly quickly, and without a reality check, you or your children can be in a panic. A living will, for example, helps everyone concerned.[11]

Our seniors deserve such a person. Adult children are often unable to provide support, as they are unfamiliar with the process and are emotionally involved. Seniors need a guide through the maze of the health care system. They could provide feedback to the hospital. This is the big gap in health care today. We take doctors at their word, but they do not know what is going on at home. Geriatric assessments are not completed, or followed up on by physicians, even when adult children request such supports. Dementia is an unseen, hidden disease covered up by those inflicted with it.

Intracranial pressure: symptoms

The Canadian Cancer Society research sent to me at my request stated that one result of the brain tumour was intracranial pressure (ICP). I know that Dad had shown these symptoms over the course of the eleven months after his tumour was re-diagnosed. The symptoms listed were:[12]

---

11   Compiled from Cancer Care Nova Scotia, 2008; Health Canada, 2002.
12   From the Brain Tumour Foundation of Canada, 2003.

1. Headache — often occurring early in the morning and made worse by coughing, bending, or straining
2. Nausea
3. Vomiting
4. Dizziness
5. Vision problems
6. Difficulty speaking
7. Confusion
8. Restlessness
9. Drowsiness and decreased consciousness
10. Trouble with coordination
11. Loss of muscle strength
12. Loss of the ability to move a body part (paralysis)
13. Seizure
14. Coma

Swallowing difficulties (dysphagia)

Swallowing is a complex process that involves twenty-six muscles. Swallowing difficulties are called dysphagia and they are a common result of neurological or neuromuscular damage. At the time, I had no idea that it was something to be expected. Large percentages of people with strokes, Parkinson's disease, and MS have this symptom. Those with structural damage included people like my dad, who had tumours. It is uncomfortable and frightening, as well as life-threatening, because dysphagia interferes with the oral intake of food and medications. *Long-Term Care Best Practices* said that up to seventy percent of residents on LTC had signs of swallowing problems. This could result in aspirations, choking, suffocation, dehydration, malnutrition, and decreased quality of life.

The Regional Geriatric Program publishes an e-zine called *BP Blogger* (the BP means "Best Practices"). One issue deals with swallowing. The Web site had a lot of information.

Signs of dysphagia[13]

- Coughing when eating or drinking
- Food or liquid spilling from the lips when eating or drinking

---

13   Reprinted with permission.

- Trouble moving food or liquid around in the mouth
- Prolonged chewing
- Trouble starting to swallow once food or liquid is in the mouth
- Clearing throat shortly after a meal
- Wet or gurgly sounding voice
- Complains of feeling that something is "stuck" after swallowing
- Shortness of breath during or right after mealtime
- Frequent heartburn or bitter taste in the mouth
- Unexplained weight loss
- Recurrent chest infections
- Refusal to eat or reluctance to have food in the mouth
- Pocketing food or liquid in the cheeks or holding food in the mouth

I had no idea that this was a common problem. It is too bad this information is not generally available. It would have explained my father's behaviour and assuaged my fears.

Canadian Cancer Society

The Canadian Cancer Society (CCS) has a wealth of services available to those fighting cancer, both human and print resources. They provided me with a peer volunteer who had gone through a situation similar to mine. They had also sent me some information on what to expect at the end of Dad's life. So much on the Web talks about care after treatment and does not provide details that would have helped me in predicting the end. I could tell that my mother was dying, although no one dared say it. There were many symptoms related to treatment: speech difficulties, communication disorders, seizures, lethargy, and depression, to name but a few. I wanted to face reality, but I had to respect my mother's right to denial. I am still trying to come to terms with her decision to protect everyone from her illness.

Geriatric assessments

Before discharge, a frail, elderly patient should receive a geriatric assessment by the health care staff. For my mother, with her medical complications (colitis, lactose and wheat allergies) and being a woman in her late seventies, with an ill husband, there should have been a physical, emotional, and social assessment of her care needs.

Clinical Assessment includes:[14]

1. Activities of Daily Living Scale
2. Instrumental Activities of Daily Living
3. Vision Test
4. Hearing Test
5. Polypharmacy: too many drugs
6. Safety of home environment
   a. Home lighting
   b. Shoes
   c. Uneven flooring
7. Balance and gait
   a. Timed tests (e.g., Get Up and Go Test)
   b. One-leg balance test for five seconds

Medical staff should be aware of a patient's need for help with Activities of Daily Living (ADL) or Instrumental Activities of Daily Living (IADL). Dad was incapable of caring for himself or my mother, and upon discharge, the nursing staff suggested that neighbours assist in their care. Such an assessment should be completed before discharge from hospital, in clinics, or at home by those charged with providing health care, including physicians and geriatric nurses. These assessments provide the means by which caregivers can determine a health care plan (Wenger, et al., 2007).

Activities of Daily Living include:

- Bathing
- Grooming
- Dressing (and undressing)
- Eating
- Transferring from bed to (wheel) chair, and back
- Mobility
- Bladder and bowel control
- Pain management

---

14   Based on Sherman (n.d.); also see: Regional Geriatric Program of Toronto at **www.helpguide.org/elder/geriatric_assessment.htm**.

Instrumental Activities of Daily Living (necessary for independence) include:

- Care of others (including selecting and supervising caregivers)
- Care of pets
- Child rearing
- Communication devices, e.g., telephone
- Financial management
- Health management and maintenance; medication management, getting Rx
- Housework: laundry, dusting, vacuuming, putting out garbage
- Meal preparation and cleanup
- Transportation: community mobility, shopping for food and clothes
- Safety procedures and emergency responses

Family members and ailing seniors

It is clear that family members face severe and potentially profound issues when caring for or advocating for family members. Unfortunately, many health care providers do not understand the various Health Care Acts that apply to both their clients and their families. Some of these include: Mental Health Act, Public Hospitals Act, Health Protection and Promotion Act, Long-Term Care Act, Occupational Health and Safety Act, Child and Family Services Act. Workers in health care continue to cite the Freedom of Information and Protection of Privacy Act (FIPPA) legislation when refusing to communicate serious and crucial safety information regarding those in their care. The Personal Health Information Protection Act (PHIPA) governs such workers. Yet, workers fail to communicate with adult children to inform them of the status of their frail parents' health. Health care providers and professionals have an obligation to inform family when they feel that seniors may be facing dementia, for example, which might put seniors at risk in their homes. This risk has an impact on the seniors, their neighbours, and the community, in that those who fall end up in hospital. Those who accidentally leave pots on the boil cause fires that tie up emergency services. Those who leave a tap on in an apartment cause flood damage to other residents' ceilings.

Dr. Ann Cavoukian, Information and Privacy Commissioner for Ontario, is on a personal mission to inform health care providers and professionals about their responsibility to include family members among those who are privy to the mental and physical health conditions of patients and clients. Health information custodians who collect, use, and disclose personal information can tell them to exercise judgment. In a conflict, PHIPA prevails over other Acts. This includes FIPPA. Health information custodians include professionals: licensed and unlicensed practitioners such as social workers, those working in LTC, or those who operate health facilities, pharmacies, laboratories, ambulance services, centres, programs, or services for community or mental health purposes.

Disclosure can be made for the purpose of contacting a relative, friends, or a substitute decision-maker for an individual who is incapacitated, injured, or ill, and unable to consent (PHIPA, sect. 38[1][c], p. 38) if it becomes necessary to eliminate or reduce a significant risk of serious bodily harm to a person or group (PHIPA, sect. 40, p. 40).

Frail seniors living on their own may be incapable of taking their medications at the right time. This is a serious risk to a senior. It is up to a health care provider to make the decision to inform family. Many family members may not understand that their ailing relatives are incapable of ADL or IADL when friends and neighbours are covering these duties. The risk of such enabling actions is great to both the senior and his or her family. Disclosure must be forthcoming to protect one and all.

Gulli and Lunau (2008) suggest that while the trend towards collaborative care is a positive one with family health teams in Ontario and Alberta, there simply are not enough health care practitioners to fill the need. Physicians are no longer willing to work the long hours or to make the house calls that used to be the norm in my parents' generation. Burnout is a huge problem, as much as the dearth of practitioners.

Quality of life and end-of-life care

Quality of life and end-of-life care policies in Canada are clear. The Canadian Bill of Rights guarantees the dignity and worth of every human being. The Government of Canada (2000) in its policy statement said the key mechanisms for improving the care of the dying include:

- Service delivery by interdisciplinary teams
- Access to services in the most appropriate location
- Availability of services when needed, whether for a few hours or around the clock
- Availability of services before death is imminent
- Services for a broad-based clientele, both with respect to cultural background and type of illness
- Awareness and skill in pain and symptom management
- Support for caregivers and family members

Access to such support varies and is dependent upon identification by family health teams, oncologists, general practitioners, and health care providers. My mother chose to die in her own home, on her own terms. She was uncommunicative and uncooperative and fought bitterly any health care support or interventions, due to dementia and complications from her cancer and her treatments. This is not an isolated case. It was a horribly difficult time, and I have not yet fully recovered from advocating for both of my parents. We had a wonderful relationship up until that time, but something happened to our family dynamics when the prognosis of cancer was made, treatment ensued, and both of my parents became ill. When dementia sets in, one's faculties begin to deteriorate. The caregiver, as much as the care recipient, needs to have emotional and physical support.

With many profit-oriented long-term care institutions around, many improvements are required. The Long-Term Care Act of Ontario is intended to improve the delivery of services in an institutional setting. Unfortunately, it is not nearly enough. Incidents of violence and abuse are legion. The private institutions do not have proper protocols in place to ensure that our seniors have access to adequate mental or physical health care. Most settings have difficulties keeping and retaining staff, which has the most profound impact on quality care. This situation affects the delivery of all services, such as the availability of staff to take residents to the toilet, to change adult diapers, to do housekeeping and laundry, and to provide adequate and timely delivery of supplies such as toilet paper and tissues.

How does one know where to turn? Doctors do not have time to help you wend your way through the system. We need people to listen to us, to explain the medical terminology, assist with making and keeping appointments, support us, give assistance with child care, transportation, lining up tests, determining a plan. This does not happen in Canada in all instances, especially in long-term care homes. Patients are discharged from hospitals with more medications than ever before. These medications require monitoring.

Conclusions and Recommendations

Whether our seniors require eldercare in the home or in long-term care, there are many issues that create barriers to success. If we keep our seniors at home, they are happier, and often healthier, but more at risk psychologically, socially, physically, and emotionally. Caregivers themselves run the risk of burnout, with its attendant physical and psychological effects. Some profit and non-profit agencies provide respite or day-away programs for senior care. This alleviates the burden of providing the quality of care that our seniors deserve. In many cases, however, if outside agencies are accessed to recruit home care, we run the risk of hiring people who are untrained and unlicensed in caring for those with complex morbidities, exacerbated by complications of complex prescriptions, physiotherapies, emotional complications of dementia, or other biopsychosocial issues.

The difficulty with parenting has been that many parents have passed through a laissez-faire phase in which the child was allowed to flourish and thrive. I remember in Grade 7 we were to self-select learning activities, with little direct guidance from the classroom teacher. I learned very little in that class and became frustrated. This philosophy of parenting had to be changed; many books were published to teach us how to say no to our children. Rabbi Shmuley Boteach offers a show called *Shalom in the Home*. He is re-educating parents in how to be fair and firm. He is teaching parents to give unconditional love with the right hand and discipline with the left. Both are necessary.

In my experiences with family and friends, I have heard endless stories of adult children who are unable to say no to frail and ailing parents. It is a reversal. Adult children have to lie and deny in an attempt to protect themselves from their parents' wrath.

Frail adults refuse the help of outside agencies, whether or not money is an issue. It is the less frail spouse who suffers. One fifty-year-old daughter, whose mother had survived breast cancer in her seventies, is trying to persuade her father to allow people to come in to help them. When he falls, the mother cannot pick him up. The mother is now fighting high blood pressure with the stress of caring for this ill man. Tough love is a concept that must be applied to adults as well as children. In this situation, it should not be up to one spouse to refuse care if family members determine that there is a need.

One family, whose father lived in the family farmhouse as he had as a boy, promised their father that his stay in the long-term care home would only last a month. They are now using more excuses to keep him in. He doesn't like his roommate, who turns up the TV too loud, and is fighting to keep his old life. Frail and ailing adults deny that they are unable to stay in their homes; they experience falls and break limbs, which land them in an LTC home. As seniors, we must make adult choices or we will not be treated as adults.

Our favourite librarian, Mari, who kindly delivered books to my mother, told me that she tried to persuade my mother to get some help with ADL. She offered to put my parents on the Meals on Wheels program, which my father and my husband delivered. Mom would not buy into any of this. Only old, sick people needed home support!

Caregiving in the home

For family caregivers responsible for seniors: remember to breathe. You are no good to anyone if you cannot breathe. Caregivers need quality of life assessments, especially for the frail spouse who is a caregiver. Demand that your doctors provide assessments and consider home support. Reassess the polypharmacy situation; contact your pharmacist for help in ensuring that prescriptions are necessary; some may even be contraindicated.

Another issue arises for seniors cared for in their own homes by outside agencies or hired professionals. They are at risk from workers, such as PSWs who can prey on them physically, emotionally, and financially. The 2007 Sue Grafton novel, *T is for Trespass*, is a mystery novel about ailing and vulnerable seniors. It demonstrates the vulnerability of seniors to those who may prey on them in their own homes. Our society has moved from a nursing model of care (nursing homes) in which the majority of staff were highly trained nurses with experience in dealing with seniors who have resistance, denial, anger, and chronic diseases and exhibit mobility and lifting issues, as well as complex pharmacologies. Only nursing staff, or those with special certificates, are legally allowed to administer medications.

Eldercare in Canada is currently an unregulated industry. In what we now call long-term care, the majority of staff are unregistered and untracked and may or may not have PSW qualifications. Whether a PSW works in the home or in a profit or non-profit agency, he or she can move from employer to employer if fired or prove to be inadequate or abusive. No controls are in place, as there are for preschool and home caregivers for children (nannies). The British system of training nannies who care for young children has an international reputation. However, those applying from other countries can forge documents and recommendations, which an unsuspecting family or agency might not think to investigate.

We are unaware of foreign practices, yet Canadian agencies continue to recruit and hire absolute strangers to live and work closely in Canadian homes with our loved ones. The agencies that hire do not keep in mind that many of our seniors are very big, and foreign workers can be small and cannot possibly lift them. However, PSWs do not necessarily have training in physical therapy, chronic diseases, and mobility and lifting issues. In Canada, with a minimal fourteen-module PSW course, there is some standardization of practices, yet without having a central registration system we have no way of knowing the type of education a worker has received, his/her previous employers, and his/her official credentials.

Strained family relations

My cousins and I were talking through e-mail. I had asked for some help in convincing Mom and Dad to hire someone to renovate their main floor two-piece bathroom. Neither of them could navigate the stairs well and, once home from hospital, could not make it up the stairs easily. One cousin asked when would be a good time to call, as she couldn't seem to get them on the phone. I explained the nap routines: Dad often slept all day, while Mom would take her hearing aids out and nap, too. I could not ever contact them by phone after they went upstairs to bed at their regular eight p.m. bedtime.

Once she managed to contact my mother, my older cousin, with experience in arranging care for her parents, suggested that we hire a live-in caregiver. They had done this and had hired a Filipino woman. I didn't feel comfortable with that as an option. Mom was not in favour of any support, I could not afford it, and many of these workers face extradition if employers do not renew their employment; nor do they necessarily treat them well.

There are agencies that publicly advertise for foreign workers on behalf of such people. Unfortunately, they are not paid well, we can assure no credentials, and there are no standards that govern such workers. Training in other countries, as with other educational systems in undeveloped countries, does not necessarily stand up as well as ours. In addition, hiring workers from other countries does not ensure that they will be able to adapt to our culture, provide the standards of care to which our seniors are entitled, and do all of the mobility and respite care, ADL, and IADL that are required for ailing seniors. In addition, seniors are vulnerable to being victimized physically, emotionally, and psychologically, and are financially vulnerable to those providing them with care.

It is often difficult for extended family members to agree on the type, quality, and level of care that elder family members should be receiving. I have heard of many situations in which disagreements between siblings occur over the care expected to be delivered to a parent. I found that my cousins were quite free with their advice, but much of it was not useful to us. When we chose not to take their advice, or tired of what we perceived as interference, we faced alienation. It added to the difficulties of a stressful time. All of our family relations between our cousins and one aunt who visited my father have ceased. As Maya Angelou says, you make the best decision you can at the time, and, whether right or wrong, you must make choices that are not always respected by others. But make them you must.

I think there are other solutions to the lack of trained staff. There is a Children's Aid program called Kinship Care. Relatives of children who must be in care are given responsibility for their nieces and nephews, for example. Why can we not facilitate such a process for aging relatives who might not have children who are able to care for them? Many seniors cannot afford to live in retirement homes, or pay for outside services, which are few and far between in rural areas. Frail seniors can be adopted by family members, adult nieces or nephews, or even by self-selected neighbours. There are many both profit and non-profit agencies, such as the Red Cross, to call upon. Money could be set aside to ensure that those aging can age at home with proper measures in place. These seniors can be adopted by friends who can act as patient navigators or simply do some light housekeeping, keep in regular contact, put out garbage, take them to appointments or the library, or pick up mail, perhaps with a small financial remuneration that would help the senior maintain his or her dignity. This would keep a senior healthy and monitored, and reduce the risks of remaining alone in the home.

Caregiving by outside agencies and support workers

Ask for information and request that your loved one be placed on a pharmacological registry to coordinate prescriptions and identify contraindications. Visit or phone the LTC at different hours. You can be proactive by identifying issues that affect a senior's mental or physical well-being, such Sundowner's Syndrome.

Health care professionals provide more specific care, and more reliable, well-documented care for infants and children than for seniors, and yet it is our seniors who are more susceptible to the ravages of age: disease, frailty, decreased range of motion, nutritional complications (difficulties with oral hygiene, anorexia, obesity), heart disease, elevated blood pressure, dementia, incontinence, polypharmacy (which can cause nausea and confusion), and depression. How many of our seniors have been attended by a geriatrician? How many of our infants and toddlers have visited a pediatrician?

Geriatricians are the lowest paid of physicians, and yet they seem to be the ones with the most complex cases that require much more time and energy, as well as expertise. More often than not, a senior will have little or no contact with a geriatrician. It is the physician who needs to be screening for physical, social, emotional, and mental health issues such as dementia. There are many ten-minute dementia tests: three-item recall, animal naming (Solomon, et al., 1998), or the clock test (Watson, 1993), to name just three. Even lawyers have a ten-item test for cognitive functioning, absolutely crucial to determine competence. In the animal test, the norm is to name eighteen animals in a minute. If a senior cannot name twelve, this indicates an abnormality. A fourth simple test is the number of IADL with which a senior requires help.

Onmemory.ca has a number of pointers. This Web site counsels family members to watch for signs such as seniors' repeating themselves, or asking the same questions over and over, becoming more forgetful (issues with short-term memory), needing reminders to fulfill ADL or IADL, depression, problems with calculations, finances, getting lost, or misusing expressive language, especially nouns.

It is predictable that a senior will have deterioration in hearing, eyesight, mobility, memory, range of motion, or cognitive abilities. These are all issues that must be addressed by caring family members, often to the detriment of their quality of life. Seniors who live alone or who have lost a spouse pose great risks to themselves, with a concomitant gradual lessening ability to manage their ADL or IADL. With the inability to perform four or more IADL, seniors are at a high risk for illness, injury, or hospitalization. Another good predictor of ill-health is an empty refrigerator (Alexopoulos, 2005). In this study, 31% of those with empty refrigerators were admitted to hospital in four weeks, compared with 8% of those with filled refrigerators. Of those surveyed (132 seniors, mean age of 81, 74 % female, 70% lived alone), those with empty refrigerators were three times more likely to be admitted to hospital.

Placing a senior in long-term care

This is a huge decision, not taken lightly by caregivers or their family members. Those who are not providing the care may disagree with the decision, since they do not understand the psychosocial impact of caring for a loved one at home. Many families report disagreements with this decision. It is up to the family to assess the risk of home care versus a private, profit, or non-profit setting.

Preparing for a move is an emotional time for both residents and caregivers. You may feel guilt in placing a loved one in care. The care recipient may feel anger, and your siblings may not agree with your decision. There is much to talk about and emotions to explore. We tried to ease Dad into the idea, but he was beyond reflecting on our inability to take care of his physical needs. Dad kept suggesting that we live with him at the house, despite our two cats, who are afraid of dogs, and despite my full-time job. It was such a battle to get him to come to terms with the move. We reiterated that there was no choice.

For those living and dying in long-term care facilities, they can pretty much bargain for a certain amount of anxiety, depression, and loneliness (Caprio, et al., 2008). To be removed from one's familiar surroundings and to be placed in a building full of "old, sick people," to quote my father, has a huge impact on quality of life. For those unused to institutionalized care, they face many risks and changes on psychological, physical, and emotional fronts that have an impact not only on them but on those who are their caregivers.

Often, being placed in LTC means that a senior will no longer have control of his or her life. Ninety percent of the residents in Dad's LTC home had been deemed incapable of decision-making through power of attorney. They must eat when told it is time; they must eat food that may or may not be palatable, or may be culturally different than what they ate at home. They are no longer in familiar surroundings. Their friends, the ones who are still alive, cannot visit easily. They lose their freedom and privacy and can no longer have their belongings around them, as security of personal items is a difficult thing to manage in LTC.

Physical and emotional pain, a result of loss of hearing and vision, failing systems, breathing issues, and anger issues, exacerbate the situation of a senior in LTC. There is a pattern of violence and violent behaviour in some situations that can be due to an increasingly complex pattern of comorbidities and the various ailments that prey on a senior.

The differences between a retirement home and a long-term care facility are in both the governing body and the access to nursing care. A retirement home is governed by the Landlord-Tenant Act and an LTC home is governed by the applicable LTC health policy of the province. The Ontario Ministry of Health and Long Term Care provided us with a lot of information. They have a publication called *Accessing a Long-Term Care Facility*. It is important to tour the agencies and ensure that they have sufficient staff and a well-run organization with a strong Family Council.

The facts you need in order to compare facilities include:

- Proportion of residents to staff
- Length of the waiting list
- Location and transportation to shopping, field trips, and health care
- Room features: size of rooms, privacy, phone or cable service, security for personal belongings, furnishings
- Number of professional care staff, e.g., RPNs, RNs
- Number of support staff such as personal support workers (PSWs)
- Meals: whether varied and appealing; flexible mealtimes; whether culturally appropriate
- Lifestyle: smoking policy, alcoholic beverages, cultural values, dietary needs, special needs
- Access to additional health care personnel as a disease requires
- Visiting policies
- The type and amount of activities
- The ability to take a resident out for a meal or an outing
- Emergency health care
- Restraint policies
- Individualized care
- Quality of care: check out the compliance reviews and accreditation reports (from: Canadian Council on Health Services)
- Available Health Care services: physiotherapy, occupational therapy, foot care, hair care

In hindsight, from the research and recommendations from professionals, I should have packed more simply when we moved my father. All of the items need to be labelled, too. I still cannot remove the industrial-strength labels they hermetically sealed to Dad's blanket, for example. A new resident needs toiletries, a housecoat, slippers, a pair of running shoes, four pairs of pyjamas, and six changes of clothes, e.g., six undershirts and pairs of underpants, six shirts, and six pairs of pants or jogging suits. All of these places offer laundry services, and this is all that would be needed. Also important: a sun hat, a winter hat, a couple of sweaters, and a seasonal coat. There is not a lot of storage space available, and many personal items, clothing included, are susceptible to disappearing forever.

Once your loved one has been admitted to an LTC home, demand regular case conference meetings. Ask about and demand geriatric and pain assessments. Ask about a treatment plan. Ask that care recipients and family members get any support that is available. Advocate and don't give up. Go to doctors' appointments with your family member. Ask questions! The ravages of old age affect the whole family, and everyone has a right to be aware of the treatment plan and prognosis. Plan ahead, but get today's answers and take small steps one day at a time.

Residents' rights and needs

It is the right of the resident to be free of pain and to be treated for the typical symptoms of being in residence in a long-term care home. Many self-care assessments exist. The Edmonton Symptom Assessment System (Bruera, 1991) is a simple 1–10-point scale with which a resident, caregiver, or medical professional can systematically assess depression, anxiety, fatigue, drowsiness, and general well-being in order to determine the needs of a resident and to improve care. This assists the caregiver to determine whether a care recipient is declining in health and helps him or her to determine whether other courses of action should be undertaken. It is a simple, effective monitoring device that will ensure that the resident is getting the best possible pain and symptom management. I used it on my father in the latter stages of his ill-health, and it motivated me to seek more pain medication.

The Cancer Society publishes numerous materials, freely available upon request, and Dad had a handbook that gave great details on the brain and brain functioning, but I do not think he was sentient enough to understand it by that point. I don't think Mom read it, either. Any information on cancer I gave her she seemed to almost ignore. At **palliative.org**, one can find several assessments, including a "Cancer Care Assessment Team Conference Summary." This provides a wide range of signs and symptoms a caregiver, whether personal or professional, should monitor in the course of a day. It includes pain, nausea/vomiting, nutritional needs, incontinence, constipation, mobility, risk of falls, skin breakdown, cognitive issues, substance abuse, edema, and spiritual, emotional, and family adjustment issues. All of the symptoms require monitoring by the health care team to ensure swift and adequate management.

Signs of impending death

Signs of death are common to many illnesses: lack of appetite, lethargy, increase in time spent sleeping, vision problems, decreased urine output, refusal of food, liquids, or water, gurgling sounds, periods of apnea (stopping breathing), cool skin, high temperature, withdrawal, change in care recipient's character, or the performance of restless, repetitive tasks (Heart's Way Hospice, 2006).

After death, the pulse stops, breathing and the heart stop, and the person's eyes become fixed, with his/her eyelids partly open. Dad spent the better part of his last two days with his eyelids like this. It was frightening not knowing that this is what could be expected and that it was a clear sign of approaching death.

One issue that concerned Elisabeth Kübler–Ross was that in some palliative care situations, the care recipient seems to hang on longer than appears possible, and well beyond that which doctors have predicted. While individual situations vary, she wrote of those times when those who are deathly ill are quite worried about those who will remain. They may be reluctant to let go. It is wise, she told us, to let the care recipient know that all will be well, and that you, as family member or friend, can manage. I did this for my mother-in-law in her final days after chemotherapy. She ended up in the hospital after her treatments in 1985, when her husband had heart attack number nineteen while trying to care for her. She had lung cancer, it had metastasized to her lymph nodes and spread to form a brain tumour, yet they chose to give her steroids and chemotherapy. It was a rough time for all of us.

While my father was in his final days, despite the fact that he could not hear me in his physical body, I knew that his emotional body needed to know that it was okay to let go. I told him that my mother was waiting for him and that he needed to find peace. I felt better for it and he let go a few days later.

The Residents' Bill of Rights in Ontario LTC

In Ontario, a Bill of Rights became law in 1987. Two groups (ACEL and CLEO, 2005) have published a Resident's Bill of Rights. This Bill of Rights must be posted in every LTC home. The same is not true for a retirement home. The Bill of Rights includes language describing:

- The right to be treated with dignity and respect and to be provided with proper physical care, food, and clothing
- The right to know who will provide medical and physical care
- The right to be afforded privacy in treatment and to have personal possessions and furnishings
- The right to be informed of medical conditions, treatment, and proper course of treatment
- The right to refuse treatment, to participate in decision-making regarding treatment, and to have private medical records
- The right to participate in activities and to be fully informed regarding restraints
- The right to visitors received in privacy and to have a twenty-four-hour family presence during palliative care
- The right to pursue social, cultural, religious, and other interests
- The right to be informed of changes in laws, rules, or policy
- The right to manage one's own financial affairs
- The right to live in a safe, clean environment

Visitors to family and residents in long-term care

One thing that brings joy to a resident is a visitor. The purpose of visiting is to provide social, physical, spiritual, or intellectual stimulation to someone living in long-term care. It can be a difficult situation for both care recipient and visitor. Shorter, frequent visits may be more suitable for the resident, depending upon his or her state of physical or emotional health. Do read up on a resident's condition or disease, if appropriate. It pays to understand cognitive or communication issues that may impact your visit. There are many publications by The Alzheimer Society that provide information for general conditions such as dementia.

It can be difficult for a visitor to see a loved one or friend with diminished capacities, but the visit brings so much to the resident, whether or not he/she provides you with evidence of this fact. I was only told later that often my father would ask for me or for my late mother. Even if communication is difficult, you are making a difference in their lives. For seniors who have lost older family members and similarly aging friends, seeing someone they love and have known brings ease to the difficult routines of daily life in long-term care. The resident misses familiar surroundings and routines. You can be a constant in their lives. You can, at least, listen to him or her.

When visiting friends and family in long-term care, there are many things you can do. It is a time to share memories and celebrate a life well lived. Having a chat and reflecting on the good old days can be a positive event. Phone ahead and plan an activity or a meal with care recipients in LTC. Many activities occur in LTC, and you can help a loved one or friend better participate in the process. You can take her a hot meal that you can eat together. It is a special treat to break bread with those you love. It shows that you honour their spirit and their life.

Find photos of familiar people and places. Looking back over shared experiences brings much joy. While it is hard to recall what we ate the day before, often distant memories are more clear for those whose bodies are fighting illness or old age. Take in newspapers, magazines, or talking books. Go to a bookstore and find a book or a magazine your loved one might find interesting. Read it to him. Often small talk is difficult. Simply listening to someone read is a relaxing, gentle time of sharing. Take in an emery board to file her nails. Take her for a walk or a stroll. Read stories or letters. Of course, all this was impossible for me and my father, due to his hearing loss, but they can be a valuable activity for those not hearing impaired. "Bring and brag," as I used to call this activity as a kindergarten teacher. If you collect something (postcards, photos, spoons), take those in to show him. Bring in photo albums to remind him of loved ones.

If she is able, bring a deck of cards or a board game. Take her out for a trip or a walk, if possible. If she had hobbies, try to find something that she can do with you. Some LTC homes now have a Wii. This is an interactive, physical video game. The player uses a wand that mimics a sports instrument such as a tennis raquet or bowling ball, and allows you to physically pretend to be playing the game. It demands eye and hand coordination and encourages some exercise on the part of the participant. It has proven to be a great stimulant for those unable to participate in regular physical activities.

It provides an approximation of particular sports: tennis, bowling, and golf. It can be a fun way to interact with a senior incapable of some of the more physically demanding entertainments.

Buy a guest book and sign your name, write a message, or write a message for the senior's loved ones who may need your support. When dementia sets in, it is the caregivers who most need you and your time and energy.

Plan ahead and phone the activity director to determine if there is a planned activity you might attend with your loved one. When my dad was first placed in the retirement home and then in the LTC, he was really upset and angry and refused to participate in anything. Eventually he came around, but with a little encouragement you can help out and participate. Many institutions have barbecues, parties, celebrations, Remembrance Day-type memorials, bus trips, or boat tours. Finally, take a book or something for you to do if your loved one is tired during the visit, or is busy with therapy or personal care. Silent companionship may be called for as well.

Family health teams and bioethics

Middle age and old age is a time when the body begins to break down, and medical issues arise that plague an individual who is used to good health. Breslin, et al. (2005), stated the top ten ethical issues that confound health care in Canada:

1. Disagreement between patients, families, and health care professionals about treatment
2. Waiting lists for treatment
3. Access to needed health care resources for the aged, chronically ill, and mentally ill
4. Shortage of family physician or primary care teams, both rural and urban
5. Medical error
6. Withholding/withdrawing life-sustaining treatment in the context of terminal or serious illness
7. Achieving informed consent
8. Ethical issues related to subject participation in research
9. Substitute decision-making
10. The ethics of surgical innovation and incorporating new technologies for patient care

These are all identified issues unresolved in health care. Many of these issues affect the elderly. The more things change, the more they remain the same. The lack of health care professionals has a huge impact on those with breakdowns in their skin, with mobility issues, or with previously diagnosed mental and physical issues.

There are three things I suggest to families regarding their health care: be active, reactive, and proactive. Never let your aging senior go to doctors' appointments alone. Do not trust that the resident LTC physician can manage your loved one's case. Ask questions, do the research, and meet or talk to the doctor regularly. Ask for an annual health care plan. Those in the medical profession are too busy; they cannot devote enough time to the complications facing ailing seniors at the best of times. With one million people in Ontario, in a population of ten million people, without a health care professional (*orphan patients*), and many seniors retiring to smaller communities, seniors are hard-pressed to find a family physician (FP). Those lofty ads for retirement communities do not mention the lack of health care you can expect as the norm in Canada. A 2005 open letter by Dr. Val Rachlis, the then president of the Ontario College of Physicians and Surgeons, tells us that his research shows that sixty-nine percent of his College members have closed their practices to new patients. The numbers of retiring physicians have added to the complications of access to health care by seniors. They are simply not being replaced by either new grads or immigration. (But that is a whole other discussion!)

Dr. Michael Rachlis's work in the area of health care calls for changes to public health policy in order to accommodate the vast numbers of seniors who will likely experience chronic care issues in the near future. Chronic diseases account for 70% of all deaths, 60% of health care costs, and 33% of deaths before the age of 65. Our health care system is not meeting the needs of those with chronic diseases; less than 30% of those with hypertension are being treated. Those with diabetes should have eye exams. Asthma is not controlled properly in 60% of our population. Sufferers of heart failure are readmitted at the rate of 20% within 60 days (Rachlis, 2006).Chronically ill family members may have an FP, but not necessarily a geriatrician who would be well-versed in the special needs of seniors with complicated comorbidities.

Suggestions for families of those in LTC

With ninety percent of residents in the LTC institutions under power of attorney (as estimated by my dad's LTC administrator), residents are not in control of their own medical care. These residents are subject to the vagaries of health care in an institution. Our seniors will continue to be at risk. There is no reason to assume that health care is as accessible in LTC as it is in a clinic or public setting. Physicians are busy and do not see every resident in an LTC facility. With a million orphan patients in Ontario, they are at risk. It is the nursing staff who control access to pharmaceuticals and make diagnoses and judgments on whether a resident should see a physician. Unfortunately, you cannot look for volunteer or profit-oriented agencies (e.g., Red Cross, CCAC) that provide in-home support to these residents, as they fall under the health care system and the LTC Act. It is difficult to get specialists to visit LTC homes. They are all very busy. It took months to find a dermatologist to visit my father's LTC home. We could not find a dental hygienist, and the massage therapist stopped visiting the facility.

Industry issues

These issues were identified from a teleconference call with Family Council Chairs from around the province of Ontario. They are common across the province. None of us on the call could agree on exactly the same issues as being the most critical, yet many themes recurred:

- More palliative care rooms
- More staff
- Better trained staff with a wide range of expertise to manage chronic disease
- Family health teams that include PSWs, nurse practitioners, physician assistants, as well as physicians, to address issues and deliver a full range of care
- More funding for staff
- Requirements for in-service training of PSWs and medical staff, including nurses and physicians, in geriatric issues: physical and mental health issues that require specific treatments

- More continuity of care, with staffing levels that permit this to occur
- An ombudsman to assist families

Violence occurs in society, and those who have been violent with their spouses or children can end up in LTC. There should be special facilities for such people. Those who are in a state of dementia can be violent. Placement in LTC results in exacerbating anger management issues, and special settings are warranted for those who cannot treat others with respect. With the closure of mental institutions fifty years ago, many of those with chronic mental disorders are either now on the streets, as they cannot tolerate being indoors, or using emergency services, or in LTC (Picard, 2008).

Suggestions for the government

There are two separate issues that face failing seniors and their families. Number one is the right to information as an adult child or caregiver. Privacy laws must not prevent outside agencies from contacting us and informing us that a senior parent has entered their client list. Many of us do not realize how ill an elderly parent is when neighbours and agencies provide care that masks the desperate ADL and IADL needs of seniors. This must be changed.

The second issue of concern is long-term care. With only two options—caring for seniors at home with extra supports, or LTC—there is nothing in the middle, or at the far end of the spectrum. LTC facilities do not do well with seniors who require chronic care. They do not have the financial and physical supports necessary.

It would appear that there is little in the way of real funding for us in LTC through the provincial budgets. This is true of education and mental and physical health care. It is a shame that we spend so much money on focus groups and invest donor-fatigued time and energy by volunteers in giving advice. Many have their own personal agendas.

We should examine the requirements of residents in LTC and determine what they need and want from the system. What is missing is a level of care that falls between the hospital and chronic care centres. We need more chronic care centres, as well as facilities in which those who have had strokes and have other treatable illnesses can be supported and their physical health improved.

LTC facilities now house those who are too healthy for the hospital, but require RN help daily. They are also filled with those whose families cannot care for them at home due to environmental, physical, or emotional barriers. An LTC home can have a variety of residents with dementia, stroke victims, cancer patients, and those with brain damage, and these folks complicate a system. Every resident is treated equally, while they are not "equal." I would like to see a care plan that determines the health care issues of each resident and finds the appropriate placement on a continuum from total care to partial care. We need group homes where those with schizophrenia or other mental disorders can be accommodated. We need homes where those who are functioning cognitively have their physical needs managed with dignity and respect. We need more resources for those who fall through the cracks.

References

Advocacy Centre for the Elderly (ACEL) and Community Legal Education Ontario (CLEO). 2005. Every Resident: LTC Bill of Rights. Retrieved February 28, 2008, from **www.cleo.on.ca/english/pub/ onpub/PDF/seniors/everyres.pdf.**

Alberta Mental Health Board. 2006. *Mending Minds: 2006 AMHB Research Showcase.* Alberta: Author.

Albom, M. 2002. *Tuesdays with Morrie.* New York: Broadway.

Alexopoulos, G.S. 2005. Depression in the Elderly. *Lancet, 365(9475),* 1961–70.

American Psychiatric Association. 1994. *Diagnostic and Statistical Manual of Mental Disorders* (4th Ed.), Washington, D.C.: Author.

Anhensel, C.S., et al. 1995. *Profiles in caregiving: The unexpected career.* San Diego: Academic Press.

Appleby, L., Cooper, J., Amos, T., & Faragher, B. 1999. Psychological autopsy study of suicides by people aged under 35. *British Journal of Psychiatry.* 175, 168–74.

Avis, N. E. 2003. Depression during the menopausal transition. *Psychology of Women Quarterly, 27* (2), 91–100.

Balducci, L., & Carreca, I. 2002. The role of myelopoietic growth factors in managing cancer in the elderly. *Drugs, 62*(1), 47–63.

Balkin, R.S., Tietjen–Smith, T., Caldwell, C., & Yu-Pei, S. 2007. The utilization of exercise to decrease depressive symptoms in young adult women. *Adultspan: Theory Research & Practice, 6*(1), 30–33.

Beery, L.C., et al. 1997. Traumatic grief, depression and caregiving in elderly spouses of the terminally ill. *Journal of Death and Dying,* 35(3).

BrainHospice.com. n.d. Symptoms Timeline (for those approaching death). Retrieved November 14, 2007, from **www.brainhospice.com/ SymptomTimeline.html.**

Brain Tumour Foundation of Canada. 2003. Retrieved June 16, 2008 from **www.braintumour.ca.**

Brant LTC Best Practices Work Group. May 2007. Reference guide for pain assessment, care planning and monitoring. Retrieved August 25, 2007, from **www.rgpc.ca/research/research.cfm.**

Bredeson, P.V. 2003. *Breaking the silence: Overcoming the problem of principal mistreatment of teachers.* California: Corwin Press.

Breslin, J.M., MacRae, S.K., Bell, J., & Singer, P.A. 2005. Top 10 health care ethics challenges facing the public: Views of Toronto bioethicists. *BioMed Central Limited, 6,* 5. Retrieved February 28, 2008, from **www.biomedcentral.com/1472-6939/6/5.**

Bruera, E., et al. 1991. The Edmonton symptom assessment system (ESAS): A simple method for the assessment of palliative care patients. *Journal of Palliative Care.* 7 (2): 6–9. Retrieved February 28, 2008, from **www.palliative.org/PC/ClinicalInfo/AssessmentTools/AssessmentToolsIDX.html**.

Burton, L.M., & Merriwether–deVries, C. 1995. Context and surrogate parenting among contemporary grandparents. *Marriage & Family Review, 20* (3.4), 349–66.

Bush, A., & Carter, P.A. 2004. The effect of cancer patients' pain and fatigue on caregiver depression level and sleep quality. *Journal of Undergraduate Nursing Scholarship, 6*(1) Retrieved January 22, 2008 from **http://juns.nursing.arizona.edu/contents6.htm.**

Callahan, C.M., Hendrie, H.C., & Tierney, W.M. 1995. Documentation and evaluation of cognitive impairment in elderly primary care patients. *Annals of Internal Medicine 122,* 422–29.

Canadian Mental Health Association 2006. Suicide. Retrieved June 28, 2007 from **www.ontario.cmha.ca/content/about_mental_illness/suicide.asp?cID=3965**.

Canadian Study of Health and Aging Working Group. 1994. Patterns of caring for people with dementia in Canada. *Canadian Journal of Aging. 13,* 470–87.

Canadian Study of Health and Aging Working Group. 2002. Patterns and health effects of caring for people with dementia: The impact of changing cognitive and residential status. *Gerontologist, 42*(5), 643–52.

Canadian Women's Healthcare Network 1998. Caregiving still in women's job description. Retrieved June 30, 2008, from **www.cwhn.ca/network-reseau/1-3/spare.html**.

Cancer Care Nova Scotia. Patient Navigation. Retrieved June 14, 2008, from **www.cancercare.ns.ca/inside.asp?cmPageID=89.**

Caprio, A. J., et al. 2008. Pain, dyspneas, and the quality of dying in long-term care. *Journal of the American Geriatric Society, 56* (4), 683–88.

Capuron, L., et al. 2002. Association between decreased serum tryptophan concentrations and depressive symptoms in cancer patients undergoing cytokine therapy. *Molecular Psychiatry, 7*(5), 468–73.

Cole, M.G. 2004. Delirium in elderly patients. *American Journal of Geriatric Psychiatry, 12,* 7–21.

Comino, E.J., et al. 2000. Prevalence, detection and management of anxiety and depressive symptoms in unemployed patients attending general practitioners. *Australian & New Zealand Journal of Psychiatry. 34*(1), 107–13.

Cotton, C. 2004. About lymphedema. Retrieved on-line, May 24, 2008, from **lymphontario.org**.

Cummings, J.L., & Jeste, D.V. 1999. Alzheimer's disease and its management in the year 2010. Retrieved August 29, 2008, from **http://www.psychservices.psychiatryonline.org/cgi/content/full/50/9/1173#R50910912**.

Depression Bipolar Support Alliance. Retrieved July 21, 2007, from **www.dbsalliance.org**.

Doidge, N. 2004. Making the Modern World. Measuring the unmeasurable: An introduction to psychology. Retrieved June 25, 2007 from **www.makingthemodernworld.org.uk/learning_modules/psychology/02.TU.04/**

——. 2007. *The brain that changes itself.* New York: Penguin.

Emick, M.A., & Hayslip, B. 1999. Custodial grandparenting: Stress, coping skills, and relationships with grandchildren. *International Journal of Aging and Human Development. 48*(1), 35–61.

Feil, D.G., MacLean, C., & Sultzer, D. 2007. Quality indicators for the care of dementia in vulnerable elders. *Journal of the American Geriatric Society, 55,* 293–301.

Forster, A. J., et al. 2004. Adverse events among medical patients after discharge from hospital. *Canadian Medical Association Journal. 170,* 345–49.

Frankl, V. 2006. *Man's search for meaning.* Boston: Beacon Press.

Gallagher–Thompson, D., & Coon, D.W. 2007. Evidence-based psychological treatments for distress in family caregivers of older adults. *Psychology and Aging, 22*(1), 37–51.

Gaugler, J.R., Zarit, S.H., & Pearlin, L.I. 1999. Caregiving and institutionalization: Perceptions of family conflict and socioemotional support. *International Journal of Aging and Human Development, 49*(1), 1–25.

Goldberg, N. 2005. *Writing down the bones*. 2nd ed. Boston, MA: Shambhala.

Government of Canada. 2000. Quality end-of-life-care: The right of every Canadian. Retrieved February 22, 2008, from **www.parl. gc.ca/36/2/parlbus/commbus/senate/Com-e/upda-e/rep-e/ repfinjun00-e.htm.**

Grafton, S. 2007. *T is for trespass*. New York: GP Putnam & Sons.

Grov, E.K., Fossa, S.D., Tonnessen, A., & Dahl, A.A. 2006. The caregiver reaction assessment: Psychometrics, and temporal stability in primary caregivers of Norwegian cancer patients in late palliative phase. *Psycho-Oncology, 15*, 517–27.

Grunfeld, E., et al. 2004. Family caregiver burden: Results of a longitudinal study of breast cancer patients and their principal caregivers. *Canadian Medical Association Journal, 170 (12).*

Gulli, C. & Lunau, K. 2008. Canada's doctor shortage worsening. Retrieved on-line June 30, 2008, from **www.thecanadianencyclopedia.com/ index.cfm?PgNm=TCE&Params=M1ARTM0013191.**

Hamilton, M. 1960. A rating scale for depression. *Journal of Neurology, Neurosurgery and Psychiatry, 23*, 56–62.

Health Canada. 2002. Investigation and assessment of the navigator role in meeting the information, decisional and educational needs of women with breast cancer in Canada. Retrieved on-line August 28, 2008, from **www.phac-aspc.gc.ca/ccdpc-cpcmc/cancer/ publications/navigator_e.html.**

Heart's Way Hospice. 2006. As death approaches. Retrieved June 14, 2008, from **www.heartswayhospice.org/as_death_approaches.htm.**

Heckman, G. 2004. The hazards of health care. Retrieved August 29, 2008, from **www.rgpc.ca/files/Hazards%20of%20Hospitalization%20 Role%20of%20Geriatrics%20Rev.ppt.**

Heru, A.M., & Ryan, C.E. 2002. Depressive symptoms and family functioning in the caregivers of recently hospitalized patients with chronic/recurrent mood disorders. *International Journal of Psychosocial Rehabilitation, 7*, 53–60.

Hodkinson, H. 1972. Evaluation of a mental test score for assessment of mental impairment in the elderly. *Age and Ageing, 1*, 233–38.

Holmes, H.M., Hayley, D.C., Alexander, G.C., & Sachs, G.A. 2006. Reconsidering medication appropriateness for patients late in life. *Archives of Internal Medicine, 166*, 605–9.

Holmes, H. M., et al. 2008. Integrating palliative medicine into the care of persons with advanced dementia: Identifying appropriate medication use. *Journal of the American Geriatrics Society.* Published article on-line: **14-May-2008 doi: 10.1111/j.1532-5415.2008.01741.x.**

Hosseini, K. 2007. *A thousand splendid suns.* USA: Penguin Group.

Human Resources and Social Development Canada. 2008. Indicators of well-being in Canada. Retrieved August 28, 2008, from **www4. hrsdc.gc.ca/indicator.jsp?indicatorid=3&lang=en**

Ingram, J. 1994. *Talk, talk, talk.* USA: Random House.

Jennett Chapel. 2007. A celebration of life. Retrieved September 2, 2007 from **www.funeralhome.on.ca/burial_cremation.htm**.

Jilks, J. 2007. The use of autobiography in therapy: A Gestalt-based approach. Retrieved February 27, 2008, from **www.jilks.com/articles/AutobiographyTherapy.htm**.

Kim, Y., Duberstein, P.R., Sørensen, S., & Larson, M. (2005). Levels of depressive symptoms in spouses of people with lung cancer: Effects of personality, social support, and caregiving burden. *Psychosomatics, 46,* 126–30.

King, S. 2006. *Pink ribbons, inc.: Breast cancer and the politics of philanthropy.* Minn.: University of Minnesota Press.

Kübler–Ross, E. 1997. *Death: The final stage of growth.* Carmichael, CA: Touchstone Books.

———. 1998. *The wheel of life: A memoir of living and dying.* Carmichael, CA: Touchstone Books.

Kübler–Ross, E., & Kessler, D. 2005. *On grief and grieving: Finding the meaning of grief through the five stages of loss.* New York: Scribner.

Kushner, H. S. 2006. *Overcoming life's disappointments.* USA: Random House.

Logsdon, R.G., Gibbons, I.E., & McCurry, S.M., et al. 1999. Quality of life in Alzheimer's disease: patient and caregiver reports. *Journal of Mental Health and Aging,* 5 (1).

Magai, C. & Cohen, C.I. 1998. Attachment style and emotion regulation in dementia patients and their relation to caregiver burden. *Journal of Gerontology Psychological Sciences,* 53B(3), 147–54.

Mausbach, B.T., et al. 2007. Depression and distress predict time to cardiovascular disease in dementia caregivers. *Health Psychology,* 26, 539–44.

Mood Disorders Association of Ontario. n.d. *Depression*. Retrieved June 28, 2007, from **www.mooddisorders.on.ca/dep.html**.

Morimoto, T., Schreiner, A.S., & Asano, H. 2001. Perceptions of burden among family caregivers of post-stroke elderly in Japan. *International Journal of Rehabilitation Research, 24,* 106.

Nease, D.E., & Malouin, J.M. 2003. Depression screening: A practical strategy. *Journal of Family Practice, 52*(2), 118–26.

Nemeroff, C.B., & Owens, M.J. 2002. Treatment of mood disorders. *Nature Neuroscience, 5*(11), 1068–70.

Nunley, K. 2003. *A student's brain: The parent/teacher manual.* Boston: Morris Publ.

Ohgaki, H., & Kleihues, P. 2005. *Journal of Neuropathology Experimental Neurology,* 64(6), 479–89.

Ontario Government. n.d. *Accessing a long-term care facility.* Retrieved January 23, 2008, from **www.health.gov.on.ca**.

O'Rourke, N., & Tuokko, H. 2000. The psychological and physical costs of caregiving: The Canadian Study of Health and Aging. *Journal of Applied Gerontology, 19*(4), 389–404.

O'Rourke, N., Cappeliez, P., & Neufeld, E. 2007. Recurrent depressive symptomatology and physical health: A 10-year study of informal caregivers of persons with dementia. *Canadian Journal of Psychiatry, 52*(7), 434–41.

Pagel, M., & Becker, J. 1978. Depressive thinking and depression: relations with personality and social resources. *Journal of Personality and Social Psychology, 52*(5), 1043–52.

Pennebaker, J.W. 2004. Writing to heal: A guided journal for recovering from trauma & emotional upheaval. Oakland, CA: New Harbinger.

Phillips, D. n.d. *Seeking peace: Brain tumour hospice care.* Retrieved November 14, 2007, from **www.brainhospice.com/index.html**.

Picard, A. 2008. The orphans of medicare. Retrieved on-line June 30, 2008, from **www.theglobeandmail.com/servlet/story/ RTGAM.20080623.wmhhospitals24/BNStory/mentalhealth**.

Pinel, J. 2006. *Basics of biopsychology.* Toronto: Pearson, Allyn & Bacon.

Rachlis, M. 2005. *Prescription for excellence.* Retrieved August 29, 2008, from **http://www.michaelrachlis.com/publications.php**.

———. 2006. *Seniors' health: We can't afford the future if we don't repeat the past.* Retrieved August 29, 2008, from **www.coaottawa.ca/ health_forum/DrRachlis.ppt**.

Rachlis, V. 2005. "Inside out": Letter from the president, Dr. Val Rachlis. Retrieved June 30, 2008, from **www.ocfp.on.ca/local/files/ Communications/Ltr2Mbrs/2005/Ltr2MbrFeb15-05.pdf**.

Redinbaugh, E.M., MacCallum, R.C., & Kiecott–Glaser, J.K. 1995. Recurrent syndromal depression in caregivers. *Psychology and Aging, 10* (3), 358–68.

Regional Geriatric Program. 2006. *BP Blogger*. Retrieved September 15, 2007, from **www.rgpc.ca**.

Reker, G.T. 2002. Prospective predictors of successful aging in community-residing and institutionalized Canadian elderly. *Ageing International, 27*, 42–64.

Rudolph, J.L., & Marcantonio, E.R. 2003. Diagnosis and prevention of delirium. *Geriatrics & Aging, 6* (10), 15–19. (**www.geriatricsandaging.ca**)

Semple, S.J. 1992. Conflict in Alzheimer's caregiving families: Its dimensions and consequences. *The Gerontologist, 32*, 648–55.

Schreiner, A.S., & Morimoto, T. 2003. The relationship between mastery and depression among Japanese family caregivers. *International Journal of Aging and Human Development. 56*(4), 307–21.

Sherman, F.T. n.d. 10 minute geriatric assessment. Retrieved February 23, 2008, from **www.sergp.org/Presentations/The 10 Min Geriatric Assessment.ppt**.

Shrank, W.H., Polinski, J.M., & Avorn, J. 2007. Quality indicators for medication use in vulnerable elders. *Journal of the American Geriatrics Society, 55*(2), 373–82.

Sigelman, C.L., & Rider, E.A. 2006. *Life span human development* (5th ed.). Belmont: Thomas Wadsworth.

Solomon, P.R., et al. 1998. Ten-minute geriatric assessment. *Arch Neurology, JJ*, March 1998, 349–55. Retrieved on-line May 14, 2008, from **www.sergp.org/toward_best_geriatric_practice.htm**.

Statistics Canada. 1997. *A portrait of seniors in Canada*, Second ed. Ottawa: Author.

Statistics Canada. 2006. *A portrait of seniors in Canada*. Ottawa: Author.

Tang, S.T., Li, C.W., & Liao, X.Y. 2007. associated with depressive distress among Taiwanese family caregivers of cancer patients at the end of life. *Palliative Medicine, 21*(3), 249–57.

Tavris, C., & Aronson, E. 2007. *Mistakes were made (but not by me): Why we justify foolish beliefs, bad decisions, and hurtful acts*. New York: Harcourt.

Taylor, J. 2008. *My stroke of insight: a brain scientist's personal journey.* New York: Viking.

Twaddle, M.L., et al. 2007. Palliative care benchmarks from academic medical centers. *Journal of Palliative Medicine, 10*(1), 86–98.

Watson, Y.L., Arfken, C.L., & Birge, S.J. . Clock Completion: An objective screening test for dementia. *Journal of the American Geriatric Society, 41*, 1235–40.

Wenger, N.S., Roth, C.P., & Shekelle, P. 2007. Introduction to the assessing care of vulnerable elders-3 Quality Indicator Measurement Set. *Journal of the American Geriatrics Society, 55*(2), 247–52.

Acronyms

ABI   Acquired Brain Injury

ACT   Assertive Community Treatment

ADL   Activities of Daily Living

ADP   Assistive Devices Program

ALC   Alternate Level of Care (hospital designation)

CAT Scan

CT Scan   Computerized Axial Tomography (takes x-rays of the brain and other body areas)

CCAC   Community Care Access Centre

CCC   Complex Continuing Care

CHC   Community Health Centre

ED   Emergency Department

ER   Emergency Room

FHT   Family Health Team (now mandated across the province in Ontario)

FIPPA   Freedom of Information Protection of Privacy Act

HHR   Human Health Resources

HSP   Health Service Plan

IADL   Instrumental Activities of Daily Living

ICE   Isolated Community Experience (to serve seniors in rural areas)

IGS   Integrated Geriatric Systems

IHSP   Integrated Health Service Plan

LHIN   Local Health Integration Network

LTC   Long-Term Care

MIS   Management Information System

MLAA   Ministry LHIN Articulation Agreement (data collection)

MOHLTC   Ministry of Health & Long-Term Care (Ontario)

MRI   Magnetic Resonance Imaging (MRI scan uses a magnet and radio waves to take pictures of the brain. It provides more detail than a CAT scan.)

NSM	North Simcoe Muskoka
OCSA	Ontario Community Support Association
PACE	Program of All-inclusive Care for the Elderly
PEC	Public Education Coordinator
PHIPA	Personal Health Information Protection Act
PRC	Psychogeriatric Resource Consultant
PSAD	Personal Services Assistance Device
PSW	Personal Support Worker
RAI	Resident Assessment Instrument (used in home care and palliative care)
RGP	Regional Geriatric Program
RISC	Regional Integrated Senior Centre
SGS	Specialized Geriatric Services
TPO	Transfer Payment Organization (governments have been outsourcing health care to various agencies, transferring money to them. They are governed by boards of directors.)

Glossary

Activities of Daily Living (ADL): bathing, grooming, toileting, dressing, eating, and other activities necessary for daily living and survival

Agnosia: failure to recognize objects

Aphasia: a disturbance in receptive or expressive language

Apnea: temporary cessations in breathing; this is a sign of approaching death in palliative care patients

Apraxia: loss of understanding of the uses of things

Assistive device: a mechanical aid to make ADL easier

Benign brain tumour: a slow-growing tumour that does not tend to invade nearby cells

Biopsychosocial issues: interrelated biological, psychological, and sociological issues

Carcinogen: a substance that has been proven to cause cancer in living cells

Caregiver: one who provides care

Care recipient: one who receives care

Comorbidities: the effect of all disorders or diseases on an individual in addition to the primary health issue

Dementia: acquired, persistent impairment in two or more cognitive areas of executive functions; profound mental incapacity

Dysphagia: choking and swallowing issues

Executive functions: planning, organizing, sequencing, and abstract thought

Frail: premorbid; at risk for biopsychosocial issues; inability to manage physical, social, and emotional needs (ADL)

Geriatric: of or relating to old age or old people

Instrumental Activities of Daily Living (IADL): caring for pets and dependents; communicating with others effectively; managing finances and health; doing housework, meal preparation, and cleanup; looking after transportation and safety procedures

Infarct: a small, localized area of dead tissue caused by an inadequate blood supply; can result from blood clots or diabetes

Incontinence: inability to control evacuation of urine or feces

Long-term care (LTC) facility/home: a health care facility for those with physical disabilities that offers 24/7 nursing staff; formerly called a *nursing home*

Malignant brain tumour: a tumour that grows quickly and invades surrounding cells; these kinds of tumours are the least likely to be totally removed surgically, since they invade and damage important structures

Metastasize: when cancer cells break off from the original site and spread to other parts of the body to cause malignancy there

Morbidity: the quality of disease; the extent of illness, injury, or disability in a defined population

Nurse practitioner: a nurse who meets primary health care needs, conducts physical examinations, selects treatment plans, and identifies medication requirements

Nursing home: now called a long-term care home; differs from a retirement home

Orphan patient: a person without a family physician

Palliative care: giving care at the last stages of life

Polypharmacy: taking too many pharmaceuticals/prescription drugs

Premorbidities: factors that may lead to death

Primary care: basic or general health care from the medical system

Registered nurse (RN): a nurse who is licensed to practise and is a registered member of a nurses' association

Registered practical nurse (RPN): a person who is registered by a professional association of nurses as having been trained to perform basic nursing tasks under the direction of a physician or an RN

Respite care: temporary institutional care of a dependent ill or handicapped person to give respite to the usual caregiver

Retirement home: a private residence for seniors (profit or non-profit); governed by the Landlord Tenant Act

Sleep apnea: intermittent failure to breathe during sleep

Subcortical issues: issues such as plaque and damaged brain cells; physical evidence manifests as dementia

Supportive living: also called assisted living, in which supports are on call 24/7

About the Author

Jennifer Jilks is an educator, writer, blogger, and an avid reader and researcher. She has developed expertise in working with a wide range of professionals in education and health care. This has helped her negotiate with medical staff while advocating for her parents as they succumbed to cancer. She sits on the Family, Youth, and Child Services of the Muskoka board of directors, which keeps her involved in the community. She holds a degree in Early Childhood Education, a B.Ed., and an M.Ed. in Curriculum and Technology, with experience in teaching students from Junior Kindergarten to Grade 8. A Special Education Specialist, she has worked with many special needs students. She has delivered workshops to peers and lectured to student teachers on a part-time basis at the University of Ottawa. For further information, visit her Web site at **www.jilks.com**.

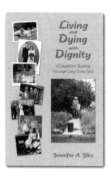